AF753229

AFRICAN POLITICAL, ECONOMIC, AND SECURITY ISSUES

LIBERIA: DEVELOPMENT AND RESOURCES

African Political, Economic, and Security Issues

Additional books in this series can be found on Nova's website under the Series tab.

Additional E-books in this series can be found on Nova's website under the E-books tab.

Countries, Regional Studies, Trading Blocks, Unions, World Organizations

Additional books in this series can be found on Nova's website under the Series tab.

Additional E-books in this series can be found on Nova's website under the E-books tab.

AFRICAN POLITICAL, ECONOMIC, AND SECURITY ISSUES

LIBERIA: DEVELOPMENT AND RESOURCES

ANYA M. MICALLEF
EDITOR

Nova Science Publishers, Inc.
New York

Copyright © 2011 by Nova Science Publishers, Inc.

All rights reserved. No part of this book may be reproduced, stored in a retrieval system or transmitted in any form or by any means: electronic, electrostatic, magnetic, tape, mechanical photocopying, recording or otherwise without the written permission of the Publisher.

For permission to use material from this book please contact us:
Telephone 631-231-7269; Fax 631-231-8175
Web Site: http://www.novapublishers.com

NOTICE TO THE READER

The Publisher has taken reasonable care in the preparation of this book, but makes no expressed or implied warranty of any kind and assumes no responsibility for any errors or omissions. No liability is assumed for incidental or consequential damages in connection with or arising out of information contained in this book. The Publisher shall not be liable for any special, consequential, or exemplary damages resulting, in whole or in part, from the readers' use of, or reliance upon, this material. Any parts of this book based on government reports are so indicated and copyright is claimed for those parts to the extent applicable to compilations of such works.

Independent verification should be sought for any data, advice or recommendations contained in this book. In addition, no responsibility is assumed by the publisher for any injury and/or damage to persons or property arising from any methods, products, instructions, ideas or otherwise contained in this publication.

This publication is designed to provide accurate and authoritative information with regard to the subject matter covered herein. It is sold with the clear understanding that the Publisher is not engaged in rendering legal or any other professional services. If legal or any other expert assistance is required, the services of a competent person should be sought. FROM A DECLARATION OF PARTICIPANTS JOINTLY ADOPTED BY A COMMITTEE OF THE AMERICAN BAR ASSOCIATION AND A COMMITTEE OF PUBLISHERS.

Additional color graphics may be available in the e-book version of this book.

LIBRARY OF CONGRESS CATALOGING-IN-PUBLICATION DATA

Liberia : development and resources / editor, Anya M. Micallef.
p. cm.
Includes index.
ISBN 978-1-61209-396-3 (hardcover)
1. Economic development--Liberia. 2. Natural resources--Liberia. 3. Postwar reconstruction--Liberia. 4. Economic assistance, American--Liberia. 5. Technical assistance, American--Liberia. I. Micallef, Anya M.
HC1075.L52 2011
338.96662--dc22

2010051535

Published by Nova Science Publishers, Inc. † New York

CONTENTS

PREFACE

Liberia held elections in October 2005, with a presidential runoff in November, a key step in a peace-building process following its second civil war in a decade. The war pitted the forces of Charles Taylor, elected president in 1997 after Liberia's first civil war, against two armed anti-Taylor rebel groups. The war also destabilized neighboring states, which accepted Liberian refugees and, in some cases, hosted anti-Taylor forces and became targets of the Taylor regime. This new book examines developments in Liberia

Chapter 1- This report covers developments in Liberia, a small, poor West African country. Liberia held elections in October 2005, with a presidential runoff in November, a key step in a peace-building process following its second civil war in a decade. That war began in 1999, escalated in 2000, and ended in 2003. It pitted the forces of Charles Taylor, elected president in 1997 after Liberia's first civil war (1989-1997), against two armed anti-Taylor rebel groups. The war also destabilized neighboring states, which accepted Liberian refugees and, in some cases, hosted anti-Taylor forces and became targets of the Taylor regime.

Ellen Johnson Sirleaf, an economist, won the presidential runoff vote, with 59.4% of votes cast and took office in January 2006, becoming the first elected female president of an African country. Her runoff rival, George Weah, a former star soccer player, conceded Sirleaf's win after initially contesting it. Most observers viewed the vote as orderly, free and fair. It fulfilled a key goal of an August 2003 peace accord that had ended the second civil war and led to an ongoing, U.S.-aided post-war transition process, which is bolstered by the multifaceted peacekeeping and development-focused U.N. Mission in Liberia (UNMIL).

Chapter 2- Portuguese explorers established contacts with Liberia as early as 1461 and named the area Grain Coast because of the abundance of "grains of paradise" (Malegueta pepper seeds). In 1663 the British installed trading posts on the Grain Coast, but the Dutch destroyed these posts a year later. There were no further reports of European settlements along the Grain Coast until the arrival of freed slaves in the early 1800s.

Chapter 3- Biomass resources meet about 99.5% of the Liberian population's energy needs so they are vital to basic welfare and economic activity. Already, traditional biomass products like firewood and charcoal are the primary energy source used for domestic cooking and heating. However, other more efficient biomass technologies are available that could open opportunities for agriculture and rural development, and provide other socio-economic and environmental benefits.

In: Liberia: Development and Resources ISBN: 978-1-61209-396-3
Editors: Anya M. Micallef © 2011 Nova Science Publishers, Inc.

Chapter 1

LIBERIA'S POST-WAR DEVELOPMENT: KEY ISSUES AND U.S. ASSISTANCE

Nicolas Cook

SUMMARY

This report covers developments in Liberia, a small, poor West African country. Liberia held elections in October 2005, with a presidential runoff in November, a key step in a peace-building process following its second civil war in a decade. That war began in 1999, escalated in 2000, and ended in 2003. It pitted the forces of Charles Taylor, elected president in 1997 after Liberia's first civil war (1989-1997), against two armed anti-Taylor rebel groups. The war also destabilized neighboring states, which accepted Liberian refugees and, in some cases, hosted anti-Taylor forces and became targets of the Taylor regime.

Ellen Johnson Sirleaf, an economist, won the presidential runoff vote, with 59.4% of votes cast and took office in January 2006, becoming the first elected female president of an African country. Her runoff rival, George Weah, a former star soccer player, conceded Sirleaf's win after initially contesting it. Most observers viewed the vote as orderly, free and fair. It fulfilled a key goal of an August 2003 peace accord that had ended the second civil war and led to an ongoing, U.S.-aided post-war transition process, which is bolstered by the multifaceted peacekeeping and development-focused U.N. Mission in Liberia (UNMIL). The next election is scheduled for 2011, and President Sirleaf has announced that she will seek reelection. Liberia's security situation is stable but subject to periodic volatility. Progress in governance under the interim government that preceded that of President Sirleaf was mixed; widespread corruption within it was widely reported. Liberia's economy and state structures remain devastated by war but, along with humanitarian conditions, are improving. Liberia has received extensive U.S. post-war reconstruction and security sector reform assistance. In March 2006, former President Taylor was arrested in Nigeria and transferred to the Special Court for Sierra Leone (SCSL) to face war crimes charges. He was later transferred to The Hague, the Netherlands, where he is on trial by the SCSL.

In addition to providing substantial support for Liberia's post-war peace and reconstruction processes, Congress has maintained a continuing interest in the status of Charles Taylor and in ensuring funding for the SCSL. Other legislation proposed in the 109th and 110th Congresses centered on immigration, debt, and tax haven issues, and the commendation of Liberia for successfully holding elections. Liberia-specific legislation introduced or acted upon in the 111th Congress has included: H.R. 1105 (Obey); H.R. 3288 (Olver); S. 656 (Reed); H.R. 2258 (Kennedy); H.R. 2410 (Berman); H.R. 2475 (Ros-Lehtinen); S. 1434 (Leahy); and H.R. 2346 (Obey).

Recent and On-Going Developments

Liberia's president, Ellen Johnson Sirleaf,[1] is expected to visit the United States in late May 2010. While her itinerary has not been released, the trip is expected to be aimed at deepening Sirleaf's high-level contacts with President Barack Obama's Administration.[2] Sirleaf, who also maintained warm ties with former President George W. Bush's Administration, may meet with President Obama. She is also expected to update U.S. policy makers, including interested Members, on Liberia's progress since her election, as well as remaining challenges in such areas as security sector reform, anti-corruption efforts, unemployment, economic growth, and legal system capacity building. Her visit is expected to include a Millennium Challenge Corporation (MCC)

Threshold Program pre-signing event and a possible U.S. Global Food Security Initiative country program.[3]

On March 18, 2010, President Obama extended for 18 months the Deferred Enforced Departure (DED) status of eligible Liberian U.S. resident aliens, which had previously been set to expire on March 31, 2010, allowing them to remain in the United States. DED is a special immigration status that effectively suspends the deportation of eligible U.S. aliens. The presidential directive ordering the extension, which had been sought by some Members, notably from districts with significant populations of Liberian origin, also authorized those eligible to work during the duration of their DED status.[4] In addition, two bills introduced in the 111th Congress would allow certain Liberian aliens to become permanent U.S. residents. (See "Immigration Issues").

The trial of former Liberian President Charles Taylor, which began in mid-2007, but was beset by procedural delays for a time, is continuing. Cross-examination of defense witnesses by the Prosecutor's Office of the U.S.-backed Special Court for Sierra Leone (SCSL), which began in November 2009, proceeded in early 2010.[5] (See "Taylor Trial").

In her late January 2010 annual address to the Liberian legislature, President Sirleaf, announced that she would seek reelection to a second term in 2011, as many observers had expected. Her announcement came in spite of a recommendation by Liberia's Truth and Reconciliation Commission (TRC) in its draft June 2009 final report that Sirleaf, as one of 49 alleged "political leaders and financiers of different warring factions" party to Liberia's civil wars, be "barred from holding public offices" or "elected or appointed" for 30 years.[6] (See "Truth and Reconciliation Commission").

In early 2010, the Unity Party (UP, President Sirleaf's party), the Liberia Action Party (LAP), and the Liberia Unification Party (LUP) were in the process of holding party conventions and were all expected to ratify an April 2009 agreement among them to merge.[7]

In mid-2010, a full-fledged Peace Corps Volunteer (PCV) country program for Liberia is scheduled to begin. It will build on the work of a special short-term humanitarian service program that began in October 2008.[8] (See "Peace Corps").

U.S.-Liberia flights by Delta Airlines are slated to begin in mid-2010. The initiation of the new route, originally planned for mid-2009 was delayed when the U.S. Department of Homeland Security (DHS) announced in June 2009 that due to security deficiencies at Liberia's international airport, it would not permit the operation of U.S.-Liberian flights. The Transportation Security

Administration (TSA), a DHS unit, is providing Liberia with assistance to enhance aviation security.[9] (See "Air and Communications Links").

In May 2009, a jury acquitted former National Transitional Government of Liberia (NTGL) Chairman Gyude Bryant and four former Liberia Petroleum Refinery Company (LPRC) executives from the NTGL period of corruption charges in a case involving the alleged embezzlement of LPRC assets.[10] Bryant faces a separate corruption case related his tenure as NTGL Chairman. (See "Post-NTGL Corruption Trials").

In late 2009, Liberia held a Senatorial by-election to fill a vacancy created by an incumbent's death in which President Sirleaf's Unity Party lost in a run-off against the opposition Congress for Democratic Change (CDC). Although the election reportedly featured a low voter turn-out, it was viewed as a dry-run of the National Elections Commission's (NEC) operational capability ahead of national elections in 2011 because nearly half of Liberia's electorate was eligible to participate in it. (See "Subsequent Elections").

The Sirleaf government is negotiating or has in recent years entered into several multi-year, large natural resource or agricultural concession deals, collectively worth multiple billion dollars worth of investment and potential exports, indicating that large foreign investors' confidence in the country's political progress and prospective stability is strong.[11]

U.S. Ties

The United States has long-standing ties with Liberia that date back to the founding of the modern Liberian state by "Americo-Liberians," black freemen and former slaves from the Americas who settled in Liberia beginning in 1821. Liberia was also a close U.S. ally, albeit a relatively minor one, during World War II and the Cold War, and the country hosted U.S. communications facilities in the 1 960s and 1970s, and received extensive U.S. development assistance. The Reagan Administration cultivated ties with the government of President Samuel K. Doe during the first half of the 1 980s, although these later soured. The United States also provided meditational support and extensive humanitarian assistance for Liberia during its first and second civil wars. It has also invested substantial amounts of aid in the current United Nations peacekeeping operation in Liberia, as well as substantial post-war rebuilding and development assistance. There has generally been strong Congressional support for these efforts. The Administration of former

President George W. Bush formed a close and cordial relationship with the Sirleaf, and similarly close relations have continued under the Obama Administration. Contemporary U.S. relations with and policy developments related to Liberia are discussed in the "U.S. Relations" section of this report.[12]

BACKGROUND

Liberia, a small, poor West African country of about 3.4 million people, is undergoing a post- conflict transition and peace-building process after its second civil war within a decade. The latter conflict burgeoned in 2000, after several minor border incursions in 1999. It pitted the forces of Charles Taylor, elected president in 1997 after Liberia's first civil war (1989-1997), against two armed anti-Taylor rebel groups: Liberians United for Reconciliation and Democracy (LURD) and the Movement for Democracy in Liberia (MODEL). The war led to an extreme deterioration in political, economic, humanitarian, and human rights conditions. It also affected neighboring states, which accepted Liberian refugees and, in some cases, hosted anti-Taylor forces. The Taylor regime also sponsored or facilitated acts of armed aggression against its neighbors, Guinea, Sierra Leone, and Cote d'Ivoire.[13]

A peace accord was signed on August 18, 2003, after months of international mediation. It was facilitated by two events: Charles Taylor's resignation of the presidency and departure from Liberia on August 11, after he was granted political asylum in Nigeria; and the early August deployment of an Economic Community of West African States (ECOWAS) military intervention force, the ECOWAS Mission in Liberia (ECOMIL). ECOMIL, with extensive U.S. and U.N. assistance, deployed to Liberia to end heavy fighting and alleviate a worsening humanitarian crisis in the wake of a failed June 2003 cease-fire. It was tasked with monitoring and securing the cease-fire, enabling the delivery of relief aid, and preparing the way for the U.N. Mission in Liberia (UNMIL).

U.N. Mission in Liberia (UNMIL)

UNMIL, first authorized by the U.N. Security Council (UNSC) on September 19, 2003, deployed to Liberia on October 1, 2003, two weeks before the National Transitional Government of Liberia (NTGL) took office on October 14. ECOMIL was dissolved and its military forces absorbed into UNMIL, which carries out diverse peacekeeping, civilian policing, and socio-economic assistance functions in support of Liberia's transition process. UNMIL provides a military guard force for the Special Court for Sierra Leone, discussed below, for which it assumed responsibility from the U.N. Mission in Sierra Leone (UNAMSIL), upon UNMIL's termination in late 2005. U.S. funding for UNMIL is covered in **Table 3**, below.

Current Strength

UNMIL has a current authorized force strength of 14,875 military personnel and 1,240 police. As of late December 2009, it had a total force strength of 10,947, made up of individual police, 480 (14.8% female); formed police units, 844 (18.2% female); military observers, 118 (7.3% female); and contingent troops, 9,505 (2.6% female). As of late December 2009, U.S. personnel deployed with UNMIL included seven individual police; four military observers; and six contingent troops.

Drawdown

A gradual, phased drawdown of the UNMIL force, guided by progress in implementing a series of benchmarks set out by the Security Council and initiated by a UNSC decision to repatriate 1,000 troops in 2006, is continuing. The benchmarks were first proposed in by the U.N. Secretary- General (UNSG) in 2006 (S/2006/159, March 14, 2006), in response to a September 2005 Security Council request for an UNMIL force drawdown plan, to include specific benchmarks and a schedule for achieving that end. The UNSG found that it was "too early for a major drawdown of UNMIL." He called, instead, for a two-year "consolidation period" during which UNMIL would implement an "adjusted mandate" defined by an 11-point agenda of "priority tasks." These centered on achieving such objectives as maintenance of a stable and secure environment; completion of ex-combatant, refugees, and internally displaced persons reintegration; security sector reform; and consolidation of state authority and governance capacity.

Notwithstanding a need to complete these tasks, he proposed that "in the absence of an immediate armed threat within Liberia," the military component of UNMIL be reduced by one infantry battalion in mid-2006 and another infantry battalion in early 2007, and that a drawdown of the Mission, beginning in early 2007, security conditions permitting, ensue.

NOTE ON UNITED NATIONS DOCUMENTS AND USAGE IN THIS REPORT

For the sake of brevity, the full titles of U.N. documents, which are often accompanied by extensive sub-titles and meeting session data, are — with some exceptions — not employed in this report. Instead, the U.N. agency source of such documents is given, followed by the item's U.N. document symbol and date of release, except with respect to Security Council documents, for which only the document symbol and date are given. Security Council documents can readily be identified by their distinct document numbers, which always begin with the symbol "S/." In this report, these primarily include periodic reports on UNMIL by the U.N. Secretary- General, Security Council Resolutions, and statements by the President of the Security Council The *Tenth Progress Report of the Secretary-General on the United Nations Mission in Liberia*, with the U.N. document symbol S/2006/159, and dated March 14, 2006, for instance, would be cited as S/2006/159, March 14, 2006. The full text and title of all U.N. documents cited in this report can be found online using the U.N. document symbol search box of the U.N. Official Document System (ODS), httpi/documents.un.org.

By mid-March 2007, the United Nations was reporting significant progress in meeting key benchmarks, including with respect to police and military training, restructuring and reform; management of natural resources; and the creation of a national security strategy and architecture — though each of these activities faced often considerable challenges. Progress toward ex-combatant reintegration and the consolidation of state authority was slower than planned, however, largely due to resource constraints. Due to these and diverse other reconstruction and development challenges, and notwithstanding areas of progress, in March 2007 U.N. Secretary-General Ban Kimoon, citing what he called "limited progress made in meeting the benchmarks for the consolidation and drawdown of the Mission," recommended a year-long extension of the UNMIL's existing mandate. [14] Assessments of and adjustments to these and a range of subsequent benchmarks, along with two associated, phased UNMIL force repatriations, have since continued. [15]

On September 15, 2009, the Security Council passed Resolution 1885 (S/RES/1 885), authorizing a third-phase drawdown, to take place between October 2009 and May 2010. It involves the repatriation of 2,029 military personnel, three attack helicopters, and 72 armored personnel carriers. Upon completion of this process, UNMIL's force will include 8,202 military personnel (including 7,952 troops in Liberia and 250 at the Special Court for Sierra Leone), while the UNMIL police component will include about 1,344 personnel (465 police advisers, 843 officers in seven formed police units, 23 corrections officers and 13 immigration officers).[16]

LIBERIA AT A GLANCE[17]

Geography: Small tropical coastal West African country about the size of Virginia

Population: 3.4 (2009)

Ann. Population Growth Rate: 2.67% (2009)

Exchange Rate Adjusted Gross National Income (GNI) Total: $634.4 mill. (2008)

GNI Per Capita: $170 (2008)

External Debt: $1.7 bill., 2010

Key Exports: Rubber, timber, iron, cocoa, gold, coffee, diamonds.

Value: $254 mill., of which $225 mill. or 88.6% of rubber (2008, IMF); and $160 mill., of which $94 million, or 58.8% of rubber (2009 proj.)

Languages: English & 29 distinct local languages

Ethnic groups: 16 indigenous groups, 95%; and freed slave descendants from the Americas, 5%

Religions: Christian, 85.6; Muslim, 12.2; Traditional beliefs, 0.6; Other/no Religion, 1.7 (LC). Note: Many observers view Liberian adherents of world religions as often being heavily influenced by traditional beliefs.

Literacy: Women, 40.8%-46.3%; Men, 65.5%-70.3%

Infant and Under-5 Mortality rate, respectively: 93 and 132 deaths/1,000 live births (2007)

HIV/AIDS adult infection rate: 1.5% (2007)

Life Expectancy, years at birth: National average. 41.84 (ave.); Male, 40.71; Female, 43 (2009)

Resolution 1885 also reauthorized UNMIL's mandate through September 30, 2010 and ordered that the post-May 2010 UNMIL force size be maintained until the completion of presidential and legislative elections in late 2011, which it authorized UNMIL to assist in administering. It also permitted UNMIL to reinforce the U.N. Operation in Côte d'Ivoire (UNOCI) on a contingency basis, if needed during anticipated elections in Côte d'Ivoire — or vice versa, should the security situation in Liberia deteriorate. The resolution called the "conduct of free and fair, conflict- free elections... a core benchmark for UNMIL's future drawdown," among others, such as the further development of "national security and rule of law institutions that are fully independently operational." It also requested that UNMIL submit to the Security Council, in collaboration with the Liberian government, a strategic plan aimed at integrating and consolidating post-conflict peace-building, stability, and development efforts in Liberia. In the meantime, the Security Council remains cautious about the extent of Liberia's post-war evolution. In passing Resolution 1903 (December 17, 2009), which renews or alters a range of Liberia-related sanctions, the Security Council declared that "despite significant progress having been made in Liberia, the situation there continues to constitute a threat to international peace and security in the region."

Sexual Exploitation and Abuse

UNMIL has implemented measures to prevent, detect, investigate, and punish acts of sexual exploitation and abuse (SEA), in line with recent reforms and renewed U.N.-wide regulations regarding sexual conduct, following abuses in several U.N. peacekeeping missions around the world, including in Liberia. U.N. Resolution 1626 (2005) bars SEA, and UNMIL has created a mission conduct and discipline team and investigatory capacity to ensure adherence to these rules. [18] In mid-March 2006, five crew members of a UN contractor, who had been under investigation for alleged rapes and the assault of Liberian police officers, left Liberia after being released on bond. According to UNMIL, their departure was "highly regretted and the matter is being brought to the attention of the authorities of the country concerned."[19] There were reportedly 12 alleged SEA incidents reported between January 1, 2009 and August 31, 2009, and six such allegations in the period between August 10, 2009 and February 1, 2010.[20]

Transition Process

The August 30, 2007 Comprehensive Peace Agreement (CPA), signed by the three warring factions and 18 political parties, laid out a peace process, provided for the creation of the National Transitional Government of Liberia (NTGL), and allocated leadership positions within it.[21] The NTGL was mandated to reestablish functioning government authority and prepare for national elections that were held in mid-October and November 2005. The elected government of President Sirleaf replaced the NTGL in late January 2006, as described below. The NTGL consisted of an executive branch, presided over by a Chairman, Gyude Bryant, and an interim parliament, the National Transitional Legislative Assembly. Bryant, a businessman and church layman who led the Liberian Action Party, oversaw the functions of the central government and various public corporations, agencies, and commissions. Bryant was given the title of NTGL "chairman" to differentiate his unelected NTGL role and authority from that of a constitutionally elected president. The transition faced many challenges, most related to the extremely destructive effects of many years of war in Liberia. Others included the dominant role within the NTGL of the three former armed factions, which were prone to internal rivalries; political discord over the allocation of state positions and resources; very limited state capacities; and reported public sector corruption.

2005 Post-War Elections

Peaceful Senate, House of Representatives, and presidential elections were held on October 11, 2005, and a presidential runoff vote was held on November 8. The 22-candidate presidential poll led to a runoff race. It pitted George Manneh “Oppong” Weah, 39 years of age, a former professional top soccer player whose star status and rags-to-riches history make him a hero to Liberian youth, against Ellen Johnson Sirleaf, then 67 years of age, a Harvard-trained economist and former businesswoman who had served as Liberian finance minister and as a United Nations and World Bank official. On November 15, 2005, the National Elections Commission (NEC) declared Sirleaf the winner of the presidential race, with 5 9.4% of votes against Weah’s 40.6%, making her the first-ever female president of an African country. Despite its declaration in favor of Sirleaf, the NEC subsequently probed and later rejected claims by Weah that the election was fraudulent. A presidential election will next to be held in 2011.

In contrast to the presidential race, election results for seats in the bicameral legislature were disparate; no party received more than 24% of seats in either chamber, and none dominated in both the Senate and the House of Representatives. The largest party in the 64-member House, in which members serve 6-year terms, is Weah's Congress for Democratic Change (CDC), which won 15 seats. The Liberty Party (LP) won nine House seats, while Sirleaf's Unity Party (UP) and the Coalition for Transformation of Liberia (COTOL) each won eight. Seven other parties each won between one and five House seats, and seven independent candidates each won a seat. In the 30-seat Senate, in which members normally serve nine-year terms,[22] COTOL won seven seats and the UP won four; all other parties won between one and three seats.[23] Political party mergers in 2009 and 2010, discussed below, have changed the allocation of seats among parties.

Notable among the newly elected legislators were several former Taylor regime officials and leaders of former armed factions or security services. These include senators Jewel Howard- Taylor, a former wife of Charles Taylor (NPP; Bong County); Prince Yormie Johnson (independent, Bong County); and Saye-Taayor Adolphus Dolo (COTOL, Nimba County). Johnson is the former leader of a faction that splintered from Taylor's early in the first civil war, and is infamous for personally presiding over the bloody, videotaped murder of former head of state Samuel Doe. He returned to run in the election from exile in Nigeria, where he had professed to have become a born-again Christian evangelist. Dolo is a former pro-Taylor militia leader, known by the nom de guerre General Peanut Butter, who reportedly committed war-time atrocities and recruited child fighters, and who is said to have aggressively opposed UNMIL peacekeeping activities. In the House, they include Edwin Snowe (independent, Montserrado County); Saah Richard Gbollie (NPP, Margibi County); and Kai G. "White Flower B-50" Farley, (CDC, Grand Gedeh County). Snowe, who was elected speaker of the House in mid-January 2006 but has since stepped down,[24] is a former Taylor in-law. He is also the former head of the Liberian Petroleum and Refining Corporation (LPRC), from which Taylor regime officials reportedly diverted significant amounts of funds, some of which may have benefitted Taylor during his exile in Nigeria.[25] Gbollie is a former Taylor fighter and Taylor administration police official accused of human rights abuses. Farley is an ex-MODEL commander and NTGL official accused of threatening the 2003 peace accord. Jewel Taylor, Dolo, Snowe, and Farley are subject to U.N. travel sanctions.

Table 1. 2005 Election: Legislative Results by Party (Seats and percentage of vote won)

Party	Senate		House	
	Seats[a]	Vote (%)	Seats[a]	Vote (%)
Congress for Democratic Change (CDC)	3	10	15	23.4
Coalition for Transformation of Liberia (COTOL)	7	23.3	8	12.5
Liberty Party (LP)	3	10	9	14.1
Unity Party (UP)	4	13.3	8	12.5
Independent	3	10	7	10.9
Alliance for Peace and Democracy (APD)	3	10	5	7.8
National Patriotic Party (NPP)	3	10	4	6.3
All Liberia Coalition Party (ALCOP)	1	3.3	2	3.1
Nation Democratic Party of Liberia (NDPL)	2	6.7	1	1.6
New Deal Movement (NDM)	-	-	3	4.7
National Reformation Party (NRP)	1	3.3	1	1.6
United Democratic Alliance (UDA)	-	-	1	1.6

Source: National Elections Commission of Liberia, 2005 Election Results, available online at http://www.necliberia.org/results.

a. This data reflects the 2005 electoral results. Political party mergers in 2009 and 2010, discussed below, have since changed the allocation of seats among parties.

Conduct of Elections[26]

With some mostly minor exceptions, the election was reportedly well-administered. About 1.35 million citizens registered to vote in April and May 2005, in a process that was marred by some minor acts and threats of violence and localized disruptions but was generally peaceful. Attempts by some NTGL ministers to try to run for office in the 2005 election, in violation of the CPA, also sparked controversy. About 1.012 million registered voters (74.9%) participated in the October 11 Senate, House of Representatives, and presidential elections, and over 821,000 (60.7%) voted in the November 8 presidential runoff poll. Results from voter registrations at 2,000 sites guided decision making about the composition of constituencies, the placement of about 2,900 polling places, and the distribution of voter education and polling materials. The large number of presidential candidates (over 50 initially, of whom 22 were ultimately registered) and registered political parties (30) reportedly proved confusing for some voters. Key election issues included national reconciliation and unity, corruption, jobs, general economic growth, and social services and physical infrastructure needs. Polling on both elections dates was peaceful.[27]

U.N. Mission in Liberia (UNMIL) elections staff and U.N. agencies provided extensive support to the NEC and other relevant agencies involved in such activities as media outreach and civic education, technical elections tasks, and electoral security coordination, as called for under the CPA. UNMIL aid for the elections reportedly totaled about $8 million, and the European Union pledged $1 million. Most of $10 million in U.S. elections assistance supported the programs of the nonprofit democracy strengthening organizations International Foundation for Electoral Systems (IFES), elections technical assistance; National Democratic Institute (NDI), civic education); and International Republican Institute (IRI), political party training. IRI and NDI, the latter jointly with the Carter Center, deployed teams to monitor the elections, as did the African and European Unions, the U.S. and many other governments, and international organizations.[28] The vote was monitored by at least 29 international organizations or governmental entities (369 individuals), as well as 52 civil society groups (over 3,500 individuals) and a roughly equal number of party observers; and 246 local journalists.

2005 Election Dispute

Weah, who had claimed to have been cheated in the first round, contested his loss in the second round and called for a re-run of the vote. He pursued his claim though a number of formal channels, but after the NEC dismissed his claim, after meeting with Sirleaf, and under heavy international pressure, in late December 2005 he agreed to drop his claim and accept the poll results. Many observers doubted that systematic or large-scale fraud had marred the election. U.S. officials viewed the process as having been orderly, largely well-administered, and free and fair, and such views were shared by most other governments and international entities that observed the vote. The United States nevertheless called for a probe of Weah's claims and for any contest of results to be carried out peacefully and through established legal channels.

Subsequent Elections[29]

In late 2009, a by-election — the fifth to be conducted after the 2005 election— was held to fill a vacancy for the Montserrado County Senate seat created by an incumbent's death. None of ten participating candidates, five independents and five from political parties, won the 51% of votes necessary to win the election outright. This outcome triggered a run-off election between the top two vote winners, a candidate from President Sirleaf's Unity Party and one from the Congress for Democratic Change (CDC), the largest opposition party. The CDC candidate emerged as the victor during the run-off, garnering 56% of votes cast against 46% for the UP candidate. Although the election reportedly featured a low voter turn-out (20% during the first round and 22.4% during the run-off), nearly half of Liberia's electorate was eligible to participate in it, given that Montserrado is the urban county surrounding Monrovia, where about half of Liberia's population lives. As a result, the election was viewed as a dry-run of the ability National Elections Commission (NEC) to conduct a large election ahead of national elections in 2011.

According to IFES, an electoral capacity-building non-governmental organization that is working with the NEC, the "process was seen as void of fraud and recognized as free, fair and transparent." IFES also reported that conduct of the "first round saw some logistical and operational challenges," but "the second round was vastly improved," and the NEC's performance was widely lauded by local election stakeholders and international observers. IFES is providing technical and financial support to the NEC under a five-year U.S. Agency for International Development (USAID)-supported project called *Building Sustainable Election Management in Liberia*. IFES supported the Montserrado by-election by providing the NEC with election administration materials and technical assistance. [30]

Sirleaf Government

Policy Agenda

President Sirleaf took office on January 16, 2006 and shortly thereafter nominated a cabinet seen as dominated by technocrats, professionals, and former opposition or policy activists. In her inaugural address, she laid out a detailed governance agenda, and launched her tenure with a series of actions to counter corruption. Sirleaf highlighted what she pledged would be "a new era of democracy" defined by political inclusion and toleration, non-violence, and safeguarding and promotion of constitutional and civil liberties and rights. She stressed the need for national reconciliation as an "urgent" and "compelling" task facing her administration. During the first 150 days of her tenure, in coordination with donors, her government also pursued diverse rapid impact projects aimed at showing "quick and visible progress." These were grouped under four (initially five) "major pillars": Security; Economic Revitalization; Basic Services and Infrastructure; and Good Governance. The same pillars continue to define her administration's medium to long term development efforts. These are spearheaded by an entity called the Liberia Reconstruction and Development Committee (LRDC), which is composed of four working committees, each of which supports a separate "pillar."

Economic Renewal

Sirleaf is pursuing an economic agenda emphasizing the creation of an investment-friendly climate; the exploitation of Liberia's rich natural resources; land tenure reform focused on increasing agricultural production; job creation, notably for youths; and expanded economic and social infrastructure rehabilitation, particularly in historically economically marginalized areas. The Sirleaf administration has consistently emphasized the importance of laying the groundwork for sustained economic growth and job creation. The latter is viewed as key by many observers, both because formal sector unemployment rates are reportedly as high because unemployment is a potential source of instability.[31] The economic and educational disenfranchisement of Liberia's large youth population is viewed as having fueled Liberia's armed conflicts, and joblessness is a continuing source of popular dissatisfaction. In mid-2007, the United Nations reported that the majority of ex-combatants remained unemployed and that thousands had regrouped in order to illegally exploit diamonds, gold, and plantation-grown rubber.

Governance

Sirleaf has vowed to take forceful action against corruption, including by requiring all key officials to declare their assets and follow a national code of conduct. She strongly endorsed and promised to "enforce" the Governance and Economic Management Program (GEMAP, discussed below) to deal with "serious economic and financial management deficiencies" and pursue an "integrated capacity building initiative." She also vowed to overhaul the "seriously bloated" the civil service, while noting that civil servant pay was poor and in arrears.[32] She promised to institutionalize a meritocratic, performance-based civil service system.

Foreign Policy

Sirleaf declared economic private sector-focused regional integration and security cooperation to be her guiding foreign policy goal. She vowed to maintain strong international bilateral and multilateral partnerships. Notably, given recent regional history, she stated that "no inch of Liberian soil will be used to conspire to perpetrate aggression" against neighboring countries.[33] Her government has also shown itself to be open to new foreign ties. Liberia now has diplomatic relations with Cuba and it established bilateral relations with China in late 2003, after the departure from power of President Taylor, who had maintained relations with Taiwan.[34]

Women

Paying homage to what she said were the special efforts of women in securing her election and the peace that made it possible—even in the face of war-related "inhumanity," "terror," military conscription, forced labor, and rape—Sirleaf vowed in her inaugural address to "empower Liberian women in all areas." She pledged to strengthen laws and law enforcement to protect women against rape, support the education of children, notably of girls, and to provide programs to enable women to play a key role in the economic revitalization process.[35] Sirleaf has nominated women to head multiple key ministries and public agencies.

Corruption

Upon taking office, Sirleaf announced an audit of the previous transitional government and dismissed all transitional government political appointees. She also laid off the entire staff of the Finance Ministry, pending a screening of employees' qualifications and level of probity. In February 2006, she revoked all existing timber concession contracts, which had been widely criticized for being let in a corrupt fashion and for being executed in an environmentally unsustainable manner. This action provided the basis, in part, for the U.N. Security Council's June 2006 lifting of a ban on Liberian timber exports. Sirleaf later initiated reviews of other contracts and concession deals granted by the transitional government. In early June 2006, she fired three sub-cabinet level officials and several mid-level civil servants accused of corruption. Her administration has also publicly released audit reports of several state agencies.

Performance

In mid-April 2006, in a document entitled *150 Day Action Plan: A Working Document for a New Liberia*, the Sirleaf administration laid out a detailed status report on short-term, quick impact policy and project implementation efforts and achievements to date.[36] The document, which was aimed both at increasing government transparency and proving her administration's adherence to Sirleaf's campaign and inaugural pledges, demonstrated that most of her plans were being implemented in a timely manner. The Executive Mansion, the equivalent of the U.S. White House, also releases similar documents pertaining to ongoing LRDC activities. Sirleaf has faced challenges in meeting high voter expectations, for instance, in relation to her election promise to provide public electricity in Monrovia within six months of being elected, despite the complexity and great cost of that an undertaking. Many voters appeared to have given the new government a honeymoon period, although expectations remained high following what many saw as disappointing performance by the transitional government. The public remains eager to see rapid job growth and rapid improvements in social services and the construction of physical infrastructure, particularly in support of education, healthcare, and transportation.

In various public comments, Sirleaf has assured Liberians that her government is successfully continuing to build the groundwork for sustained growth, but has counseled Liberians to be patient, since many ongoing investments in infrastructure, basic services capacity building and foreign investment business projects will take time to generate jobs and incomes. Several road building projects are currently underway and the government is examining options for large-scale electricity generation and long-distance power transmission. Despite the fact such projects, which are largely donor-financed, may not generate general economic growth for some time, Liberia's economy is growing rapidly. In December 2007, the Economist Intelligence Unit (EIU) reported estimates and projections showing a sharp jump in Liberia's gross domestic product, from 5.3% in 2005, to 7.8% in 2006, to 8.5% in 2007, with rates of 9.5% and 11% projected for 2008 and 2009, respectively.[37] In March 2008, Liberia is expected to publish a Poverty Reduction Strategy Paper (PRSP), which expected to guide economic policy and provide the basis an agreement with the International Monetary Fund (IMF) for a credit and technical assistance program for 2008-10, as well as ongoing cooperation with the World Bank. Liberia is also in the process of awarding offshore oil exploration contracts.

President Sirleaf has also been an active participant in African Union activities, sometimes taking stances at odds with other African leaders — e.g., overtly criticizing the June 2008 elections in Zimbabwe as "not credible" and urging the AU to "declare the results unacceptable" — as well as those of ECOWAS and the Mano River Union (MRU).[38] She has been particularly been involved in efforts to strengthen the MRU and in efforts to resolve the political crisis in neighboring Guinea.[39]

Sirleaf Administration: Criticisms and Challenges

The general public largely gave Sirleaf a political honeymoon in her first years in office, but she has since been the target of some criticism, both of a routine political nature by opposition parties (including Taylor supporters upset by his SCSL trial) and by some human rights and transparency policy advocates. Although many Liberians and international human rights advocates have praised Sirleaf's strongly stated support for such rights and the rule of law, some criticized her nomination of Kabineh Janneh as a Supreme Court Justice, who was later confirmed in the post.[40] Her administration had also been criticized for not creating an Independent National Commission for Human Rights (INCHR), an institution called for under the 2003 peace agreement. In June 2009, however, the president ratified an amended act passed by the legislature in May 2009, and in mid-August 2009 forwarded to the Senate seven INCHR nominees. Criticism has since shifted to the Senate for failing to confirm the nominees.[41]

In 2006, there were several reports of assaults or harassment of journalists by members of the Special Security Service (SSS), a Liberian executive branch security agency, and by regular police. In response, the Press Union of Liberia (PUL) threatened to launch a "news black-out" of coverage of the government. President Sirleaf reportedly responded to the allegations by stating that "those who violate the rights of the Liberian people or journalists for that matter will be dealt with and punished appropriately" and that her "government will not tolerate violation of the rights of people, including journalists."[42] Information Minister Johnny McClain also met with the PUL and reemphasized that the Sirleaf administration "is committed to press freedom and that there is a standing policy of respect and cordiality toward the press."[43] The international press rights advocacy organization Committee to Protect Journalists (CPJ) stated in an open letter to President Sirleaf that it was "troubled" by the alleged attacks on the press and that "despite an Information

Ministry statement [...] affirming the government's commitment to press freedom, there has been no evidence of an investigation into these incidents nor any public effort to punish those responsible." The CPJ also stated in an open letter to President Sirleaf that

> While there is no evidence that these incidents are the result of government policy, your administration has a responsibility to restrain security forces from attacking or harassing journalists who are trying to do their jobs. As an organization of journalists dedicated to defending the rights of our colleagues worldwide, CPJ respectfully urges you to make good on your pledges to uphold press freedom by ensuring a prompt and transparent investigation into these cases.[44]

Some critics have alleged that the Sirleaf government, like its predecessors, is corrupt, but the Sirleaf Administration rejects such accusations, citing its record of anti-corruption actions.[45] Given the historically embedded presence of public sector corruption in Liberia, the government' approach to addressing the problem combines a continuing series of law enforcement actions, institutional reforms, and education and training programs. It may, however, face difficulties in prosecuting indictments, given the limited capacity of Liberia. Another challenge is to ensure that it pursues enforcement actions in a professional and apolitical manner, as recent Liberian history has been marked by the use of corruption prosecutions as a tool for achieving political retribution.

The Liberian government under the Sirleaf Administration has recorded a number of successes in fighting corruption, but it remains a key, abiding challenge. In late August 2008, President Sirleaf signed into law a bill establishing a Liberia Anti-Corruption Commission (LACC). In September 2008, she appointed as its chair Frances Johnson Morris, a former minister of Justice and Commerce and the former head of the National Elections Commission, and a Sirleaf relative.[46] Her Administration has also highlighted apparent progress in fighting corruption, for instance by citing the country's rapid positive progress as measured by the World Bank Institute's *Worldwide Governance Indicators*.[47] The government as also strongly supported the Governance and Economic Management Assistance Program (GEMAP) and the Liberia Extractive Industries Transparency Initiative (LEITI), both discussed below. A government Public Procurement and Concessions Commission (PPCC) is also pursuing a range of efforts to ensure transparency and accountability in government purchases and contracts.

Despite such efforts, some Sirleaf Administration officials have periodically been accused of corruption. In September 2008, President Sirleaf appointed a special seven-member independent corruption commission, the so-called Dunn Commission, named after its chair, Dr. D. Elwood Dunn. It was charged with investigating allegations that certain current and former Sirleaf Administration officials had received contract renewal bribes from the U.S. head of the Liberian International Ship Corporate Registry (LISCR) aimed at preventing a competitive bid for the work, as well as allegations of other corrupt actions, in several cases associated with former Acting State and Presidential Affairs Minister, Willis Knuckles. The Administration also faced allegations that it had attempted to cover up the issue by bribing journalists not to report the story.[48] The Commission, which hired the James Mintz Group as an expert technical investigator, issued a public report of its findings in January 2009.[49]

There have also been a series of other cases of apparent actual or alleged corruption involving top officials, in many cases uncovered by investigations by the independent General Auditing Commission (GAC). Led by Auditor-General, John Morlu, who has publicly criticized the Sirleaf Administration's record on corruption, the GAC has released reports indicating several million dollars worth of unaccounted spending within the Health, Education, Mines and Finance ministries.[50] Prominent cases involving key officials, among others, include:

- the suspension in October 2009, resignation in January 2010, and current prosecution of the former information minister, Lawrence Bropleh, over allegations of his involvement in a "ghost worker" fund diversion scheme;
- a procurement irregularities case that led to the February 2010 resignation of the then-internal affairs minister, Ambulai Johnson, Sirleaf's brother, and questions over the origins of his personal assets;
- the September 2009 dismissal of Harry Greaves, a former Sirleaf advisor, as managing director of the Liberian Petroleum Refinery Corporation (LPRC) over a case involving Greaves' alleged involvement in the allocation of a contract to a firm in exchange for compensation more than double as large as the estimated value of the contract by another bidder, and allegations of bribery pertaining to an ensuing investigation of the contract award;
- the resignation in 2009 or removal of serving ministers, including Agriculture Minister Christopher Toe, Public Works Minister Luseni

Donzo, and Justice Minister Philip Banks, in cases involving alleged fiscal mismanagement, administrative irregularities, or other matters, and there have been allegations of mismanagement and possible corruption regarding the administration of county development funds, of which, as a result, the presidency has taken control.[51]

SECURITY ISSUES

Security Conditions

Liberia's security situation has improved markedly since August 2003. It is currently "generally stable, but fragile," and is subject to periodic volatility and localized instability.[52] Public security and police authority are formally entrusted to the Liberia National Police (LNP), who are advised and supported by UNMIL civilian police (CIVPOL). LNP patrols in the capital reportedly increased in the latter half of 2009, leading to a marked decrease in armed robbery, but rates some other serious crimes, including rape, notably of juvenile females, have remained high.[53]

Despite increasing LNP capacity, the LNP continues to face serious challenges, and the public often perceives public security as being guaranteed by UNMIL CIVPOL, who earlier during UNMIL's deployment played more direct roles in ensuring that end. The LNP is reportedly making progress in building up its capabilities, but reportedly remains beset by operational deficits and absenteeism, has a limited presence and mobility in many rural areas, and some LNP members reportedly engage in acts of bribery. In addition, the capacity of the judicial sector remains limited, and public confidence in the judicial system is low; according to the State Department, the "Liberian public views the police and other formal justice institutions with fear, skepticism, and mistrust."[54] There have also been clashes between police, other security agency units, and Armed Forces of Liberia (AFL) and. Some AFL members have reportedly violently assaulted or robbed civilians. As a result of public mistrust in the capabilities and of the LNP, other security agencies, and the judicial sector, vigilantism and periodic mob violence present continuing problems.[55]

A key post-war source of instability in Liberia, former fighters associated with various armed factions, was largely neutralized in the year after the August 2003 peace agreement was signed. More than 101,000 ex-combatants

(22% women and 10.8% children), were demobilized under a disarmament program administered by UNMIL and the NTGL that ended in late 2004. Some demobilized fighters remain a periodic source of sometimes violent protest, mostly related to the status of generalized joblessness among ex-combatants and the demands of those who are owed reintegration job training and subsistence assistance. A small minority of ex-combatants have reportedly turned to crime, including armed robbery and the illegal exploitation of natural resources.[56]

Public protests relating to severance and pension payments by former members of the Liberian military and members of security services not included in demobilization programs have generally subsided. Other public security threats include a wave of armed robbery in Monrovia, which the government is attempting to suppress, and periodic civil unrest related to socioeconomic grievances, predominantly involving students, workers, civil servants, and jobless youth. Price increases for rice, fuel, and cement are also sources of public dissatisfaction. In her annual address to the legislature in January 2008, Sirleaf stated that she would temporarily suspend a $2 tax on bags of rice, the Liberian staple food, pending consideration of a legislative tax reform proposal. Periodically, ritual-related killings by so-called "heartmen" provoke public safety fears and sometimes mob violence against alleged perpetrators.[57]

Community-level property dispute conflicts have repeatedly occurred throughout Liberia, but notably in Nimba County in northern Liberia between members of the Gio/Mano and Mandingo ethnic groups. Contested claims over home and land occupancy and ownership rights are often at the center of such disputes, which sometimes take on ethnic dimensions. Such disputes often have origins in property occupations and appropriations that occurred as a result of war-time population displacements and movements. Lack of land rights documentation, property fraud, often involving state officials, and the absence of effective dispute resolution mechanisms have aggravated such problems. A Presidential Commission created to probe such disputes in Nimba County recommended that a process of community reconciliation and dispute resolution be pursued, and President Sirleaf ordered that contested properties in Nimba be returned to their legal owners. In addition, an act creating a national Land Commission charged with pursuing reforms in land tenure and ownership policy, laws, and administration, in part to resolve and prevent land conflicts, was signed into law in August 2009. The Commission, which was formed in late 2009 and became operational in early 2010, has a five-year mandate. It is receiving capacity-building assistance from the U.N. Human Settlements Program (UN-HABITAT).[58]

Political parties who lost in Liberia's elections and the attendant realignment of Liberian political forces remain a potential source of instability or violent acts. The family of a witness in the SCSL trial of former president Charles Taylor (see "Taylor Trial" below), for instance, was reportedly targeted with death threats in early 2008. Prior to his capture, U.N. and U.S. officials and many Members of Congress had been concerned about persistent, credible reports that Taylor had periodically interfered in Liberian affairs from exile in Nigeria through a network of political, military, and business associates, which Taylor denied. These alleged actions were seen as destabilizing and threatening to the consolidation of peace (see section on Taylor below). There had been some speculation that former Taylor administration officials would make large gains in the 2005 elections and that he would be able to use them as proxies to influence the new government. There was no such general outcome, but several close Taylor associates were elected (see "2005 Post-War Elections," above). In July 2007, George Koukou, the transitional government house speaker, Charles Julu, a top military officer under former president Samuel Doe who was accused of wartime human rights abuses, and several associates were arrested and charged with treason for allegedly plotting the ouster of the Sirleaf government. They were acquitted, however, in May 2008.

Liberia remains under U.N. sanctions, which were first imposed to counter the Taylor regime's alleged regional destabilization efforts and other activities counter to international law and U.N. policy goals. Under the current sanctions, individuals associated with the Taylor regime's activities remain subject to a U.N. travel ban and, in some cases, asset freezes.[59] Liberia also remains subject to a partial arms embargo.[60] Bans on the export of Liberian timber and diamonds have been lifted. The threat to Liberia from instability in neighboring Côte d'Ivoire, which posed a significant external threat to the stability of Liberia and to sub-regional security for several years, according to United Nations reports, waned after the signing of a political accord in that country.[61] Widespread violent general strikes in neighboring Guinea in early 2007 and political instability in Guinea in 2009, following a coup d'état in late 2008 after the death of then- President Lansana Conté, was also viewed as potential external threat to Liberia. The appointment of a new transitional government in Guinea following the signing of an early 2010 accord, however, appears to have substantially lessened any threat to Liberia.[62]

Although there have been currently no specific publicly reported personal security threats against President Sirleaf, the United States provided her with a personal State Department Diplomatic Security team at the start of her tenure and supported training efforts for the Special Security Service, Liberia's presidential and VIP protection service; see below. An electrical fire in the Executive Mansion in July 2006 during a visit by neighboring heads of state highlighted Liberia's general lack of emergency services. Firefighters from UNMIL, the Firestone rubber company, and the international airport, the latter two based about 45 minutes out of the capital, were called in to fight the blaze, since National Fire Service largely lacks the capacity to respond to fires in the capital. That lack of capacity was again illustrated in August 2006, when the U.S. Navy's *Apache*, an ocean tug boat, helped to extinguish a fire on a commercial freighter in the Port of Monrovia, and later rescued a fishing crew at sea. The Apache crew was in Monrovia to conduct repairs on the city's main commercial pier and survey the harbor. Following the *Apache*'s departure from Liberia, marine safety experts from the International Maritime Organization (IMO) undertook an assessment of Liberia's search and rescue capabilities.[63]

Rubber Sector Reform

Rubber has traditionally been a key source of state export revenues and employment in Liberia. The presence, however, of ex-combatants on several rubber plantations, some armed, undermined the industry's post-war redevelopment. In the years after the 2003 peace agreement, rubber workers and local residents near plantations reported that former fighters robbed them and coerced them into selling rubber latex at sub-market prices, in the process earning revenues that were reportedly not taxed.[64] Ex-combatant control of plantations also reportedly resulted in unsustainable harvesting practices, various human rights abuses, and environmental degradation.

To address this situation, in 2006 the government and armed UNMIL troops took possession of Gutherie, a major rubber tree plantation in western Liberia, from former LURD ex-combatants who had squatted on it, tapping rubber and in some cases controlling local rubber sales. Gutherie was reportedly the site of forced child labor and diverse violent crimes against persons. The repossession was one of the objectives of a joint government-U.N. task force created to make the rubber industry transparent, environmentally sound and sustainable, subject to state governance and regulation, and a source of legal jobs — including for the ex-combatants from whom control of Gutherie was seized. UNMIL plans called for a similar seizure of another key ex-combatantoccupied rubber plantation in the southeast county of Sinoe, though ex-combatants at the plantation reportedly met with local officials and agreed to vacate the site peacefully.[65] In May 2006, the UNMIL Human Rights and Protection Section (HRPS) studied Liberia's rubber sector and published a series of key findings and recommendations pertaining to the sector.[66] Issues that it examined included human rights concerns pertaining to the industry; post-conflict business practices and corruption; the status of and role of commercial rubber concession and management agreements; worker, child, and community rights; implications of plantation agriculture and sectoral industrial practices for the environment; and the rule of law within the rubber sector, including issues relating to ex-combatant occupation of plantations.

While the normal peacetime functioning of the rubber sector has largely resumed and the sector has been brought under state regulatory control, in February 2010 UNMIL reported that

> The situation in and around Liberia's rubber plantations continued to be of concern. Labour disputes, including over salary and severance payments, prompted demonstrations at the Guthrie and Cavalla plantations, with the conflict over control of rubber at Sinoe Plantation continuing to be a major security concern.[67]

In addition, in November 2009 the president and general manager of a large-scale rubber plantation and rubber processing firm, who also served as the chairman of Liberia's national Public Procurement and Concession Commission was murdered, "allegedly by disgruntled workers" near the firm's work site. [68]

Security Sector Reform

New Military Created

With U.S. assistance, Liberia has created a new military made up of approximately 2,000 initial recruits.[69] The force is commanded, on an interim basis, by officers from other countries in West Africa, including Nigeria, Ghana, and Benin.[70] The recruit pool was drawn from across Liberia and includes members from diverse ethnic groups to ensure ethno-regional balance. A goal that 20% of the total force be female was not met; less than 5% of the force is female.[71] Selection of volunteer enlistees, for purposes of screening out human rights abusers, began in early 2006, and less than 20% of applicants were accepted. Prospective recruits underwent a vetting process administered by U.S. contractors that included reviews of selectees' records by personnel from the U.S. embassy, UNMIL, and other donor governments, and Liberian civil society and government representatives.[72] As of late January 2009, recruiting of 2,057 personnel had been completed, and basic training for all elements was completed in late 2009.[73] As of mid-August 2008, 45 recruits had been commissioned as officers. [74] Despite having received commissions and training, in mid-2008, UNMIL officials viewed the "command effectiveness" of the officer corps as limited and in need of further development. Military restructuring was initially hindered by a need to demobilize and verify the severance pay eligibility of over 13,000 irregular forces and Armed Forces of Liberia (AFL) soldiers. Funds for this purpose were initially scarce, but all irregular and regular forces were demobilized.[75]

U.S. assistance for these post-war military security sector reform (SSR) activities was administered by the State Department and carried out primarily by the defense services contractors DynCorp International and Pacific Architects and Engineers (PAE). DynCorp was charged with helping to vet, recruit, and provide basic training and equipment for the new force. It also refurbished and provided operations and maintenance services for two AFL bases, Camp Sandee Ware (formerly known as VOA Camp) and Barclay Training Center (BTC), and provided O&M for the two bases.[76] PAE provided construction services and specialty training, equipment, logistics, and base services.

State Department expenditures for U.S. assistance for military SSR and the training of the reconstituted post-war AFL are estimated at $240.56 million through the end of FY 2009, when the bulk of new AFL training had been completed. Part of this funding supported base reconstruction and operations and maintenance. Additional funding for these and related purposes may be provided in FY 2010 and FY 2011, respectively; $5.2. million had been obligated as of early FY 2010 (see below). FMF and IMET Defense Security Cooperation Agency (DSCA)- administered assistance programs for Liberia, which are not formally a component of U.S. military reform/restructuring assistance programs, have bolstered and complemented these efforts.

U.S. assistance for military restructuring was also accompanied by efforts to help Liberia build the capacity of its Ministry of Defense (MOD) and establish a defense policy framework, although lapses in funding for this effort reportedly resulted in mixed results and a loss of capacity-building opportunities.[77] Two results of these efforts were the approval of a new

Liberian national security strategy in January 2008 and the passage in August 2008 of a new national defense act.

Defense Sector Reform and the AFL: Current Issues and Challenges

In early 2010, U.S. assistance for defense sector reform, which is in general facilitated by the existence of a U.S.-Liberia military cooperation agreement, entered a new phase.[78] Initial training of the founding units of the new AFL ended in December 2009, by when the force had achieved operational status and undergone an Army Readiness Training Evaluation Program (ARTEP). The Liberian MOD assumed full formal control of the newly trained force in early 2010.[79] U.S. support to the new AFL has shifted from a program of contractor-based basic training and capacity building to one centering on military-to-military mentoring and advice, bolstered by some continuing assistance in support of AFL base operations and maintenance (O&M) and certain other functions. DynCorp International has been contracted to provide $5.2 million worth of support for electrical power generation, water supply, waste disposal, and vehicle maintenance at two AFL bases during the first half of 2010.[80] The Army Corps of Engineers also tentatively plans to fund the "design, construction, upgrade and revitalization of several arms storage and ammunition storage facilities" at AFL bases.[81] UNMIL troops are also pursuing joint training with specialized AFL units, e.g., engineering, military police, and signal and headquarters staff.[82]

The mentoring mission, supported with State Department Foreign Military Financing (FMF) funding under a program dubbed Defense Sector Reform (DSR) Phase I, began in early 2010 and is slated to run for five years. It is being undertaken by a Marine-led team of approximately 60 U.S. Africa Command military personnel drawn predominantly from the Marines but also incorporating members of other services. Their collective deployment and activities are known as Operation Onward Liberty. Activities under the DSR program are vetted and authorized by the U.S. Ambassador to Liberia, Linda Thomas-Greenfield, although day-to-day work is undertaken by the designated AFRICOM officer in charge (a Marine Forces Africa [MARFOAF] officer), who reports to AFRICOM and the Ambassador via the embassy-based DoD Office of Security Cooperation (OSC). The objective of Operation Onward Liberty is to help the Liberian government "build a professional military that is apolitical, subordinate to civilian leadership, and respectful of human rights."[83] Team members will advise AFL units at various command levels as they pursue continued locally-led training, particularly at the unit level. Such continuing training is viewed as a critical follow-up to previous basic training;

according to the UNSG, "it is assessed that the Armed Forces of Liberia will not be independently operational before 2012, given that the Force's officer corps needs significant additional experience before it is able to take command."[84]

The DSR program is to be complemented by a program of assistance by the Defense Department's Defense Institution Reform Initiative (DIRI) that is slated to focus on improving the capacity of the MOD and Liberia's defense policy structure.[85] The DIRI Liberia program is currently being formulated. An initial consultative DIRI team visit to Liberia (part of what DIRI terms its "Requirements Determination") took place in September 2009 and a follow-up program assessment and implementation visit (part of a DIRI "Program Development" process) followed in March 2010. The Liberian MOD has established a Liberian working group to collaborate with the U.S. DIRI team, which DIRI officials interpret as indicating "strong Liberian interest in, and ownership of, the project." A key initial area of planned activity is work to finalize National Defense Strategy (NDS), integrating inter-agency and AFL inputs, "that would empower the Ministry to effectively develop policy, budgets, and resource management plans, and manage logistics, personnel issues, and public relations." A further U.S. DIRI team was slated to take place in mid-April and at six-week intervals thereafter. A longer-term program roadmap, with associated benchmarks, will also be designed and implemented. These activities will be assessed every 12-18 months.[86]

While the United States is currently continuing to provide operations and maintenance support to the AFL, as defense sector capacity-building proceeds, the long-term success and sustainability of the effort will increasingly rely on the ability of the Liberian government to adequately manage and fund the new AFL. Funding, in particular, may pose a significant challenge, given Liberia's modest annual national budget.[87] Defense Minister Brownie Samukai, Jr., however, has asserted that the government intends to keep the defense budget at a 9% or less share of the overall national budget, suggesting that the government is taking measures to ensure that defense reform is both adequately funded and fiscally sustainable.[88] Competing development and reconstruction priorities in the long-term, however, may decrease the availability of resources for the defense sector, particularly if advocates of increased social welfare expenditures successfully argue that non-defense investments are more likely to produce larger and more productive, tangible benefits for a larger number of Liberians than the defense sector.[89]

While some may contend that Liberia can ill afford to unilaterally fund a national military, the need for continued AFL and MOD professionalization is widely viewed as crucial, for multiple reasons. Prominent among these is a core national defense rationale: Liberia lies within a subregion that has experienced substantial political instability and cross-border armed conflict in recent decades, and must be able to defend its territorial integrity. Such investments are also seen as being necessitated by a need to prevent a recurrence of the politically destabilizing role that Liberia's military and state security forces have played in the past. Training and constitutionally- based military institution-building are seen as necessary in order to ensure that the new AFL does not intervene in civilian politics or engage in other extra-legal activities.

While there are no indications that the new AFL — which is explicitly designed to function as an apolitical, professional force — is a likely to reprise such a destabilizing role, there have been occasional problems of AFL absenteeism, rank and file protests about living conditions, and some reports of indiscipline among some AFL members, in some cases of a violent or criminal nature, or involving intoxicants.[90] While the scope of such phenomena have been limited to date and do not threaten state stability, the contemporary history of civil-military relations in the West Africa suggests that, if not addressed, they may have the potential to develop into more serious threats. Military absenteeism and indiscipline, both within Liberia and in the surrounding sub-region, have historically underpinned negative outcomes ranging from military ineffectiveness to abuse of civilians by diverse military units, and military protests over pay and living conditions have spurred state instability and played a causative role in several coups d'état and putsches. It is notable that, as of early 2010, while U.S. defense equipment has been donated to the Liberian MOD, weapons and ammunition reportedly continued to be under U.S. control.[91]

Sector Reform: Challenges of Balancing Foreign Support for and National Ownership of Security

As described elsewhere in this report, the Liberian security sector reform (SSR) process has relied heavily on U.S. and other external assistance, which has often been provided through the use of foreign contractors. Adapted U.S. institutional models, norms, and policy objectives have also played an influential role in shaping the SSR process. In the view of a number of observers, such external inputs were essential because rapid military reform was widely seen as crucial to building long-term stability, and post-war Liberia largely lacked requisite financial, human, and other resource capacities. Similarly, the strong American role was seen as apropos because Liberia has long drawn from U.S. legal and institutional models in defining its state structure. The extensive foreign role in Liberia's SSR process, however, may also pose challenges for the long-term sustainability of the outcomes of the SSR process since, while historically U.S.-influenced, Liberia's state and society are the unique product of local history, ethno-social make-up and culture, and geographic scale, among other factors. As a result, to the extent that the institutions and processes that SSR produces were not initially organically or integrally defined by local cultural norms and socio-political authority, interests, and needs, over the long-term, these influences may reshape the resulting institutions, potentially in a manner at odds with their original formal purposes. Similarly, to the degree that their design did not incorporate adequate public input, their political legitimacy might be called into question.92 Furthermore, while many criticisms and problems associated with SSR in Liberia have been cited in the research literature, including lack of adequate participation by the broad public, sequencing of institution-building and associated law and policy-making, a number of researchers have also pointed out that substantial efforts were undertaken to ensure that the SSR process was shaped by Liberian interests and views. For instance, while some observers were concerned that a 2006 U.S.-funded report by the RAND Corporation was overly influential in shaping the design of national security structures, after it was released, the Liberian government facilitated a "participatory and democratic security reform process."93 This included a "widely consultative" national security review led by a Liberia's Governance Reform Commission (GRC).94 While not without its critics and problems, the review included input from a range of civil society and political actors, and reportedly critically informed a subsequent government-drafted national security strategy.95

Coast Guard[96]

In order to protect Liberia's 360 mile coast line and associated 200 nautical mile exclusive economic zone against periodic poaching by foreign trawlers, potential drug trafficking, human trafficking, piracy, and illicit maritime dumping, as well as the need for search and rescue capacities, Liberia is developing a coast guard. The effort is dependent, in large part, on the provision of U.S. training and technical assistance funded primarily with State Department Foreign Military Financing (FMF) funding through Defense

Security Cooperation Agency in collaboration with AFRICOM. The field program is coordinated and carried out by the U.S. Coast Guard (USCG), with some assistance from U.S. Navy elements.

In August 2008, in response to a 2007 request from the Liberian government and a subsequent request from AFRICOM, and in coordination with the U.S. embassy in Monrovia, a USCG team conducted an in-country technical needs assessment to identify Liberia's potential coast guard needs and capacities. It subsequently produced an assessment report and recommendations based on its findings, which it presented to the U.S. embassy in Monrovia and the Liberian Minister of Defense in early 2009. Following this presentation, the Ministry of Defense (MOD) identified a pool of Liberian Coast Guard (LCG) personnel composed of new AFL members who had already undergone background vetting and basic military training. In February 2009, a delegation of Liberian MOD and U.S. Embassy personnel visited USCG facilities in Washington and Virginia to discuss prospective LCG development plans and to make field visits to small-scale USCG stations viewed as comparable in size and function to future LCG stations.

The assessment report, which was comprehensive and included a number of core recommendations, was intended to function as a guideline for the creation of a more detailed LCG development plan.[97] It provided a discussion of common pitfalls often associated with nascent coast guard development efforts, and recommended, in the interest of program sustainability, that Liberia take a staged approach to developing and initiating LCG operations. It urged that Liberia fully construct and staff LCG primary headquarters facilities at Freeport, Monrovia's main port, prior to establishing additional LCG stations, and that the LCG carefully coordinate the timing of training, facilities and infrastructure preparation, and equipment acquisitions. A crucial overarching recommendation was that LCG development be guided by a full-time, well experienced advisor or advisory team. The Liberian government concurred with these recommendations and initiated development of a LCG with a mission to carry out scaled down versions of applicable USCG functions (e.g., law enforcement, fisheries protection, and search and rescue).

As a result of consultations between the Liberian government, AFRICOM, U.S. embassy personnel, and the USCG, an AFRICOM-funded USCG maritime/LCG advisor was deployed to Monrovia in September 2009.[98] LCG personnel, who number under 50 members, subsequently began basic maritime operations, law enforcement and engineering training provided by USCG Mobile Training Teams (MTT) in Liberia. Further MTT training is expected to continue for multiple years and may be periodically supplemented by U.S.

Navy training. A small cadre of selected LCG members, both officers and enlisted, are undergoing additional USCG technical and managerial training in the United States. An activation ceremony for the new LCG attended by President Sirleaf was held in February 2010.[99]

U.S. training efforts have been complemented by a U.S. Navy Construction Battalion (Sea Bee) team, which is building waterfront facilities (e.g., a boat ramp and a related pier) at Freeport.[100] The Liberian government has also rehabilitated or constructed a headquarters and barracks at Freeport. Two 25-foot Defender-class boats for use in harbor and near-coast operations are expected to be provided to the LCG by the United States in late 2010, along with approximately two years worth of associated equipment. The duration of U.S. assistance to the LCG will depend on LCG development progress, and has not been determined; informal projections, based on the record of similar U.S. assistance programs in Georgia and Haiti, however, suggest that the effort is likely to last at least five years.

National Guard State Partnership Program

Liberia was added to the National Guard State Partnership Program (SPP) in 2009, making it the eighth African SPP partner country out of 62 globally. Liberia has been twinned with the Michigan National Guard (NG).[101] The SPP pairs U.S. state National Guard contingents with foreign militaries in support of diverse civil-military and security cooperation partnership, training, and exercise activities, depending on mutual partner needs and capacities. [102] The program is designed "to concentrate a small component of the U.S. defense structure — a state's National Guard — on a single country or region in support of U.S. Government policies" in support of "the development of long term personal relationships and interagency coordination mechanisms that would not otherwise exist."[103]

The Michigan-Liberia SPP partnership program remains at a formative stage. The process leading to its creation began in May 2009, when after agreeing to a Liberian request for an SPP state partner, AFRICOM requested that the NG Bureau (NGB) recommend a state to fulfill the request. The NGB provisionally decided to make Liberia a SPP partner in August 2009, and Michigan was selected as Liberia's U.S. state SPP partner in October 2009.[104]

While a specific Michigan-Liberia SPP country engagement plan has yet to be finalized, it is anticipated that the partnership program would build on and complement existing AFRICOM and State Department/U.S. Embassy-Monrovia country plans. A next step in creating an SPP engagement plan, based on past SPP experience in other countries, is likely to include a

Michigan NG field visit to Liberia, during which Michigan NG would consult with U.S. embassy-based State and DoD officials and Liberian MOD officials. Based on provisional findings and planning, a Michigan Bilateral Affairs Officer (BAO) would then be assigned through AFRICOM to the embassy's DoD Office of Security Cooperation (OSC). The BAO would act as a key liaison and consultant in further formulating a SPP engagement plan. Reciprocal senior leadership country consultative visits between the Michigan NG and Liberian MOD would then occur, and a partnership plan would be finalized.[105]

Other Defense Cooperation

The Liberian government has voiced support for the new U.S. Africa Command, and offered to host it in the region, although most observers see this as unlikely, given the poor state of Liberian infrastructure and limited state capacity and resources.[106]

Liberia has received multiple U.S. Africa Partnership Station (APS) ship visits, most recently in the fall of 2009. Missions have included Liberian Coast Guard Assistance (see above), U.S. Marine training for the AFL, humanitarian and development material and medical services donations, and cultural programming.[107] A U.S. Navy-led effort, the APS program conducts ship visits to ports in the region during which a variety of training, capacity-building, humanitarian, and cultural activities are undertaken. The APS program, housed on U.S. navy ships, is designed to function as a "maritime university" housing diverse training and assistance resources.[108] It integrates personnel from other U.S. armed services, civilian agencies, and non-governmental organizations to provide diverse types of maritime safety and security training, as well as humanitarian and development assistance.[109]

Liberia is the signatory of a ship boarding agreement with the United States under the Proliferation Security Initiative, a U.S. effort to prevent trafficking of weapons of mass destruction and related materiel "to and from states and non-state actors of proliferation concern."[110]

Police and Justice Sector Assistance

The United Nations reports that police reform and restructuring efforts have made significant progress but that significant challenges remain. As of mid-August 2008, 3,661 Liberian National Police (LNP) officers, of which 9% were female, had been trained as part of an effort to complete recruitment and training of an initial target of 3,500 police officers by July 2007. While a full complement of LNP officers has been trained, the United Nations has reported that LNP operational capacity remains weak. LNP deployment to the field, particularly up-country, is limited and has faced constraints, such as lack of basic infrastructure and police equipment, including vehicles, fuel, and communication gear, for which the LNP is largely dependent on donor support.[111] In recent years, the United Nations has also reported that there are high rates of LNP absenteeism and other disciplinary problems, such as corrupt practices involving judicial and law enforcement officials, and that LNP leadership and specialized skills are limited. In part due to limited police and broad justice sector operational weaknesses, incidents of mob violence and vigilante justice remain common.[112] The "practical import" of such weaknesses, the UNSG reported in mid-2008,

> is that the United Nations police advisers and formed police units are daily called upon to support the Liberian National Police in mounting operations critical to the maintenance of law and order and to sustain the emerging peace and stability in Liberia.[113]

While the challenges facing the LNP remain substantial, diverse efforts to address them are being pursued, including the development of a Professional Standards Division to effectively investigate complaints of LNP misconduct and efforts to prevent absenteeism by vetting LNP payroll records and the duty status of officers. In mid-2008, the LNP, in collaboration with U.N. partner agencies, held a workshop to examine the long-term strategic development of the LNP, including with regard to professional standards, logistics and maintenance systems, human resource development, and effective management.[114] In mid-2009 and again in September 2009, the LNP presented to donor government a strategic plan and 18 proposed capacity building projects estimated to jointly cost $18 million. Little donor support had been provided to fund the plans as of early 2010, but in 2009 the UNDP established a Liberia Justice and Security Trust Fund, and some donors are reportedly interested in funding police needs though it or on a bilateral basis.[115]

Due to previous U.N. Security Council arms embargos, the LNP is unarmed, with the exception of a Police Support Unit (PSU) and an Emergency Response Unit (ERU).[116] The PSU, originally slated to include 600 personnel, currently has a force size of 200. It is intended to provide armed backing for regular LNP officers and respond to situations of public disorder. The ERU is designed to provide mobile capacity to respond rapidly and robustly to critical threats to internal security or public safety, particularly in anticipation of the eventual departure of UNMIL from Liberia. The ERU has a current strength of 287, with an additional 47 staff expected to join the force after completing training in March 2010. Originally envisioned as a 500-person force, in response to the current level of tactical demands on the unit, it will not be further expanded in the short-term. While the ERU has been a key recipient of foreign capacity building assistance, its long term sustainability and effectiveness may be curtailed by resource constraints and lack of equipment and vehicles necessary to reach remote parts of Liberia, notably after the eventual termination of UNMIL. Due to very poor road conditions in many parts of Liberia, the unit is heavily "dependent on UNMIL air assets to deploy quickly, particularly during the rainy season."[117]

The United States is continuing to provide the LNP and its ERU with training assistance through UNMIL, as it has for several years, primarily through U.S. civilian police (CIVPOL) seconded to UNMIL, who provide training, mentorship, and advice. The U.S. police training contingent, the size and focus of which has varied from year to year, has typically consisted of 10 to 20 U.S. CIVPOL officers, as well as equipment and contractor-based logistical support, in addition to other police capacity-building support.[118] This aid, which is administered by the State Department's International Narcotics and Law Enforcement Affairs Bureau (INL), is aimed at developing the LNP "into a credible and competent police service that respects human rights and the rule of law" and "bolstering the operational and administrative capacity of the LNP," which the United States views as "a critical precursor" to eventual draw-down of UNMIL. Improved police-community relations and human rights abuse prevention are keystones of this training. A another component of INL support is the deployment of a U.S. police Senior Advisory Team (SAT), which works with UNMIL "to help the LNP leadership improve and establish personnel policies, internal affairs, logistics, payroll, discipline, promotion, and civilian oversight" both through the provision of technical advice and through leadership mentoring. In FY 2010, the Obama Administration plans to deploy additional ERU advisors to provide field training and mentoring program for the ERU; provide training and equipping for the PSU; and provide nonlethal equipment and support police infrastructure improvements.[119]

U.S. and UNMIL assistance efforts also support the rehabilitation of the judicial and penal systems. U.S. efforts are provided under the INL-administered Justice Sector Support Liberia (JSSL) project, as well as by USAID-funded rule of law programs. The general aims of the JSSL program are to improve the administration of justice and bolster adherence to the rule of law generally and respect for human rights. The JSSL deploys justice sector legal and technical advisors, provides training, professional mentoring, and equipment, and helps develop and strengthen justice sector effectiveness and infrastructure. The program focuses on the judicial system broadly, including the Ministry of Justice, the corrections system, and other rule of law organizations. It has helped create Liberia's first ever public defender program, train prosecutors, renovate the main judicial building in Monrovia, create a case-numbering system slated to be scaled up nationally, and enhance LNP-prosecutor linkages, as well as providing some vehicles and equipment in support of such functions. Current efforts seek to expand capacities outside of Monrovia.[120]

Special Security Service

The Special Security Service (SSS), which provides executive branch and VIP close protection services, is undergoing a process of restructuring and professionalization. It was a roughly 1,252- member presidential protection unit that functioned under the NTGL and the Taylor government. Under Taylor, the SSS—which was run by Benjamin Yeaten, a former Taylor militia commander who is currently being sought by the Sirleaf government for alleged treasonous activities—gained a reputation for brutality. The SSS has continued to have a sometimes troubled reputation. Some members of the leadership that initially served under the Sirleaf Administration were viewed by informed observers as unprofessional and corrupt. Multiple acts of arbitrary violence committed by SSS officers have been reported.

As part of the restructuring process, a substantial number of SSS members were decommissioned; on May 1, 2006, UNMIL announced that 841 SSS members had accepted U.S. and UK-funded buyout packages and been deactivated in April. There are press reports, however, that allege that some decommissioned SSS officers had not received their severance packages, and there have been protests associated with such claims. Some protesting claimants, however, are reportedly ineligible to receive severance payments.

The restructuring process, which seeks to correct reported leadership weaknesses and professionalize all aspects of SSS organization and operations, is being undertaken with the assistance of the State Department's Diplomatic Security Service (DSS). Using a mix of Nonproliferation, Antiterrorism, Demining and Related Projects (NADR) and other foreign assistance funds, DSS directly provided close protection services for President Sirleaf during the first few months of her tenure, while about 100 SSS agents underwent specialized DSS close protection training in Liberia and in the United States.

About 300 SSS agents received basic close protection support and perimeter training in Liberia. About 600 SSS officers have also reportedly received general UNMIL police training.[121]

HUMANITARIAN CONDITIONS

Humanitarian conditions are much improved from the context of severe and widespread post-war need that was prevalent in the years after the war, but high rates of poverty remains endemic. Liberia continues to receive substantial international food aid and is highly donor-dependent. International assistance is, however, increasingly supporting resettlement and socio-economic recovery, rather than emergency humanitarian needs. According to a U.N. High Commissioner for Refugees (UNHCR) briefing note, about 200,000 Liberian refugees had repatriated by mid- February 2006. By late April 2006, over 321,000 Liberian internally displaced persons (IDPs), including over 59,000 families, had returned to their places of origin or resettled. Most had received resettlement assistance, usually consisting of basic non-food items, transport aid, and two months of food supplies. U.N. agencies, together with non-governmental organizations (NGOs) and NTGL ministries have implemented a wide range of reconstruction and capacity building projects relating to nutrition, water and sanitation, primary health care services, and transport infrastructure. Numerous schools have reopened nationwide, with extensive assistance from UNICEF.

Nearly all child ex-combatants were reportedly been reintegrated into their communities of origin, and many received follow-up aid in the form of social services. In mid-March 2006, the U.N. Secretary-General reported (S/2006/159, March 14, 2006, *op. cit.)* that 65,000 of 101,495 demobilized ex-combatants had benefitted from donor-financed reintegration and rehabilitation projects, and that about 37,000 were still waiting to be placed in such programs. The Secretary- General reported that although funding was available for most of these ex-combatants, about $5 million was “urgently needed” to provide such assistance to some 5,125 ex-fighters.

Health Issues

Liberia faces substantial public health challenges. Malaria is endemic, water-born stomach illnesses are common, tuberculosis cases often go uncured, and there are periodic outbreaks of diseases like Yellow Fever, measles, and cholera, but Liberia lacks an adequate health infrastructure for combating such illnesses.[122] Medical supplies and trained staff are in chronic short supply. A number of donor-backed initiatives help improve health care capacity, however. UNICEF is aiding the reopening of health clinics nationwide, and a UNICEF/WHO polio vaccination campaign that began in October 2004 has reached some 1.2 million children. WHO coordinates a U.N./government/NGO/USAID technical group that is working to improve the national health system, notably regarding HIV/AIDS, malaria and tuberculosis (see below). WHO and FAO are also helping the government to create an avian flu surveillance and response plan.

AIDS

The threat of HIV/AIDS in Liberia is gaining increasing attention, though recent survey information indicates that HIV prevalence rates are lower than had been commonly assumed previously. A 2007 demographic and health survey showed that the national adult HIV infection rate was 1.5%, and indicated that infection rates varied from 2.5% in urban areas to 0.8% in rural ones, with the highest prevalence rate, 2.6%, in and around Monrovia.[123] Previous estimates of infection rates, albeit not based on national surveys, had ranged between 5.9% and 8.2%, with some observers positing that the rate could be as high as 12% in some population sub-groups.[124] The UNMIL HIV/AIDS Adviser's Office is supporting public education-related AIDS prevention and national planning efforts focused on care of orphans and vulnerable children, among other activities. The World Health Organization, in coordination with other U.N. agencies and the NTGL, is developing project proposals to fight AIDS, malaria, tuberculosis and build health system capacity. The U.N. Population Fund supports several AIDS awareness and prevention programs. Liberia receives Global Fund assistance, but its application for further assistance under the Fund's recent Round 5 funding project assessment process was reportedly rejected.[125]

USAID implements several AIDS-related programs in Liberia on behalf of the Office of the U.S. Global AIDS Coordinator (OGAC). These include the

2007 demographic health survey, in partnership with other donors, which includes HIV surveillance; targeted behavior change efforts focusing on youth and other groups; and support for home-based care and related assistance. In her inaugural speech, in which she cited a 12% HIV infection rate, President Sirleaf vowed to "tackle this national scourge." At a February 2006 House International Relations Committee hearing on Liberia (see below), Members suggested to then-USAID Assistant Administrator for the Bureau for Africa Lloyd O. Pierson that Liberia be considered for U.S. assistance under the Presidents Emergency Plan for AIDS Relief in South Africa (PEPFAR). Liberia has received about $.7 million a year in Global HIV/AIDS Initiative (GHAI) account funds in recent years.

GOVERNANCE: BACKGROUND

Liberia's supreme law is its 1984 constitution, effective since 1986. It provides for a political and legal system that is substantially modeled on that of the United States, though not entirely; for instance, federalism is absent. Liberia's government is made up of three branches that exercise separate powers and authorities: a bicameral legislature, which consists of a 64-member House and a 30-member Senate; a presidentially led executive branch that controls multiple line ministries and several independent agencies; and a judiciary. Legislators are directly elected by voters in each of Liberia's 15 counties, while the president is directly elected by universal suffrage. The President and House Members are each elected to six-year terms, and Senators serve nine-year terms, except in cases of irregular vacancies of elected positions. Presidents may serve up to two terms. Although the Sirleaf government's mandate is derived from the constitution, that of the NTGL was extra-constitutional. During its tenure, those provisions of the Constitution and laws of Liberia that were inconsistent with the provisions of the 2003 Comprehensive Peace Agreement were suspended, though all other provisions of the constitution remained in force.

Although Liberia's constitution provides for a system of checks and balances among the three branches of government, in practice the executive branch has historically exerted extensive influence over the legislature, the judiciary, and local governments. Historically, Liberian presidents have wielded exceptional, sometimes extra-constitutional powers and closely controlled the legal system, the security forces, and the economy, as well as headed majority ruling parties. Liberia has also long suffered from the effects of public sector corruption and a tradition of political patronage. This often resulted in uneven, urban-centered socio-economic development and often deprived large segments of the population, notably the rural indigenous majority, of access to public goods and services.

Given this history, President Sirleaf could have attempted to aggregate predominant power in her office, but doing so would have run counter to her emphasis on building national unity, constitutional and institutionally robust governance, fighting corruption, and institutionally developing the state. Her emphasis on developing state institutions and processes, rather than exerting presidential command authority may mean that she is both less likely and less able to rule in the largely unilateral manner of her predecessors. However, she also came to power with a weaker electoral mandate than those of past presidents; neither Sirleaf's Unity Party nor any other party commands a legislative majority. Similarly, no candidate was able to command majority support in the initial 22-candidate presidential first round presidential vote.

The relative strength of opposition parties in the parliament initially led some observers to hypothesize that Liberia's legislators might bridge their party differences and cooperate in furtherance of their collective institutional power vis-à-vis the executive branch, and take on a more engaged and assertive role in policy-making than has been traditional. To date, however, President Sirleaf has often been able to dominate the national policy agenda. This is attributable, in part, to a tradition of strong executive leadership; limited capacity within the legislature; the limited legislative experience of many current legislators; the fractionalized party make-up of the legislature; and to the governing experience of Sirleaf and many in her cabinet. Most bills continue to be originated by the executive branch and passed with presidential priorities intact. A notable exception to this pattern was the legislature's September 2007 rejection of the asset seizures bill targeting former president Taylor and his associates.

Transitional Government

A key impetus for the Sirleaf administration's policy emphasis on anti-corruption initiatives was the mixed governance record of its predecessor, the NTGL. The NTGL was able to successfully carry out most of the basic functions assigned to it under the August 2003 peace accord, but its efforts to restore state authority and the rehabilitate state institutions were hampered by central government ministry inefficiencies, widespread resource constraints, and lack of institutional and financial system capacities and trained manpower. Despite such challenges, it did make significant progress during the last half of its tenure. During this time, many revenue, customs, immigration, and local officials were deployed to sites outside Monrovia. Regional Central Bank offices were also opened, permitting salary payments without recourse to time-consuming travel to Monrovia. The process of deploying government officials upcountry was supported by USAID, which has supported the rehabilitation of administrative buildings in several key counties.

Among the most challenging issues facing governance capacity-building efforts were persistent reports of corruption within the NTGL, in some cases on a large scale. Alleged acts were particularly notable in the context of import-export transactions, government contracts and budgeting, and the issuance of commodity marketing or land, natural resource, and associated concession rights.[126] The U.N. Secretary-General reported in mid-March 2005 that there was a "lack of [NTGL] transparency in the collection and use of revenues and the resistance of some government and public corporation officials to reforms and audits aimed at fighting corruption" (S/2005/177). The World Bank and bilateral donors made similar observations and called for transparency measures. National fiscal and budget obligation mechanisms and voucher record- keeping systems under the NTGL were chaotic and subject to manipulation by key officials in some cases.[127] In some government agency budgets, the miscellaneous expense budget account category "Other" was reportedly substantial in many cases, and expenditures of such "Other" funds were said to have been carried out in an ad hoc manner, with few controls. Actions by the transitional legislature either to appropriate for private use or pay very nominal lease fees for expensive vehicles that each legislator was given drew local and foreign condemnation. In November 2005, the U.S. Embassy in Monrovia stated that the U.S. government was

> shocked and disappointed by the recent incidents of transfers of Liberian Government property and resources into private ownership. This drains vital government resources that could otherwise be used for critical developmental programs, and sends the wrong signal to international donors who finance such programs. It also perpetuates the culture of abuse of public trust and impunity that has contributed to two decades of decline in Liberia. The U.S. Embassy considers these transfers unscrupulous, irresponsible, and contrary to the public interest of the people of Liberia. Liberian government resources are for the benefit of the Liberian people and should not be misappropriated for private use.[128]

Citing a 2004 presidential proclamation, it stated that Liberian government officials who engage in "violations of the public trust" and persons who abet such actions might, along with their families, be ineligible for U.S.-funded programs and services, including consideration for Diversity Visa, Immigrant Visa, and other visa services.[129]

Post-NTGL Corruption Trials

In January 2009, jury selection began in a corruption case involving the alleged embezzlement of Liberia Petroleum Refinery Company (LPRC) funds by former National Transitional Government of Liberia (NTGL) Chairman Gyude Bryant and four former LPRC executives from the NTGL period.[130] Bryant is separately being tried on charges of economic sabotage relating to the alleged embezzlement of $1.3 million during his tenure as chairman. The charges stem from a Sirleaf administration investigation that began in January 2007 in the wake of an Economic Community of West African States (ECOWAS) audit probe of the NTGL. Bryant pled innocent to the charges, which were laid against him in February 2007 and carry a possible 10-year prison sentence. At trial in April 2007, Bryant unsuccessfully claimed constitutionally derived sovereign immunity from prosecution on the basis that he was a serving head of state at the time his alleged crimes took place. In August 2007, Liberia's Supreme Court approved his trial, ruling that he was not eligible for immunity because the NTGL, over which Bryant presided, was a product of the extra- Constitutional August 2003 peace accord that authorized creation of the NTGL. Other NTGL officials, such as former Finance Minister Lusinee Kamara, have also faced corruption charges linked to their NTGL duties. The charges against Kamara were spurred by the findings of the ECOWAS audit. Court proceedings in all of these cases have often been slow and protracted.

Concession Deals

Natural resource and land concession contract deals drew attention during the NTGL's tenure because of their financial significance and potential long-term effects on national development. U.N. experts and donor governments questioned the propriety of a March 2005 monopsony diamond concession deal with a previously unknown firm, which was later canceled. Some observers also questioned the NTGL's award of offshore oil exploration permits to three relatively small firms just prior to elections.

The NTGL also signed two major long-term natural resource concession deals. One, with the Firestone group of companies, extends and amends a previous series of concession agreements, first signed in 1926, giving Firestone rights to large plantation areas for the cultivation of rubber.[131] The contract was amended, in part, because Firestone contended that it was unable to exploit its holdings due to fighting over the last decade and a half, and in order to boost foreign investment in Liberia. The deal gave the Firestone group surface rental and other rights to nearly 200 square miles of active or proposed rubber plantation land for 36 years in exchange for $.50 per acre per year and various investments, tax payments, social and infrastructure development outputs, and various other commitments. It was extendable for an additional 50 years after renegotiation. Another deal, with Netherlands-based Mittal Steel Holdings, provided for the rehabilitation or construction of diverse mining, administrative support, processing, and transport infrastructure intended to support the extraction and shipment of iron ore from northern Liberia. It gave Mittal a variety of surface rental, mineral license, iron ore extraction, transport infrastructure construction, and other rights in exchange for diverse capital investments, totaling about $900 million, and royalty, lump sum, tax, and other payments to the government. The initial term of 25 years was extendable for an additional 25-year term, if certain criteria were met.

Both deals drew criticism from some civil society groups that contended that the NTGL lacked a legal mandate to negotiate long-term concessions, that such functions could only be carried out by a duly elected government, and that such deals should be negotiated in a manner more favorable to Liberian economic and other national interests.[132] The contracts were also politically controversial. The Mittal deal was the subject of rival bids by the large mining firms Global Infrastructural Holdings Limited (GIHL), BHP Billington and Rio Tinto, and its ratification was contested legally and in parliament. Some civil society critics have alleged that the deals were not undertaken in a transparent manner.[133] Mittal denied that charge and maintained that the contract was won in a "transparent and competitive bid process" and will bring significant foreign investment and infrastructure development to Liberia.[134] The former U.S. Ambassador to Liberia, John Blaney, reportedly pushed for a deal that would require that a major railroad that was to be rehabilitated as part of any proposed iron ore investment arrangement would be made into a multi-use railroad, regardless of what firm was awarded mining rights.[135]

The Firestone contract has also drawn attention for other reasons. Some Firestone plantation workers have complained about poor working conditions and high production quotas. Some environmental advocacy groups and residents living near Firestone rubber processing facilities have alleged that chemicals used in latex processing are polluting wells and the water and aquatic life of the Farmington River, and damaging these resources or preventing their use by local residents.[136] A Firestone spokesperson has denied that "effluent—the by-product that comes out into the water from our operations" pollutes the Farmington River. A Firestone spokesperson reportedly stated that Firestone "consistently" samples water from the Farmington River, is in compliance with relevant Liberian environmental laws, and has developed multiple safe drinking wells areas in its plantation concession area.[137]

The Firestone group is the subject of a class action suit brought in California by the International Labor Rights Fund, an advocacy organization that says its goal is to counter child, forced, and other abusive labor practices internationally, including through litigation. The suit alleges that Firestone employs children, practices forced labor, involuntary servitude, and negligent employment practices. Firestone categorically denies these charges, describing the suit as "outrageous" and "completely without merit." It maintains that its operations comply fully with Liberian laws and asserts that its workers are all adults of legal working age, are union- represented, are paid well above prevailing wages, and are provided with social services, and that Firestone is bringing much needed investment to Liberia.[138]

In June 2007, a U.S. District Court (Indianapolis Division, Southern District of Indiana) judge granted Firestone's motion to dismiss 11 of 12 counts in the case, but denied the motion with regard to one count, a child labor claim made under international law and the Alien Tort Statute (ATS).[139]

In late April 2007, Firestone production was decreased as a result of a labor strike that reportedly concerned worker benefits, rivalry over leadership control of the union, and issues related to talks on a collective bargaining agreement.[140] In late 2007, the Liberian Supreme Court reportedly ratified the election of a new Firestone workers union. Labor activists had long contended that the previous Firestone union, whose leadership had launched a court case to prevent the new union from being legally recognized, was a company-controlled entity. Firestone reportedly refused to recognize the new union prior to its legitimation in court.

New Contracts

Upon taking office, President Sirleaf vowed to review and renegotiate concession contracts signed by the NTGL to ensure that they were fair, provided Liberia with favorable terms, and did not cede national financial or other interests to foreign firms, or give such firms undue control over variables such as future prices or regulatory powers. A renegotiated contract with ArcelorMittal (the name of the firm after a 2006 merger) took effect in May 2007. In late 2007, the Liberian government announced that ArcelorMittal had agreed to increase its proposed investment in Liberia from $1 billion to $1.5 billion over ten years or so, and that the firm expects to ship the first consignment of ore in mid-2009. The government projects that the new contract will eventually generate as many as 20,000 jobs for Liberians.

The Liberian government has released a detailed summary comparing the old Mittal contract and the new one. [141] According to Global Witness, a non-governmental organization critic of the original Mittal contract, improvements in the revised contract include:

- Provisions requiring iron ore prices under the contract to be set by the ore market, in contrast to the first contract, which gave Mittal the right to set the price, "thereby giving it control of royalty rates and tax payable, and encouraging transfer pricing";
- A limited five-year tax holiday for Mittal, in comparison to an indefinitely extendable one;
- Liberian national control over two key public infrastructure assets, the port of Buchanan and the railway to Yekepa (a major iron ore mine site);
- The non-exemption of Mittal from future human rights or environmental laws passed by Liberia;
- Recognition of the Mittal parent company's responsibility for liabilities faced by its operating affiliate in Liberia; and
- Increased balance between the rights of existing property holders and Mittal regarding the latter's right to expropriate new concession land.[142]

Global Witness, however, continues to criticize what it asserts is the contract's "precedence over Liberian law on income tax, royalties and other payments due to government." It also views in a negative light a contractual confidentiality clause "which will make it very hard for Liberian citizens to monitor revenue flows from Mittal and ensure the government uses the money wisely to reduce poverty."[143] Such challenges may subject to change as a result of Liberia's joining of the Extractive Industries Transparency Initiative (EITI) in 2009; see below.

The re-negotiation of a new contract with Firestone was finished in early 2008, and the agreement is slated to be submitted to the legislature. According to President Sirleaf, the agreement:

> includes aggregate investment on the order of $130 million in replanting, and the establishment of a rubber wood processing plant. This model agreement subjects Firestone, for the first time in its eighty-two year history of operations, to the payment of taxes of general application; to a five year plan of providing better living conditions for workers and employees; and to limited land holdings.[144]

The Sirleaf government also plans to use the new Firestone contract as a model agreement in separate renegotiations of other rubber and palm oil plantation concession agreements.

NTGL Anti-Corruption Efforts

The NTGL took some steps to halt corrupt practices. It established a Task Force on Corruption and a Cash Management Committee and attempted to eliminate bribe-taking in relation to commodity imports, notably by better managing Monrovia's port, of which UNMIL took temporary control in late April 2005. In addition, the National Transitional Legislative Assembly (NTLA) created a committee to investigate allegations of administrative and financial irregularities by its leadership, which eventually led to the removal of key NTLA leaders. Some observers, however, saw the NTGL Task Force as lacking the capacity or political will to achieve significant results, and some Liberian officials resisted donor and ECOWAS-backed transparency and audit measures. An African Development Bank loan was reportedly not disbursed in 2005 because Liberia failed to provide required fiscal data, and an ECOWAS-sponsored auditing mission was opposed by Liberian auditors and certain government officials, who cited concern over a violation of Liberian sovereignty, despite the publicly-stated support of Chairman Bryant for the audit. In July 2005, Chairman Bryant suspended two officials over their alleged diversion of funds paid by the satellite communications firm Inmarsat to several Liberian state entities, and the NTGL suspended three Bureau of Maritime Affairs officials, including the Commissioner, and Liberia's International Maritime Organization representative for fraud.[145]

To help the NTGL tackle corruption, the United States sent several Treasury Department experts to advise the Liberian government in the areas of budget and tax policy, management, and administration and in central bank operations and fiscal policy and regulation. These U.S. experts have also assessed Liberia's financial enforcement (financial crime and corruption) capacity. A resident U.S. legal advisor and a temporary duty team of prosecution experts have been deployed to Liberia to assist in building Liberia's judicial capacity. Similar efforts have continued under the Sirleaf administration.

Concerns over transparency produced a sometimes halting and often highly conditional provision of pledged aid by donor governments and agencies to NTGL-led Liberia, as well as some reticence to offer new funding. This negatively affected the scale and pace of resettlement, reintegration, and socio-economic rehabilitation. Nonetheless, a network of national, international, U.N., and private development and relief organizations has made considerable progress in these areas. Most of them participate in an inter-sectoral, U.N.-coordinated initiative, the Results-Focused Transitional Framework (RFTF). An April 2005 NTGL/U.N./World Bank assessment of the RFTF found that it has been effective in "addressing short-term, stabilization priorities," but that medium- to long-term post-transition institutional and reconstruction development will require a more robust, coherent, and comprehensive strategy.

KEY GOVERNANCE ISSUES

Anti-Corruption Efforts under Sirleaf

Liberian-donor government relations have improved under President Sirleaf, in large part due to her strong support for anti-corruption and other economic governance efforts. In late January 2006, she announced a financial audit of the outgoing transitional government, which had repeatedly been accused of corruption. Sirleaf has also suggested that she may seek a review of other public contracts and concession deals granted by the NTGL.[146] The Liberian government is also working to reform its key export-earning forestry and diamond sectors.

Forestry Sector

In early February 2006, Sirleaf adopted the recommendations of the Liberian Forest Concession Review Committee, an entity comprised of Liberian civil society, government agency, UNMIL, and donor government representatives. It reviewed the legality and propriety of logging concession contracts and recommended diverse logging sector reforms. Sirleaf's action effectively canceled all existing logging concessions and created a Forestry Reform Monitoring Committee (FRMC) to regulate future concession contracts. The natural resources and human rights policy advocacy group Global Witness, which has tracked abuses and corruption in Liberia's forestry sector for several years, praised the move. It called, however, for "greater support" by UNMIL "to the Forestry Development Authority ... to ensure that it is able to operate in a secure environment" as a prerequisite to the removal of then-current U.N. timber sanctions on Liberia. [147] UNMIL, along with a consortium of donor governments and specialized agencies known collectively as the Liberia Forest Initiative (LFI), is assisting the Liberian government to implement timber reforms.[148]

The FRMC is tasked with carrying out its functions by applying or establishing the following:

- land-use planning principles;
- a timber production and export chain-of-custody tracking system;
- a market value-based tax system timber tax system defined by "equitable sharing of the benefits with local communities;"
- revised contract requirements;
- transparent forest concession allocation procedures, based on Liberia's Public Procurement and Concession Act of 2005, which allows the suspension of participants who abet civil disturbances or default on their financial obligations— a key aim in light of alleged patterns of abuse under the Taylor administration;
- a regulatory and law enforcement regime to counter financial and tax fraud, human rights abuses, economic sabotage, and violations of labor and other laws relating to the misuse and mismanagement of forest resources; and
- an environmental impact assessment process.

It was also given the tasks of advising on the implementation of GEMAP goals (see below) as they pertain to the Liberian Forestry Development Authority; ensuring the full and transparent participation of communities and civil society in forest management, conducting a full review of the forestry laws and regulations; and recommending legislation to implement forestry reforms.[149]

Sirleaf's cancellation of prior logging concessions and creation of the FRMC were seen as key steps prompting the U.N. Security Council to pass Resolution 1689 on June 20, 2006, which lifted the ban on Liberian timber exports first imposed under Security Council Resolution 1521 (2003). In passing Resolution 1689, the Security Council cited the Sirleaf administration's "commitment to transparent management of the country's forestry resources for the benefit of Liberians and its reforms in the timber sector." It warned, however, that it would reinstate the timber ban if the government does not adopt FRMC-proposed forestry reform legislation. Global Witness opposed the Security Council's lifting of sanctions, contending that the Liberian government lacks full control over forest lands and has not yet adequately reformed the forestry sector.[150] Some other experts have expressed concerns that echo those of Global Witness. [151] The U.S. Treasury's Office of Foreign Assets Control is reportedly currently preparing updated regulations to allow the import of Liberian timber into the United States.

In early October 2006, President Sirleaf signed into law the National Forestry Reform Law of 2006, passed by the legislature in mid-September 2006 in one of its first major legislative actions. In doing so, she fulfilled the U.N. Security Council's criteria for lifting its ban on exports of Liberia timber. Among other measures, the new law divided Liberia's forest lands into three categories: protected areas, areas where community logging and wood processing can be pursued, and commercial logging concession areas. It also requires that logging firms publicly disclose their revenues and that 30% of commercial timber concession lease revenues be used to fund education, healthcare, and other basic community social services. The law reportedly does not, however, clearly define how revenues for such services are to be divided among beneficiaries, which may make decision making processes pertaining to that end politically controversial. Liberia's Forestry Development Authority has formulated a timber concession bidding process, based on the new forestry law, which was initially implemented in early 2007. Environmental activists are monitoring this process to ensure that it meets the forestry management, conservation, and other goals of the new law.[152]

Liberia's forests are the home to diverse species of flora and fauna, some rare or endangered. According to U.N. research findings, in 2000, Liberia's forests "constitute[d] approximately 45% of the remaining Upper Guinea Forest, which spans 10 West African States from Guinea to Cameroon" and were "variously assessed as [occupying] between 31.3% and 50% of the total territory of Liberia." Estimates of the contribution of timber exports to Liberia's foreign exchange earnings vary. They declined after the imposition of sanctions on such exports in 2003, but U.N. research findings indicate that for 2002, such earnings totaled "at least $146 million" and could have been as high as "$180 to 200 million."[153] Although precise data on the value of pre-war timber revenues vary, such revenues are generally thought to have comprised as much as half of all export earnings.

Depending on such factors as price, rates of cutting, and relative use of sustainable forestry practices, future export levels could vary widely from those estimated for 2002, when forestry concessions were administered by the Taylor regime and harvested by commercial interests with allegedly close links to the Taylor administration. The Taylor regime was accused of allowing the use of unsustainable forestry practices and illicitly diverting earnings from the timber sector. It also allegedly used some timber firms' transport and trade activities as cover for arms trafficking and turned the security forces of some firms into pro-government militias.[154]

Diamonds

On May 4, Liberia was admitted into the Kimberley Process[155] following the U.N. Security Council's passage on April 27, 2007, of Resolution 1753, which lifted an export ban on Liberian diamonds imposed by the Council in late 2003 (Resolution 1521).[156] In passing Resolution 1753, the Council also announced its intention to review Liberia's admission to and general compliance with the Kimberley Process.[157] In May 2007, ten diamond screening and evaluation offices were opened across Liberia, and in July began to offer mining, selling and broker licenses. The first post-embargo diamond exports began in September 2007.

In order to meet Kimberley Process certification criteria, the Liberian government had suspended the issuance of diamond mining licenses, all of which expired at the end of December 2005, making diamond mining effectively illegal in Liberia pending its accession to the Kimberley Process. As part of its efforts to implement the Kimberley Process, the government now has a diamond office in Monrovia and several regional diamond certification offices. Liberia's Kimberley Process-related capacity building and a technical training effort have been substantially aided by the United States. In addition to constructing the Government Diamond Office and providing it with gemology equipment and office furnishings, U.S. assistance in this area has included the following:

- Training of Liberian diamond evaluators in South Africa (three staff) and Dubai (two staff);
- Training of Ministry of Lands, Mines, and Energy staff to manage ten regional offices and related material and salary assistance, including vehicles, to support the establishment and future functioning of these posts throughout Liberia;
- Salary support for five diamond evaluators;
- Provision of specialized technical training to multiple ministry staff in the areas of Stream Sediment Studies, database applications, and GIS and remote imagery;
- Production of a comprehensive geological assessment of Liberia's diamond production capacity, and digitization and reproduction of geological maps of Liberia;
- Provision of software and hardware components of a database for tracking diamond production and Kimberley Process admission and program compliance; and
- Production of 1,000 Kimberley Process rough diamond export certificates.[158]

Much of this assistance was provided under a $1.44 million FY2005 ESF funding tranche under a U.S. Geological Survey-implemented contract with the Constella Futures International, a social development technical assistance firm. The U.S. Treasury's Office of Foreign Assets Control is reportedly currently preparing updated regulations to allow the import of Liberian rough diamonds into the United States.

Diamond deposits in Liberia are mostly alluvial, that is, found on or near the surface after having been deposited by water flows, often far from their point of origin. In January 2006, however, the firm Diamond Fields International (DFI) Ltd. announced that it had discovered strong indications of a kimberlite, or pipes of igneous, volcanic, often diamond-bearing material, in Grand Cape County.[159] If the kimberlite is verified as being richly diamondiferous, Liberia's future production of diamonds could rise substantially, potentially to the level of neighboring Sierra Leone.

GEMAP

The Sirleaf Administration strongly supports the Governance and Economic Management Assistance Program (GEMAP), an agreement signed in September 2005 by the NTGL and the International Contact Group on Liberia (ICGL), an international policy coordinating group of donor and regional governments and multinational institutions.[160] The aims of GEMAP are to secure Liberia's revenue base; improve budgeting, expenditure management, procurement practices, and concession grant-making; establish mechanisms to control corruption; build the capacity of government agencies involved in financial management and economic governance reform, e.g., the General Auditing Commission (GAC,) General Services Agency (GSA), Governance Reform Commission (GRC), and Public Procurement and Concessions Commission (PPCC) will be strengthened through international assistance, as well as the ability of line agency activities in these areas. GEMAP also supports public accountability-focused access to government information by journalists, civil society, and citizens.

A key component of GEMAP was the provision of contract-based management of the revenue and expenditure flows of key public sector entities, notably the main port, airport, and fuel refining firm, among others, in order to strictly enforce central government controls over state revenues and to improve public fiscal capacities.[161] Under this component of the program, international financial comptrollers with co-signing authority regarding key fiscal management mechanisms, assumed duties at the Central Bank of Liberia and other key ministries, notably the Ministry of Finance, the Ministry of Lands, Mines, and Energy and the Bureau of Budget, and as well as key revenue-earning agencies, including ports, airports, customs offices, and the forestry sector.[162] A key GEMAP benchmark was met in September 2009, when GEMAP's international comptrollers relinquished co-signatory authority to their government counterparts in those agencies that had not previously "graduated" from GEMAP, i.e., met their goals under the program.[163] GEMAP also involves donor-assisted support for diverse economic governance, financial management technical assistance, and judicial capacity-building efforts to institutionalize transparent state management capacity-building goals and related reforms.[164] The United States and other donors are continuing to provide financial management technical assistance aimed at consolidating gains made under GEMAP.[165]

Liberia Extractive Industries Transparency Initiative (LEITI)

Liberia is a signatory of the Extractive Industries Transparency Initiative (EITI), an international effort to foster transparent and accountable governance in resource-rich countries through the publication of verified government revenues derived from extractive industry company payments. In October 2009, Liberia became the second EITI signatory to be judged an EITI Compliant Country, i.e., a country that has undergone EITI "validation," a formal assessment process that verifies compliance with EITI transparency standards, goals, and processes that signatories agree to implement and uphold.

Liberia committed to join EITI in October 2006, and formally agreed to participate under a Memorandum of Understanding (MoU) signed in April 2008, shortly after the formation of the Liberia Extractive Industries Transparency Initiative (LEITI), a national EITI group of government, civil society, and private business stakeholders. The MOU formally committed LEITI members to full implement EITI principles in Liberia. Like most EITI-signatory countries, Liberia's EITI program addresses revenues from oil, gas, and mined commodities, but is unique in that it is the first one to include forestry as a sector subject to EITI compliance. Agricultural production is also subject to LEITI reporting.

Among other actions taken to implement the LEITI program, a forestry scooping was produced in June 2008; a presidential proclamation was issued in September 2008 making the LEITI program a key, binding government policy; a LEITI public communications strategy was initiated in October 2008; and two EITI validation reports were published (in February of 2009 and 2010). In addition, in July 2009 Liberia a public act was signed into law that formally established LEITI as an independent state entity, albeit made up, in part, of non-governmental actors, and laid out its legal and functional mandates; it was the second country to pass such a law. Significantly, the act requires public access to all contracts subject to LEITI reporting compliance.[166]

LEGISLATIVE BRANCH

As discussed elsewhere in this report,[167] Liberia's current Congress could potentially play a more prominent role in governance than have its predecessors, in part because President Sirleaf's party does not enjoy a majority in either chamber of the legislature. Many Members are enthusiastic about their representative role and are determined to assertively exercise the constitutional powers and responsibilities of the legislature.[168] A range of challenges may, however, impede the realization of such goals. A key impediment is the relative inexperience of many of Liberia's legislators. Although a number of Members are professionals with varying private or public sector experience and a few served previously in the legislature as

Members or staff, the vast majority have never previously held elected office and have no lawmaking or policy-making experience. In meetings attended by the author in July 2006, many Members expressed a need for instruction or information regarding the basic functions of being a legislator, the workings of the committee system, and the legislature's oversight, appropriations, authorizing, and constituent relations roles.

In many cases, Members are unable to turn to their personal staffs to provide expertise on legislative functions because, as is common across the public sector in Liberia, many staff lack appropriate training or job-specific skills. In many instances, the professional work of the legislature is carried out by university students, reportedly because pay levels are viewed as too low to attract trained, professional staff. In other cases, staff reportedly lack appropriate skills because they were hired "based solely on contacts and family relationships," with little regard to competence or training, "rendering [many offices.. .]dysfunctional."[169]

There is also a paucity of institutional resources available to Members. Committee staff are virtually nonexistent, and the legislature as a whole lacks many of the assets necessary to independently carry out its principal roles. The two chambers largely lack bill drafting expertise, and most bills are drafted by the executive branch or by outside organizations. Parliamentary record keeping capacity is also limited; legislative debates and votes are recorded by hand, in part due to a lack of audio or stenographic recording equipment. Legislative debates and decisions, therefore, are reportedly often documented incompletely and sometimes erroneously.

The manner in which legislative resources are allocated also appears to curtail the institution's potential effectiveness. In comparison to many countries, the size of Liberian Members' office staffs is large, and a high proportion of Members' staffs perform non-legislative services, such as food preparation, gardening, and driving. Similarly, despite a general lack of resources, the two chambers of the legislature maintain duplicate services; each, for instance, has its own research department. These institutional challenges are compounded by a dearth of office space and equipment. The legislature's Capitol building, which was looted and suffered decay due to neglect during the civil war, lacks most basic functional infrastructure elements, such as water and electricity, though it is currently undergoing an upgrade (see below).

Some Liberians, including some legislators, as well as outside observers are also concerned that legislators' lack of knowledge regarding their normative and constitutional roles as representatives of the public might cause some to seek use their offices for purposes of private gain, rather than to serve the public. Such concerns were highlighted in October 2006 when, just prior to the slated start of a U.S.-supported project to rehabilitate the Capitol building (see below), several Liberia news reports described acts of alleged "looting" of the Capitol building by some Members and staff of the legislature, who were reported to have removed and appropriated government property for personal use from the Capitol.[170] Similar concerns reportedly arose in relation to legislative negotiations relating to the recently enacted forestry law reforms. According to informed observers, during talks prior to the passage of the forestry reforms, some legislators made remarks suggesting that they viewed a successful outcome of the reform process as being one in which they personally—as persons representing the public, in contrast to the general Liberian public itself—would directly benefit from processes at issue, such as the allocation of forestry concessions or revenues.

A certain amount of on-going public skepticism about government transparency in general may be attributable to public perceptions formed of the NTGL and of the transitional legislature, the decision-making conduct of which was often opaque and sometimes allegedly corrupt (see "Transitional Government," above), and to widespread reports of corruption under previous Liberian governments. Such views may be spurred by on-going investigations of alleged corruption under the NTGL.[171]

U.S. Legislative Assistance

To help overcome the challenges faced by the legislature, the United States supported a $1.8 million USAID project to rehabilitate the Capitol and is providing legislative capacity-building assistance through the U.S. democracy-building organization, the National Democratic Institute (NDI). This follows on an earlier post-elections governance capacity-building effort undertaken by NDI, the International Republican Institute (IRI), and the International Foundation for Election Systems.[172] NDI describes its current work as follows:

> NDI is implementing a 14-month USAID-funded program to support the modernization of the Liberian legislature by: developing sustainable systems and institutional practices that improve the effectiveness of the legislature; improving the ability of legislative staff to respond to current members' requests and manage the day-to-day operations of the legislature; and

enhancing the capacity of legislators to fulfill their representative, lawmaking, and oversight roles. The Institute has been working closely with the Joint Legislative Modernization Committee (JLMC), a group of legislators tasked with identifying institutional challenges and recommending viable remedies. Additionally, NDI provides support to the Women's Legislative Caucus of Liberia (WLCL) to strengthen its organizational structure and refine its strategic plan. NDI is also providing technical and financial support to a local radio partner to connect lawmakers with their constituents and disseminate information nation-wide on legislative activities.[173]

Congressional Role

In addition to appropriating funds to assist Liberia, Congress is taking a direct role in supporting governance capacity-building in Liberia. In July 2006, following a visit by a congressional delegation and a parliamentary assessment by a House Democracy Assistance Commission (HDAC) staff team, Liberia was selected to participate in a multi-year HDAC House Democracy Partnership (HDP) program. HDAC partnerships provide "technical assistance to the parliaments of newly democratic countries on a peer-to-peer basis, with Members of Congress working with Members of Parliament and congressional staff working with their parliamentary counterparts."[174]

HDAC 's goal is to help partner legislatures improve "fundamental capabilities of legislatures to serve as effective, independent, representative bodies of government." Key HDAC activities include Member Outbound Programs, in which U.S. Members and staff delegations hold discussion on topics such as "essential legislative capabilities, policy questions, bilateral relations and regional issues" and constituent relations with their counterparts in partner legislatures. HDAC Staff Institutes, in which HDAC and other Congressional staff hold U.S. and overseas- based training sessions for partner legislature staff focusing on such areas as "budget analysis, committee operations, research, and administration" are another key activity, as are Member Inbound Programs. In the latter, Members of partner legislatures travel to the United States for "training focusing on Congressional operations and constituent services." Specialized trainings focus on such areas as defense oversight, in cooperation with the Department of Defense, ethics, and budget committee work. HDAC provides limited material assistance "in areas where it can achieve immediate impact," such as planned legislative research and library capacity-building in Liberia. [175]

WAR CRIMES, HUMAN RIGHTS CASES, AND TRANSITIONAL JUSTICE

Taylor Trial

Former Liberian President Charles Taylor is defending himself against an 11-count war crimes indictment first brought against him in 2003 by the Prosecutor of the U.S.-supported Sierra Leone-based Special Court for Sierra Leone.[176] The indictment against Taylor alleges that he violated international and Sierra Leonean law by actively aiding and abetting activities in furtherance of the armed insurgency against the government of Sierra Leone by the Revolutionary United Front, a now defunct Sierra Leonean rebel group.

Taylor's trial is being conducted by the SCSL in the Hague, the Netherlands, where under a special agreement the SCSL is using the premises of the International Criminal Court (ICC).[177] The trial, which had originally been slated to begin in April 2007, opened in early June 2007, but proceedings were delayed after Taylor boycotted his trial and later fired his initial defense team. A new defense team was later hired. It successfully requested increased funding for his legal defense and in mid-August 2007 won a postponement of Taylor's trial on the basis that the team must be allowed adequate time to review extensive evidence that has been submitted in the case. The trial resumed in January 2008, with testimony by 91 witnesses for the Prosecution, which wrapped up its case in February 2009. The defense opened its case in July 2009. Cross- examination of defense witnesses by the Prosecutor's Office of the U.S.-backed Special Court for Sierra Leone (SCSL), which began in November 2009, proceeded in early 20 10.[178]

Taylor was taken into the custody of the SCSL following his arrest on March 29, 2006, at a border checkpoint in the northern Nigerian state of Borno, as he tried to cross by road into Cameroon. He was apprehended by Nigerian security forces after fleeing the southern Nigerian city of Calabar, where he had lived with an entourage of aides and family members beginning in August 2003, when he was given asylum by Nigeria's government. He reportedly fled on March 27, two days after Nigeria's government announced that Liberia was "free" to take Taylor "into its custody," while not specifying how that end could or would be achieved, or moving to arrest him. After his capture, Taylor was extradited to Liberia in a Nigerian presidential jet. He was then immediately flown by UNMIL helicopter to the premises of the SCSL in Freetown, the capital of Sierra Leone, where he was taken into SCSL custody.

On April 3 he was arraigned and pled not guilty, though he qualified his plea by questioning the SCSL's "jurisdiction over me, as the 21st President of the Republic of Liberia."[179]

Trial Venue

In June 2006, Taylor was transferred from the headquarters of the SCSL, in Freetown, Sierra Leone, to the prison premises of the International Criminal Court (ICC) in the Hague, the Netherlands. The ICC, with the agreement of the Dutch government, agreed to allow the SCSL to use ICC facilities in order to conduct the Taylor trial.[180] Dutch authorities agreed to allow Taylor to be tried on Dutch soil after Britain offered to imprison Taylor if he is convicted.[181] The SCSL will retain legal and institutional control over the Taylor case but will use the physical premises of the ICC in the Hague, the Netherlands, to conduct his trial and related hearings. Taylor's transfer to the Netherlands was made for reasons of security and to prevent potential instability in Sierra Leone and Liberia, where his trial could prove politically controversial and emotive.[182] The decision to transfer him to the Hague remains a topic of debate.

The decision to transfer the trial to a venue outside of Sierra Leone or the continent of Africa stimulated debate over the over the implications for justice of the transfer.[183] Some have contended that Taylor's trial should have been conducted in the country where his alleged crimes took place. Such an outcome, in this view, would demonstrate—both to victims and perpetrators of international human rights and laws of war violations in Sierra Leone and the surrounding subregion—that accountability for such actions can be achieved in the same social and geographic contexts in which they were committed. Similarly, some have argued that the didactic and symbolic value for the region of a local public trial would be greater than one conducted abroad, in part because it would allow more direct and proximate access to the court proceedings by the local population. Some observers have worried that because many Sierra Leonean journalists lack the ability to cover the trial directly due to cost or other factors, Sierra Leoneans would be deprived of a key channel of information and analysis accessible to them in the local patois (*Krio*, an English-based Creole) and responsive to local concerns. Sierra Leoneans lack widespread access to television and print media, particularly western media sources that are more likely to have the resources to cover a trial in the Hague. Other factors cited in favor of holding a trial locally have included concerns about the logistical, legal, financial, and bureaucratic barriers that an overseas venue might pose for witness participation in the trial, as well as for its general organization and staging.[184] Such concerns continue, and may potentially imperil the reputation of the SCSL as a novel, cost-effective international judicial model.[185]

Others have supported the transfer on the basis that any factor that might spark political unrest or conflict—such as Taylor's trial—should be avoided, given the relatively fragile and recent transition to peace in Liberia and Sierra Leone, both of which have extended histories of political instability. In this view, moving the trial to the Hague has decreased the chance that political controversy prompted by Taylor's trial may lead to local unrest, and has undercut his ability to directly appeal to or rally potentially armed followers, should he attempt to use the trial as a political platform. Some have also maintained that holding the trial in a distant location would help Sierra Leoneans and Liberians overcome the legacies of war. A local trial, according to this point of view, might present too immediate and visceral a reminder of the wartime suffering that many in these two countries have only recently overcome. Sierra Leoneans, this line of reasoning emphasized, are weary of war and its effects and want to "move past" their experiences of wartime brutality and focus on peace and socio-economic reconstruction.

Sirleaf Administration Role

Taylor's SCSL case and extradition have been delicate matters for President Sirleaf, because her government was not party to his asylum deal or indictment, but was charged with resolving issues arising from them. Prior to his transfer to the court, some observers had raised concerns over the hypothetical possibility that the stability of Sirleaf's government might be undermined if Sirleaf were to alienate or anger supporters of former President Taylor, particularly given that he won the presidency with 75.3% of the vote in 1997, and because he is a former warlord whose factional fighters had a reputation for brutality. Prior to her mid-March 2006 visit to the United States, Sirleaf had stated that her administration would eventually seek the repatriation of former president Charles Taylor from Nigeria or his transfer to the SCSL under certain conditions. These included consultations with and the assent of "regional leaders who managed the process of leading to his exile;" accommodation for certain unspecified timing considerations; and a transfer process that would "not undermine the security" of Liberia. She also reportedly said that she did not view it as an immediate priority. She specifically stated that any solution would require the concurrence of the European Union, the African Union, and West African leaders, with whom she met during a regional pre-inauguration consulting tour, in part intended to address "certain national and regional sensitivities." Notwithstanding these actions, in March 2006 her government formally requested Taylor's extradition from Nigeria, prompting the sequence of events leading to Taylor's capture.

In mid-July 2007, .the Sirleaf Administration submitted a bill to the national legislature that would have allowed it to seize and seek international cooperation in "tracking, freezing and confiscating the funds, properties and assets" allegedly misappropriated and/or controlled by Taylor and certain of his relatives and associates.[186] The bill was considered controversial because Taylor has not been convicted of any crimes in Liberia or by the SCSL. In September 2007, the legislature rejected the bill on ground that it would unconstitutionally deny due process rights.[187] The government has pledged to attempt to continue to pursue efforts to effect such seizures, and may amend and resubmit the bill.

SCSL: U.S. Views and Assistance

The United States strongly supports the SCSL's mandate to try those responsible for war crimes in Sierra Leone. The court is also seen by some as providing an alternative institutional model to the International Criminal Court and is viewed as a smaller, leaner organization compared to the more administratively extensive and costly international criminal tribunals for the former Yugoslavia and Rwanda, though questions have recently been raised about its costeffectiveness.[188] Court officials, however, point out that per-capita "justice" cost comparisons with larger war crimes and related courts are misleading, since the latter can achieve efficiencies on the basis of larger economies of scale and because the SCSL had to invest in substantial initial fixed costs, even though the number of plaintiffs was relatively small. They also point out that the court has been able to maintain a relatively rapid trial and appeals process, which has kept down costs. They also point out that the court is expected to provide a substantial legacy, in the form of buildings and institutions, that is expected to bolster the rule of law in the region after the court has completed its activities. Lastly, they point out that the SCSL has achieved several milestones in the administration of international justice, as the first international court to:

- Indict a sitting African head of state for war crimes;
- Derive its funding from voluntary contributions;
- Be established in the country where the alleged crimes at issue took place; and

- Issue rulings on the recruitment and use of children in the context of a war crimes trial and the treatment of forced marriage as a war crime separate and distinct from crimes of sexual slavery and rape.

Table 2. U.S. Assistance for the Special Court for Sierra Leone ($ millions)

Account[a]	Amount	Fiscal Years by Appropriation and Obligation
ESF	2	FY2000[b]
DFA	3	FY2001[c]
ESF	5	FY2002
ESF	10	FY2003[d]
K Fund	2	FY2005
ESF	13	FY2006[e]
ESF	13	FY2007f
ESF	12.4	FY2008
ESF	9	FY2009
ESF	7.5	FY2010
Total through FY2008	76.9[g]	
ESF	5	Requested FY2011 level

Source: State Department information provided orally or in writing. Notes:

[a] K Fund: Emergencies in the Diplomatic and Consular Service; DFA: Development Fund for Africa; ESF: Economic Support Fund.

[b] Funds provided in FY2001.

[c] No-year funds de-obligated from prior year funds. Funds provided in FY2001.

[d] $5 million provided in FY2003 and $5 million provided in FY2004.

[e] P.L. 109-102, which contained appropriations for FY2006 foreign operations, stated that $13 million "should" be provided to the SCSL.. The State Department reports that this amount was, in fact, provided to the SCSL in FY2006.

[f] The $13 million figure was composed of $3 million in FY2007 supplemental ESF account funds provided under P.L. 110-28 (passed as H.R. 2206/Obey) and $10 million in ESF appropriations provided under P.L. 110-5 (passed as H.J.Res. 20/Obey).

[g] $69.309 million transferred to the SCSL as of March 9, 2010. FY 2010 contribution to be provided after annual foreign operations appropriations funding allocation notification to Congress.

Currently the SCSL is facing a severe funding shortfall that could critically impair its ability to both complete its judicial activities and wind up its operations on schedule. The court also faces the prospect of difficulties in financing its long-term residual activities, which are expected to pertain to witness protection; archival activities, including record keeping associated with future legal and financial documents of the court; a residual registrar's capacity required for enforcing court sentences and maintaining relations with countries hosting imprisoned convicts of the SCSL; legal decision-making regarding future appeals, conditions of prisoner treatment, or contempt proceedings; and financial matters pertaining to such activities.

There was occasional friction between the Bush Administration and the SCSL with regard to the effect that certain of the court's actions have had on political events and U.S. policy goals in West Africa. Some State Department officials in private, for instance, questioned the political prudence or timing of certain actions taken by former SCSL Prosecutor, David Crane, such as his unsealing of the indictment against Taylor at a critical juncture during Liberian peace talks held in Ghana in June 2003. Some critics also faulted the Administration for not pushing harder to obtain the extradition of Taylor from Nigeria after the latter provided him with asylum in August 2003. In 2006, however, the United States began to pursue this goal more urgently, explicitly, and directly, and such criticisms declined.

Transitional Justice in Liberia

Potential for War Crimes Tribunal in Liberia

There have been some calls for a special court to try crimes committed during Liberia's civil wars.[189] Many Liberians who suffered the death of loved ones or personal attacks and other crimes, and some have expressed a desire to see those who committed such deeds punished.[190] Some observers have suggested, however, that President Sirleaf does not, in general, support prosecuting those who committed war time atrocities during the 1989-2003 civil wars because such tribunals might reignite old antagonisms and conflict. Such sentiments may be held by many Liberians, in part due to personal or familial linkages to parties involved in the conflict, and due to concerns similar to those cited in favor of moving the Taylor trial to the Hague. Some have argued that the current legislature might not support the creation of a tribunal because some of its members might be targets of subsequent prosecutions. The creation of a tribunal could face legal barriers, as well as political ones. Some peace agreements covering Liberia first civil war contain amnesty provisions for war-time crimes. There is no apparent legal barrier to one that might cover Liberia's second civil war, however. The 2003 Comprehensive Peace Agreement provided for a "recommendation for general amnesty to all persons and parties engaged or involved in military activities during the Liberian civil conflict that is the subject of this Agreement" but did not explicitly provide for one. It did, however, endeavor to "address issues of impunity, as well as an opportunity for both the victims and perpetrators of human rights violations to share their experiences" by providing for the creation of a Truth and Reconciliation Commission (TRC).

Truth and Reconciliation Commission

While no war crimes tribunal special tribunal has been established, in late February 2006, President Sirleaf inaugurated the Liberian TRC, which the transitional legislature created in 2005. She also pledged to support and strengthen the TRC, which has a mandate to investigate crimes and human rights abuses committed from 1979 until 2003.[191] The TRC formally began operations in early June 2006, but did not begin to collect testimony until October 2006 and had to halt operations about a month later due to financial shortfalls. In mid-2007, after having undertaken a fund-raising effort, it launched a multi-month project to collect testimony from the substantial Liberian community living in the United States, in part supported by Minnesota-based Advocates for Human Rights and Northwestern University's Center for Human Rights Law, which had begun to collect diasporic statements for the TRC in early 2007.[192] In October 2007, it relaunched field hearings in Liberia after receiving assistance from the U.N. Development Program and USAID, among other donors. In FY2006, USAID provided $.5 million in support to the TRC.

In June 2009, the TRC released a draft of its final report, which was formally published in its final form in December 2009. It examined the root causes and social effects of armed conflict in Liberia, and presented findings regarding gross violations of human rights, violations of international human rights and humanitarian law, and "egregious domestic law violations."[193] It laid out recommendations for public sanctions, including lists of alleged perpetrators of human rights violators and economic crimes whom the TRC "recommended for prosecution" or further investigation, and for non-judicial public sanctions, such as a prohibition on holding public office" or "elected or appointed for a period of thirty (30) years."[194] The latter included a list of 49 persons named "for their role in supporting, financially and otherwise, various warring factions." Numerous other recommendations in the report related to diverse issues, "including public integrity, corruption, human rights, economic empowerment, good governance, national identity and reparation, amongst others intended to resolve past conflicts as part of a national progression towards lasting peace and reconciliation."[195]

The TRC report was controversial, in part, because President Sirleaf was included on the list of alleged leaders or key supporters of armed civil war factions whom the TRC recommended be barred from holding public offices" or "elected or appointed for a period of thirty (30) years." The basis for the recommendation was not explained in detail in the report, but appears to have been rooted in Sirleaf's short-lived support for Charles Taylor at the start of his effort to oust Doe. In early 2009, Sirleaf, who was imprisoned by former President Taylor, had testified that she had not been party to any armed group during Liberia's civil wars. She said, however, that she had "to apologize to this nation" for initially supporting Taylor after being "fooled by" him. [196]

President Sirleaf appears to have rejected the TRC's recommendation that she not hold public office. In addition to not resigning her position, during her annual message to the legislature in January 2010, she announced that she would seek reelection to a second term in 2011, as many observers had expected. In the same speech, she raised questions over the legal standing and import of the TRC's recommendations. She stated that the TRC's recommendations on "criminal tribunal, criminal sanctions and public sanctions and economic crimes and investigations" had "been the subject of great debate since the TRC Report was made public" and that

> To deal with this, I propose amendments to the Independent National Human Rights Commission (INHRC) Act of 2005 to enable that body to seize itself of those aspects of the TRC Report, and to work in collaboration with the Ministry of Justice to determine those recommendations that are implementable or enforceable under the Constitution and laws of Liberia.[197]

Cases against "Chuckie" Taylor

In mid-September 2006, former President Taylor's Boston-born son, Roy M. Belfast Jr. (AKA Charles McArthur Emmanuel and Charles "Chuckie" Taylor, Jr.) pled guilty to a federal passport fraud relating to his official submission of false data regarding his father's identity. He had been arrested at Miami International Airport by U.S. customs agents while attempting to enter the United States from Trinidad on March 30, 2006, one day after his father was apprehended in Nigeria. Belfast, who reportedly has an extensive U.S. juvenile criminal record, was sentenced on December 7, 2006 to 11 months in prison for the fraud.[198]

Hours after being sentenced in the passport fraud case, Belfast pled not guilty to a separate indictment brought against him by a U.S. federal Grand Jury. It charged Belfast with torture, conspiracy to torture, and of using a firearm during an act of violent crime while serving as the head of the Liberian Anti-Terrorist Unit (ATU, known informally as the "Demon Forces") during his father's presidency. The ATU was a state security unit staffed primarily by members of Taylor's former civil war faction. Belfast is reportedly the first person ever to have been charged under a statute that allows U.S. courts to hear criminal cases involving acts of torture committed abroad by any person present in the United States.[199]

The initial charges against Belfast, in his capacity as an ATU official, related to the alleged 2002 torture of one person, but other self-identified victims publicly accused him of having committed similar crimes against them after he was indicted. In November 2007, he was charged under a superseding indictment with torturing at least seven Liberians "under color of law" and in furtherance of a conspiracy to maintain and protect his father's political power. The charges included violent acts, such as burning, beating, stabbing, and the application of electrical shocks, in some cases in association with murder, committed between April 1999 and July 2003. Belfast's initial indictment followed efforts by the advocacy group Human Rights Watch (HRW) to persuade the Justice Department to investigate him "for torture and war crimes." HRW submitted a dossier to the Justice Department in support of its allegations against Belfast.[200] In early July 2007, a U.S. Southern District of Florida judge denied a defense motion to dismiss the case. After several continuances, Belfast's trial was held over a period of six weeks in September and October, 2008. He was convicted on October 30, 2008 on five counts of torture, one of conspiracy to torture, one of using a firearm while committing a violent crime, and one of conspiracy to use a firearm while carrying out such an act. In January 2009, he was sentenced to 97 years in prison for these crimes.[201]

In May 2009, five plaintiffs who sued Belfast in civil court for damages that they claimed to have sustained as a result of the torture that he was convicted of committing won a default judgment in the case. In February 2010 they were collectively awarded $22.4 million in compensation for physical pain and mental suffering, and as a punitive measure against Belfast.[202]

Like former President Taylor and many of his associates, Belfast is also subject to a U.S. asset freeze under Executive Order 13348 (July 22, 2004) and to a United Nations travel ban. These measures were originally imposed to halt support by the Taylor government for the Revolutionary Front of Sierra Leone (see "Taylor Trial," above). Some press reports suggest Belfast may have abetted such activities.[203]

U.S. RELATIONS

The United States and Liberia have a long-standing historical relationship.[204] The United States has long provided Liberia with substantial assistance, and U.S.-Liberian bilateral ties have often been close, with some exceptions, including the final years of late president Samuel K. Doe's regime and during the tenure of former President Charles Taylor. Official U.S. interactions with the NTGL were also guarded, due to real or perceived problems of corruption within the NTGL and due to the participation in it of members of the armed parties to the conflict, some suspected of human rights abuses.

Current U.S.-Liberian relations are warm, as they were during the Administration of former President George W. Bush.The Sirleaf Administration's close working relationship with the Bush Administration began with her inauguration in 2006, which former U.S. First Lady Laura Bush and former Secretary of State Rice attended, among other prominent U.S. guests.[205] Former President Bush — whose Administration had played key roles in ending Liberia's second civil war and in stabilizing and helping the country to rebuild in the immediate post-war years, backed by substantial, Congressionally-supported U.S. post-war rebuilding assistance[206] — admired Sirleaf's leadership and achievements, and awarded the U.S. Presidential Medal of Freedom to her in November 2007.[207] In February 2008, then-President and Mrs. Bush traveled to Liberia, among other African countries.

Diverse U.S. officials have repeatedly voiced support for President Sirleaf's government since her election, most recently in April 2010, when Under Secretary of State for Political Affairs William J. Burns visited Liberia. During his visit, he stated that it was "remarkable to see how far the country has come since it held its first free and open post-conflict election in 2005," but added that it is "equally evident is that much work remains for Liberia to fully recover after years of horrific civil war." Burns stated that the core purpose of his trip was to send the message that "the United States will stand by Liberia as it continues to make progress towards reaching its full potential as a democratic state." His comments echoed those of Secretary of State Clinton, who, after meeting with President Sirleaf in April 2009, stated that Sirleaf's leadership had "been exemplary and extraordinary" and had "made an enormous contribution" to Liberia's advancement, and that "President Obama and I are very committed to the future of Liberia and to President Sirleaf's continuing leadership."[208] During his trip, Burns also announced a U.S. commitment to "provide $19.75 million in funding to further advance Liberia National Police force training," which, he said fulfilled "a promise made by Secretary Clinton during her visit last August."[209]

Clinton's 2009 trip was the second most recent visit by a high-level U.S. official to Liberia, and the most senior leadership visit to date to the country during the Obama Administration. During the visit, in a speech to the Liberian parliament, she related the importance of expanding democratic participation and institution-building to Liberia's prospective success in meeting its substantial challenges, among the most pressing of which she cited as corruption and the need for land tenure reform, and lack of access to jobs, electricity, housing, education, and law enforcement. She specifically called on the legislature to develop its budgetary oversight role, counter corruption and promote transparency, and pass a code of conduct in order to ensure "ethical standards that guide the pursuit of the common good."[210] She also called on the legislature to help ensure "credible... free and fair elections in 2011," in part by passing a threshold bill.[211] In remarks delivered at the Liberian National Police (LNP) Academy, she discussed the importance, challenges, and achievements of U.S., multilateral, and Liberian partnership in rebuilding Liberia's police force during the on-going post-conflict period. In particular, she emphasized the importance to the United States of its investment in assisting in the development of the LNP Emergency Response Unit, and announced a prospective increase in U.S. financial support for LNP training (discussed previously in this report).[212]

President Sirleaf has made several official visits to the United States, including one in February 2007, when she attended a World Bank-organized Liberia Partners' Forum donor meeting in Washington D.C.[213] She made another such visit in March 2006, during which she addressed a joint session of Congress on March 15 and met with President Bush on March 21.[214] She reportedly closely consulted with U.S. officials regarding her priorities for Liberia and the status of Charles Taylor. During a pre-inaugural December

2005 trip to the United States, Sirleaf also met with key U.S. and international financial institution officials.[215]

President Sirleaf is expected to undertake a further official visit the United States in late May 2010. While her itinerary has not been released, the trip is expected to focus on deepening Sirleaf's high-level contacts with Obama Administration officials. Sirleaf is expected to update U.S. policy makers, including interested Members, on Liberia's progress since her election, as well as remaining challenges in such areas as security sector reform, anti-corruption efforts, unemployment, economic growth, and legal system capacity building. Her visit may occasion the announcement of a possible Millennium Challenge Corporation (MCC) Threshold Program and a possible U.S. Global Food Security Initiative country program (see "Development Assistance and Related Bilateral Cooperation").

111th Congress

Liberia-related activities in the 111th Congress have focused on Liberian U.S. immigration issues; support for Liberian female legislators; transparency in Liberia's natural resource sector; and the appropriation of U.S. assistance for Liberia and the SCSL (on the latter, see Table 2, above).

Other Liberia-related issues matters likely to continue to draw the attention of some Members in the 110th Congress include Liberia's relative progress with respect to security sector reform, anticorruption and transparency efforts, and democratization; its economic growth prospects; and its politico-military stability in relation to the relative need for continued UNMIL operations and funding.

Appropriations

In addition to appropriating funds for foreign operations that are normally allocated, in part, for programs of assistance to Liberia, the 111th Congress laid out several Liberia-related provisions in its FY 2009 and FY 2010 appropriations.[216] The Explanatory Statement accompanying P.L. 111-8, Omnibus Appropriations Act, 2009 (passed as H.R. 1105, Obey):[217]

- specified that Marquette University be made eligible for consideration as one of multiple potential recipients of funding for "exchanges between United States and Liberian officials" under a one-time $6 million international exchange grant program;

- allocated $90.3 million in Economic Support Fund (ESF) assistance for Liberia;
- directed, with respect to ESF funding for Liberia, that "USAID should support efforts to increase access to electricity, and should expand programs that promote and strengthen the rule of law, consistent with country plans" and "consider the work of North Carolina State University."
- Stated that "USAID and the Department of State should support international efforts to trace and freeze assets allegedly confiscated and controlled by former Liberian President Charles Taylor, and by his family members and associates. Funding is encouraged to support programs that work with the Liberian Solicitor General to identify and recover these funds"; and
- Stated that the Trade and Development Agency "should consult with the Committees on Appropriations on the next phase of work related to the Mount Coffee Hydro Power Station and the construction of a proposed fiber optic ring around Monrovia."

P.L. 111-117, Consolidated Appropriations Act, 2010 (passed as H.R. 3288, Olver) allocated for Liberia $153 million in ESF assistance and $10 million in regional Peacekeeping Operations funding.[218] It also directed that funds appropriated in the law

> that are available for assistance for Liberia... shall be made available to promote and support transparency and accountability in relation to the extraction of timber, oil and gas, cacao and other natural resources, including by strengthening implementation and monitoring of the Extractive Industries Transparency Initiative and the Kimberley Process Certification Scheme.

Immigration

As in previous Congresses, some Members have argued in favor of measures to allow certain Liberian refugees to reside in the United States, either on a temporary or permanent basis. Most recently, some Members have urged that Deferred Enforced Departure (DED; see text box), a special immigration status under which certain eligible Liberian aliens may legally reside and work in the United States, be extended by President Obama for such persons upon its current scheduled expiration on March 31, 2010. Two bills would also provide permanent residence status to Liberian refugees in the United States.

Deferred Enforced Departure (DED) and Temporary Protected Status (TPS)

Deferred Enforced Departure (DED) is established by discretionary presidential fiat based on the president's constitutional power to conduct foreign relations. It is not a specific immigration status under the law; rather, it has the effect of suspending enforcement of certain immigration laws for eligible persons, primarily by deferring or preventing the deportation of persons subject to a loss of Temporary Protected Status (TPS). TPS is a temporary "safe harbor" immigration status granted to qualified persons from countries affected by various types of crises, such as ongoing armed conflict, natural disaster, or other severe challenges. Aliens who enjoy TPS and DED status may also apply for authorization to work in the United States, which is sometimes granted automatically. Eligible Liberians were first given TPS after the start of Liberia's first civil war in 1991. This status was terminated and they were granted DED in 1999. Their TPS status was later renewed several times. Upon its expiration in late September 2007, former President George W. Bush, citing the continued fragility of "the political and economic situation in Liberia," granted affected Liberians DED status for 18 months, effective October 1, 2007. Upon the expiration of President Bush's directive, President Barack Obama, citing "compelling foreign policy reasons" and pursuant to his "constitutional authority to conduct the foreign relations of the United States," extended DED status for such persons through March 31, 2010.[219]

On March 10, 2010, a Liberian National Immigration Conference was held on the Capitol to "highlight the need for an immediate extension of DED for the approximately 3,600 eligible Liberians living in the United States and ... efforts supporting the extension." In a Dear Colleague letter announcing the forum, Representative Donald M. Payne invited Members to participate in the event. He also stated that he would be "sending a letter to President Obama urging an extension of DED."[220] In late February 2010, over 20 Members also wrote a similar letter to President Obama.[221]

Two bills, S. 656 (Reed), the Liberian Refugee Immigration Fairness Act of 2009, introduced March 19, 2009, and H.R. 2258 (Kennedy), the Liberian Refugee Immigration Protection Act of 2009, introduced May 5, 2009, seek to adjust the immigration status of various categories of Liberians in the United States. S. 656 would direct the Secretary of Homeland Security to adjust the

U.S. residency status of qualifying Liberian aliens to that of lawful permanent residents. The bill would require qualifying applicants to be non-criminals, as defined in the bill; to be present in the United States since January 1, 2009; and to apply for adjustment before April 1, 2011, among other criteria. It would also authorize the Secretary to authorize applicants to work in the United States while their cases are pending and would not trigger a reduction in the number of immigrant visas available to Liberians not eligible for adjustment under the Act. H.R. 2258 provides for a broadly similar immigration status adjustment process for qualifying Liberians as those that set out in S. 656, but defines eligibility differently, and similarly provides that such adjustments will not offset the number of immigrant visas otherwise available to Liberians. In contrast to S. 656, eligibility for adjustment under H.R. 2258 would be limited to Liberian U.S. alien residents who were granted TPS on or after March 27, 1991; or were eligible to apply for TPS on or after March 27, 1991.

Other Bills

Liberia-related bills or measures introduced in the 111th Congress that have not been passed into law include the following:

- As passed by the House, H.R. 2410 (Berman), the Foreign Relations Authorization Act, Fiscal Years 2010 and 2011, introduced May 14, 2009, would establish a new State Department exchange program, to be undertaken in cooperation with the Liberian Women's Legislative Caucus. It would fund scholarship-based exchanges for female legislators and congressional staff from Liberia in order to increase active female participation in Liberian politics and democratic processes. H.R. 2475 (Ros-Lehtinen), the Foreign Relations Authorization and Reform Act, Fiscal Years 2010 and 2011, introduced May 19, 2009 contains an almost identical measure. According to H.Rept. 111-136, which accompanies H.R. 2410, the Congressional Budget Office estimates that this program would cost under $.5 million per year, and total $1 million between 2010 and 2014.
- S. 1434 (Leahy), Department of State, Foreign Operations, and Related Programs Appropriations Act, 2010, introduced July 9, 2009 would mandate that assistance funds appropriated under the Act for Liberia, among three other West African countries, "be made available to promote and support transparency and accountability in

relation to the extraction of timber, oil and gas, cocoa and other natural resources, including by strengthening implementation and monitoring of the Extractive Industries Transparency Initiative (EITI) and the Kimberley Process Certification Scheme," and prohibits such funds from being used to support "industrial-scale logging."

- The House report (H.Rept. 111-105) accompanying P.L. 111-32 (passed as H.R. 2346, Obey) called for Liberia, among nine other countries, to "receive priority consideration" with respect to receiving a potential portion of a $300 million FY 2009 ESF appropriation to assist developing countries affected by the global financial crisis. Such language, however, did not appear in P.L. 111-32 or the conference report accompanying it.

110th Congress

Liberia-related activities by the 110th Congress built on those pursued by the 109th Congress. Congress continued to monitor the activities of the SCSL and, in particular, the Taylor war crimes case, and provide funding for the SCSL. Congress's focus on Liberia also centered on aiding Liberia's efforts to consolidate its post-war governance and economic rebuilding processes. Issues that drew particular congressional attention included:

- Efforts to rehabilitate schools, clinics, roads and other public facilities;
- Progress under the GEMAP transparency initiative;
- Progress of U.S.-backed security sector restructuring, and possible expansions of related assistance, e.g., for the creation of a quick reaction gendarme unit; increased mobility capacity building for the police and military; and maritime waters and land border monitoring and interdiction capacity building.
- Consideration of potential continued support for UNMIL and the pace of its projected draw-down; and
- U.S. decision-making on debt relief for Liberia and the status of future Brooke Amendment restrictions on Liberia.[222]

The 110th Congress provided continuing appropriations for the purpose of assisting Liberia's postwar rebuilding process when it passed P.L. 110-5 (H.J.Res. 20/Revised Continuing Appropriations Resolution, 2007), which provided approximately $120.81 funding for FY2007 foreign operations.[223] The Congress also provided $48.95 million in supplementary FY2007 funding for Liberia under P.L. 110-28 (H.R. 2206/U.S. Troop Readiness, Veterans' Care, Katrina Recovery, and Iraq Accountability Appropriations Act, 2007). In FY 2008, Congress allocated $125.35 million in FY2008 Liberia funding for Liberia, as laid out in its joint explanatory statement for P.L. 110-161 (H.R. 2764/Consolidated Appropriations Act, 2008). The final amount allocated to Liberia, which included funds allocated for Liberia from central appropriation accounts under the law, totaled $163 million in FY 2008.

The Liberia Stabilization, Economic Empowerment, Development and Security Act of 2008 (Liberia SEEDS Act of 2008, or H.R. 6655, Jackson, 110th Congress) would have authorized assistance to Liberia for the following: (1) roads and bridges; (2) rehabilitation of Monrovia Freeport; (3) water and sanitation; (4) the electricity sector; (5) vocational education programs for war-affected youth and ex-combatants; (6) establishment of a government employee training institute and enhancement of government accountability and effectiveness; (7) narcotics control and law enforcement; (8) educational exchanges; and (9) the Truth and Reconciliation Commission of Liberia.

Other Liberia-related bills introduced in the 110th Congress include the following.

- H.R. 1941 (Kennedy), Liberian Refugee Immigration Protection Act of 2007;
- H.R. 1591 (Obey), U.S. Troop Readiness, Veterans' Care, Katrina Recovery, and Iraq Accountability Appropriations Act, 2007;
- H.R. 3123 (Kennedy), To extend the designation of Liberia under section 244 of the Immigration and Nationality Act so that Liberians can continue to be eligible for temporary protected status under that section;
- S. 396 (Dorgan), A bill to amend the Internal Revenue Code of 1986 to treat controlled foreign corporations in tax havens as domestic corporations;
- S. 554 (Dorgan), Act For Our Kids;
- S. 656 (Reed), Liberian Refugee Immigration Fairness Act of 2007;
- S. 965 (Byrd), U.S. Troop Readiness, Veterans' Care, Katrina Recovery, and Iraq Accountability Appropriations Act, 2007;
- S. 1508 (Dorgan), Clean Energy Production Tax Incentives Act of 2007; and
- S. 1903 (Reed), A bill to extend the temporary protected status designation of Liberia under section 244 of the Immigration and

Nationality Act so that Liberians can continue to be eligible for such status through September 30, 2008.[224]

Immigration Issues

H.R. 1941 and S. 656 would have provided permanent residency status to certain Liberian nationals who were granted or were eligible for TPS, while H.R. 3123 and S. 1903 would have extended the status of persons eligible for TPS. On July 30, the House passed H.R. 3123, which was received in the Senate on August 3. On September 12, 2007, President Bush, citing the continued fragility of "the political and economic situation in Liberia," directed that eligible Liberians resident in the United States and subject to a loss of TPS as of October 1, 2007 be granted DED for 18 months, until March 31, 2009. He also directed that such grantees be allowed to work in the United States. His action fulfilled basic underlying aims of the TPS-related bills discussed above.

In December 2008, a number of House Members co-signed a letter to former President Bush and similar one to the Transition Team of then-President-Elect Barack Obama calling for an extension of DED for eligible Liberians resident in the United States and subject to a loss of TPS on March 31, 2009.[225]

U.S. Assistance Summary

U.S. assistance to Liberia, which is broken out by accounts and amounts for FY2004-FY2010, appear in **Table 3**. The Obama Administration's assistance agenda for Liberia, which continues many of the same kinds of activities that had been pursued by the Bush Administration, centers on "fostering peace and security, strengthening democratic institutions, and rebuilding the economy in a country recovering from 14 years of civil war."[226]

Development Assistance and Related Bilateral Cooperation[227]

In addition to security sector assistance, which is discussed elsewhere in this report, current USAID and State Department assistance is focused on increasing good governance and democratization; advancing economic growth through assistance to capacity-building and investments related to agriculture, sustainable natural resource management, energy, and infrastructure; and investments in the education and health sectors.

Apart from elections support and legislature strengthening, which are discussed elsewhere in this report,[228] focal governance-strengthening activities center on rule of law judicial system strengthening and in creasing access to justice through support for magistrate and legal assistance training, notably through a long-term American Bar Association program called the Judicial Training Institute (JTI), and alternate dispute resolution, notably with regard to land disputes. Efforts to bolster government transparency and accountability are another key component of such programs. Such assistance is provided through support for the Anti-Corruption Commission and USAID follow-on support for GEMAP (discussed elsewhere in this report), under a USAID program called the Financial Management and Capacity Building Program (FIMCAB) and other civil services training programs.[229] There are also USAID-supported civil society and media capacity building efforts to increase human rights education.[230]

Economic growth and related programs center on agriculture capacity-building and the small business sector (e.g., tree crop rehabilitation, livestock re-stocking, and small business training and credit programs, notably in rural and farm areas); and food-for-work initiatives targeting rural areas and food aid for vulnerable groups. Another key program provides capacity-building assistance to the Ministry of Agriculture. Programs in this area also support community-based land and forest management; transparent regulation and governance of commercial forest management; and support for biodiversity conservation goals. According to the FY 2011 CBJ,

> As part of the new Global Hunger and Food Security Initiative, the United States will help Liberia design and implement a country-led comprehensive food security strategy to help the country increase long-term food security and provide support to entire value chains, in order to bring produce to markets and enable Liberia's farmers to feed all the country's citizens.[231]

USAID energy and infrastructure assistance is another key component. Activities in this area focus on rebuilding roads and bridges to enable farm to market transport; rehabilitation of government buildings, e.g., schools, clinics, and training institutions; and increasing access to electricity. The latter centers on increasing access to electricity through increased power distribution and generation, notably through the use of clean and renewable energy technologies, e.g., solar, water-based and biomass power generation, and technical energy efficiency use gains. Support is also provided to enhance energy-related government policy-making capabilities and public utility effectiveness. Micro-power generation, particularly in rural areas and in support of other USAID activities, is also a key focus of these efforts.

Health and education programs form the final two main pillars of U.S. development assistance in Liberia. Health assistance seeks to rebuild and improve basic health services through support for staffing, equipment and supplies, and training, and facilities upgrades, notably in rural areas; ensure child welfare, notably for orphans and other vulnerable or special needs children; and increase access to clean water and sanitation. There are special programs for family planning and reproductive health; nutrition; and for prevention and intervention programs aimed at combating malaria, tuberculosis, and HIV/AIDS. USAID also supports efforts to bolster the program planning and management capabilities of the Ministry of Health. Education programs center on teacher training, with a special program aimed at improving reading instruction and testing; increasing professional public service worker access to higher education; providing financial support and mentorship to poor children and programs to facilitate the access of older youth to access formal education and life skills training; and a book distribution program. USAID also supports Ministry of Education policy-making, program management, and financial capacity- building, and broader community outreach education programs pertaining to health, nutrition, hygiene, and sanitation.

Millennium Challenge Corporation

Liberia has been eligible for Millennium Challenge Corporation (MCC) Threshold Program assistance since late 2008. As of early April 2010, MCC and USAID were working with Liberia's Ministry of Planning and Economic Affairs to develop a country Threshold Program, for which an agreement may be signed by mid-2010. The program is currently conceived of as a three-year program (2010-2013) that would focus on girl's primary education; land rights and access; and trade policy.[232]

Peace Corps

The Peace Corps is expanding its presence in Liberia. In August 2008, the Peace Corps—which had deployed over 3,832 Peace Corps Volunteers (PCVs) to Liberia from 1962 to 1990, when war-related security conditions led to a suspension of the program—officially reopened its program in Liberia. In October 2008 the first group 12 volunteers, of an eventual total of 13, deployed to Liberia under the new program, which was initiated under the

Peace Corps Response (PCR) program (formerly called Crisis Response), a special short-term humanitarian service deployment program. Under the program, veteran PCVs called Peace Corps Response Volunteers (PCRVs) deploy to countries that have special needs, typically ones recovering from armed or political conflict or natural disasters, but which may eventually host a regular Peace Corps country program. In Liberia, PCRVs have worked on health and education system reconstruction, mentoring teacher trainers, training health professionals, and supporting Parent Teacher Associations and resource libraries for teachers, among other education capacity-building projects. The program helped lay the groundwork for a transition to a full Peace Corps country program that is expected to receive its first group of PCVs in July 2010. The new PCVs, whose services will overlap with the continuing PCRV program, will support secondary education, working as English, science, and math teachers. Funding for Peace Corps activities in Liberia is estimated at $1.44 million in FY 2010 and projected to rise to $2.45 million for FY 2011, when the program is expected to support 41 volunteers.[233]

Trade Benefits

The United States is also supporting President Sirleaf's market-based economic growth agenda in a variety of other ways. In late February 2006, the U.S. Trade Representative announced that President Bush had reinstated duty-free Generalized System of Preferences (GSP) trade benefits for Liberia. USTR said that the action was intended to provide "strong support to recently elected President Ellen Johnson Sirleaf's efforts to increase employment, diversify exports, and stabilize society." It was made, according to the USTR, because Sirleaf had repealed a decree prohibiting strikes and invited the International Labor Organization (ILO) to help Liberia to conform with ILO obligations, thus making "improving worker rights a high priority."[234] On January 1, 2007, Liberia became eligible to receive U.S. trade benefits under the African Growth and Opportunity Act (AGOA).[235] In February 2007, Liberia and the United States signed a bilateral Trade and Investment Framework Agreement (TIFA). Its aim is to bolster bilateral economic cooperation, primarily by creating a U.S.-Liberia Council on Trade and Investment charged with monitoring bilateral trade and investment developments and opportunities, related policy problems, and identifying and working to remove impediments to bilateral investment.[236]

Economic Cooperation and Investment

In February 2007, the U.S. Trade and Development Agency (USTDA) announced that it would provide a $400,000 grant to the Liberian Ministry of Lands, Mines and Energy to fund a technical and economic feasibility study of the rebuilding and expansion of the Mount Coffee Hydropower Station. The station, once a key national source of electricity, was destroyed during the first civil war. USTDA had first announced plans to support such a study in mid-May 2006.[237] This announcement had been preceded by a February 2006 announcement by the U.S. Export-Import Bank (Ex-Im) stating that it had renewed its Short-Term Insurance Pilot Program for Africa (STIPP) for three years beginning March 31, 2006, and that Liberia had been added to the program.[238] Similarly, in March 2006, the Overseas Private Investment Corporation (OPIC) had announced that "following the election of President Ellen John Sirleaf and the conclusion of its long civil war," it had "reopened its programs in Liberia for the first time since 1990" as part of an effort of "[r]eaffirming U.S. government support for Liberia."[239]

OPIC is now involved in a public-private commercial and investment business development lending project, the Liberia Enterprise Development Fund (LEDF), together with the RLJ Companies of Black Entertainment Television founder Robert L. Johnson, CHF International, and the U.S. African Development Foundation (ADF). The purpose of LEDF is to create a projected $30 million loan portfolio aimed at supporting small businesses in Liberia. OPIC has committed to provide $20 million in debt financing to LEDF, and Mr. Johnson and the ADF have committed, respectively, to provide $3 million and $1 million annually over three years. CHF International will administer the program in Liberia.[240] OPIC also co-sponsored a Liberia Private Sector Investment Forum in February 2007.

Air and Communications Links

Another effort aimed at fostering bilateral ties, including commercial ones, was the February 2007 signing of an Open Skies aviation agreement between the United States and Liberia.[241] In October 2008, Delta Airlines announced plans to initiate U.S.-Liberia flights, an outcome that would fulfill some of the goals of the Open Skies agreement.[242] Flights were originally slated to begin in mid-2009, but Delta's plans faced delays, and flights are now slated to begin in mid- 2010.[243] Delta's initial plans were deferred in June 2009, when the U.S. Department of Homeland Security (DHS) announced that it would not authorize the operation of the planned route, pending further DHS evaluation of Delta's request to initiate the flights. The decision followed an assessment of Roberts International Airport (ROB), outside Monrovia, by the Transportation Security Administration (TSA), a DHS unit. It indicated that ROB did not meet international security and International Civil Aviation Organization (ICAO) standards.[244]

TSA is providing Liberia with technical assistance to enhance aviation security and compliance with ICAO standards. It has deployed an Aviation Security Sustainable International Standards Team (ASSIST) to Liberia to assess local needs and help build national capacities in this area, and is slated to conduct a reassessment of ROB capabilities in these areas.[245] ROB services and infrastructure are also being upgraded, in part with the U.S.-supported, contract-based assistance of Lockheed Martin Global Services.[246] Another key benchmark necessary prior to the initiation of flights to Monrovia was met in October 2009, when the TSA reportedly gave provisional approval for the operation of Delta flights at Amilcar Cabral International Airport in Cape Verde, which is slated to function as a refueling stop for Delta's planned flights to Liberia and other African destinations.[247]

The U.S. Postal Service (USPS), in cooperation with the Departments of Defense and State, is also helping to boost U.S.-Liberian communications and help rebuild Liberian government capacity. USPS has donated postal equipment to Liberia, trained Liberian postal workers, and provided recommendations regarding its future development.[248]

Debt Relief, Donor Cooperation, and Related Issues

In February, 2007, the United States, other governments, and several multilateral organizations co-hosted the Liberia Partners' Forum, a meeting between the Liberian government and Liberia's public sector creditors and bilateral assistance donors in Washington, D.C.[249] The aim of the event, following a similar one held in July 2006, was to review Liberia's achievements and challenges in the areas of economic governance, fiscal policy implementation, general economic development, and related matters. During the meeting, Bush Administration officials announced their intention to cancel $391 million in debt owed by Liberia to the United States, both under the Heavily Indebted Poor Countries (HIPC) Initiative and in cooperation with other donors, such as the World Bank, the African Development Bank, and the International Monetary Fund.[250] In early June 2008, the United States acted on its pledge, writing off $394 million of Liberian debt under HIPC and Paris Club agreements. The U.S. Treasury has also provided over $185 million to support Liberian IMF debt relief financing and provided $17.5 million to clear Liberia's African Development Bank debt. As of mid-2009, official bilateral debt owed to the United States, slated to be cancelled after Liberia completes the HIPC process, totaled $29.26 million.[251]

Table 3. U.S. Bilateral and Related Assistance to Liberia, FY2004-FY2011 ($ millions; actual, estimated, or requested levels; errors due to rounding)

Account[a]	FY2004 Actual	FY2005 Actual	FY 2006 Actual[b]	FY2007 Actual[c]	FY2008 Actual[d]	FY2009 Actual[e]	FY20 10 Estimat[e]	FY2011 Request
CSH[f]	2.82	3.97	2.87	8.50	-	-	-	-
GHCS[f]	-	-	-	-	24.04	25.7	35.65	34.15
DA	-	6.85	23.73	30.50	29.86	32	-	-
ESF	-	24.8	92.72	30	43.19	104.3	153	137.34
FMF	-	2.98	1.98	1.52	.30	1.50	6	9
GHAI[f]	-	.70	.70	.95	-	-	-	-
IDFA-Supplemental[g]	200	-	-	-	-			
IDFA/IDA[g]	.04	9.71	3.71	2.46	-	-	-	-
INCLE	0	5	0.99	1	4.10	4.13	6	17
IMET	0	0	.13	.21	.38	.44	0.5	0.53
NADR-SALW	0.16	-	.22	5	-	-	-	-
PKO	-	25	20	53.25	51.66	49.65	10	5
P.L. 480, Title II/Food for Peace Title II[g]	21.53	22.55	26.97	16.47	9.41			
TI[h]	3.072	2.58	6.39	5.60	.06	-	-	
MRA[g]	27.89	28.19	31.65	22.5	-	-	-	
Sub-Total: Bilateral and Emerg. Aid	**255.51**	**132.33**	**212.06**	**177.96**	**163.00**	**224.02**	**226.15**	**218.02**
UNMIL/ CIPA[i]	290.34	235.42	77.17	177.21	154.28	123.40	135.40	135.40
Totals - All Funding	**545.85**	**367.75**	**289.23**	**355.17**	**317.28**	**347.42**	**361.55**	**353.42**

Sources: State Department, *Congressional Budget Justification for Foreign Operations [CBJ] and Department of State Congressional Budget Justification* for FY20 11 and prior fiscal years, and information from USAID/OFDA, State/PRM, State/OGAC, and State/Political-Military Affairs officials.

Notes:

a Account names: CSH: Child Survival and Health Program Fund Account; GHCS: Global Health and Child Survival Account; DA: Development Assistance Account; ESF: Economic Support Fund Account; FMF: Foreign Military Financing Account; GHAI: Global HIV/AIDS Initiative; IDA: International Disaster Assistance (former IDFA account; renamed IDA in FY 2008); IDFA: International Disaster & Famine Assistance Account (once known as the IDA account, which it was again renamed in FY 2008); INCLE: International Narcotics Control and Law Enforcement ; IMET: International Military Education and Training Account; NADR-SALW: Nonproliferation, Antiterrorism, Demining and Related Projects-Small Arms and Light Weapons; PKO: Regional Peacekeeping Account; TI: Transition Initiatives Account; MRA: Migration and Refugee Assistance Account; and CIPA: Contributions for International Peacekeeping Account

b Reflects regular FY2006 appropriation allocations and FY2006 supplemental appropriation under P.L. 109- 234. The Administration requested $13.8 in MRA funds for Liberia but did not request the $50 million in ESF support that the law provided. The purposes for which the ESF appropriation were used are listed on page 125 of the FY2008 CBJ. Regular and supplemental FY2006 bilateral and emergency aid totals $208.35 million; that assistance plus CIPA funding for FY2006 totals $280.77 million.

c Reflects regular FY2007 appropriation allocations and FY2007 supplemental funding levels as described in the FY 2009 *Congressional Budget Justification* and in State Department, *Congressional Budget Justification - Foreign Operations*, FY 2010. Supplementary FY2007 funds were provided to assist Liberia under P.L. 110-28 (passed as H.R. 2206 [Obey], the U.S. Troop Readiness, Veterans' Care, Katrina Recovery, and Iraq Accountability Appropriations Act, 2007, which former President Bush signed into law on May 25, 2007). Under P.L. 110-28, $40 million in regional Peacekeeping Operations (PKO) funds were allocated to support security sector reform in Liberia; $3 million in Economic Support Fund (ESF) supported the Special Court for Sierra Leone; and $5 million in regional Nonproliferation, Anti-Terrorism, Demining and Related (NADR) Programs were provided "for the protection of the Liberian President." P.L. 110-28 also authorized the U.S. Treasury to use FY2007 appropriated Bilateral Economic Assistance to aid Liberia in retiring its international financial institution debt arrears. Some of the Liberia-related language in P.L. 110-28 is contained in the joint explanatory statement in H.Rept. 110-107, which Section 3807 of P.L. 110-28 mandated guide the foreign assistance allocations, reporting requirements, and directives for which it provided appropriations. H.Rept. 110-107 accompanied H.R. 1591, which was vetoed by former President Bush. For background, see CRS Report RL3 3900, FY2007 *Supplemental Appropriations for Defense, Foreign Affairs, and Other Purposes*, coordinated by Stephen Daggett.

d FY 2008 spending allocation notification to Congress, including appropriations designated for Liberia under P.L. 110-161, and State Department, *Congressional Budget Justification - Foreign Operations*, FY 2010.

e All FY 2009 funding from regular FY 2009 foreign operations appropriations except for $10 million in DA funding from the FY 2009 Bridge Supplemental (P.L. 110-252, the Supplemental Appropriations Act, 2008) and $24 in ESF from the FY 2009 Spring Supplemental (P.L. 111-32, the Supplemental Appropriations Act, 2009). Several acts funded regular FY 2009 appropriations; for background, see CRS Report RL34552, *State, Foreign Operations, and Related Programs: FY2009 Appropriations*, by Susan B. Epstein and Kennon H. Nakamura.

f The Global Health and Child Survival account, created in FY 2008, integrates funds formerly allocated under the CSH and GHAI designations. In FY 2008, these were allocated between USAID and OGAC in the amounts of $23.235 million and $.8 million, respectively. In FY 2009, $24.9 million was allocated to USAID and $0.8 million to OGAC.

g Funding under some accounts, such as IDFA/IDA, MRA, and P.L. 480/Food for Peace Title II, often rises during a given fiscal year because these accounts are appropriated in a global lump sum and allocated throughout the year in response to emergent needs. Therefore requested amounts may differ substantially from actual disbursements, and in some cases, no country-specific level is requested. Congress officially designated food assistance that had long been referred to as P.L. 480 Title II, in reference to P.L. 83-480 (the Agricultural Trade Development and Assistance Act of 1954, as amended), as the Food for Peace Act in the 2008 farm bill (P.L. 110-246). This assistance provides U.S. food aid in response to emergencies and disasters overseas and non-emergency, development-focused programs that help improve food insecurity globally. For background, see CRS Report R4 1072, *International Food Aid Programs: Background and Issues*, by Melissa D. Ho and Charles E. Hanrahan.

h TI entries for FY2004, FY2005, and FY2006 reflect levels reported in USAID's Budget Justification to the Congress FY2007 and the Administration's combined Congressional Budget Justification for Foreign Operations for FY2008. Internal OTI data reflect annual funding levels that differ from those reported in the Budget Justifications listed above. OTI reports the following actual TI funding levels for Liberia: FY2004: $4.067 million; FY2005: $2.15 million; and FY2006 $7.57 million. The FY2007 and FY 2008 levels reflects data in the FY 2009 Congressional Budget Justification.

i CIPA entries for FY2004 and FY2005 reflect levels reported in the State Department's *Budget* in Brief. Entries for FY2007 and FY2007 reflect information received by CRS from the International Organizations Bureau of the State Department. The FY2008 level reflects information provided by the State Department's International Organizations Bureau.

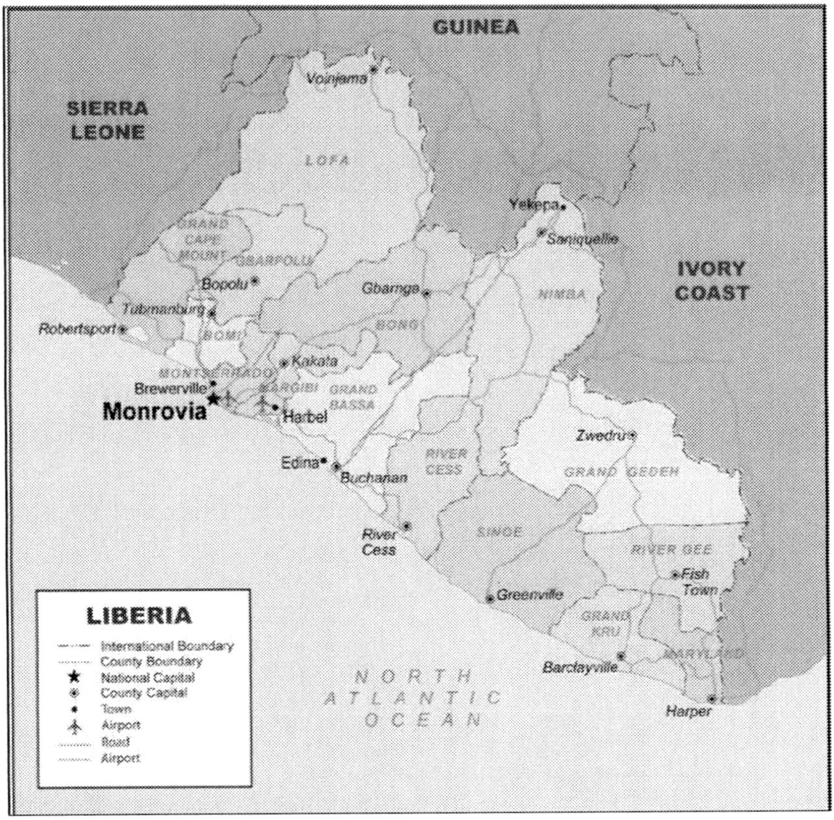

Source: Map Resources. Adapted by CRS.

Figure 1. Map of Liberia.

Several multilateral and bilateral creditor deals both prior to and after the U.S. action had also reduced Liberia's debt substantially, and as April 2010, bilateral debt reduction deals with all with all Paris Club creditors except Switzerland had been reached. In April 2009, Liberia was able to finalize negotiations to buy back $1.2 billion in outstanding government commercial debt held by hedge funds and other distressed debt investors (sometimes called vulture funds) at a deep discount of 97.5%, after the World Bank and several bilateral donors, including the United States, agreed to provide $38 million to pay off 25 outstanding commercial claims. The balance of its sovereign debt, $1.7 billion, was expected to be written off when Liberia reaches its HIPC Completion Point. The IMF also reported in April 2010 that the Liberian government planned to reach agreements with remaining official non-Paris

Club creditors, holding debt of $129 million, and private creditors holding $21 million of commercial debt, and was on target to reach its HIPC completion point in mid-2010, providing it met certain conditions. The $21 million (reported elsewhere as $20 million) is held by two vulture funds, Wall Capital Ltd. and Hamsah Investments, who were awarded a claim for that amount by a UK court after suing the Liberian government for repayment. The government has announced that it would be unable to pay the award, as doing so would violate its HIPC commitments, although it was seeking a waiver to do so. The original debt associated with the claim totaled $15 million, and had been resold several times.[252]

U.S. Assistance Levels

Levels of U.S. bilateral and U.N. peacekeeping assistance for Liberia, for FY2004 through FY2011, appear in **Table 3**.

End Notes

[1] Although her name is widely cited as Johnson-Sirleaf, the Liberian president does not employ a hyphenated form of her last name. See Wil Haygood, "For Liberia's 'Iron Lady,' Toughness Part of Territory," *Washington Post*, December 16, 2005.

[2] Such contacts have included an April 2009 meeting with Secretary of State Hillary Rodham Clinton, an official visit to Liberia in August 2009 by Secretary Clinton, and an April 2010 visit to Liberia by Under Secretary of State for Political Affairs William J. Burns, which are discussed below; see section on "U.S. relations."

[3] Liberian Government, "President Sirleaf To Meet US Government Officials in Washington," May 14, 2010.

[4] Administration of Barack H. Obama, *Memorandum on Deferred Enforced Departure for Liberians*, March 18, 2010.

[5] Taylor is being tried by the SCSL on war crimes and related charges under an amended, 11-count indictment first brought against him in 2003. The Prosecutor alleges that he directly aided and abetted diverse crimes allegedly committed in Sierra Leone by the RUF. Open Society Institute, "Trial Proceedings," http://www.charlestaylortrial.org; and SCSL press releases and court documents.

[6] TRC, *Consolidated Final Report* (unedited), Volume II, June 29, 2009.

[7] These party realignments are viewed as part an effort to create a strong political coalition in support of the reelection of President Sirleaf in 2011. Just prior to the LUP convention in mid-February 2010, a number of politicians from several smaller parties, some former LUP members, agreed to join the party. The Informer, "Several Cross Carpet to LUP," February 12, 2010 via AllAfrica.com; Nana Adu Ampofo, "Major Liberian Parties Merge Ahead of 2011 Election," *Global Insight Daily Analysis*, April 2, 2009; and Economist Intelligence Unit, *Country Report Liberia*, June 2009.

[8] Peace Corps, "Liberia," December 17, 2009.

[9] Delta Air Lines, "Delta Expands Africa Presence with First-Ever Flight between Atlanta and Monrovia, Liberia," October 22, 2008; Dow Jones News Service, "TSA Blocks Delta Flights To 2 African Cities On Security," June 3, 2009; and TSA, "TSA and Liberia Partner to Enhance Aviation Security," April 7, 2009.

[10] Two of the other LPRC accused include the former speaker of the incumbent Liberian House of Representatives, Edwin Swone, Jr., and Senator Richard Devine. C. Emmanuel Johnson, "Court Continues Jurors Selection," *The News* (Monrovia) via AllAfrica.com January 6, 2009; Agence France Presse (AFP), "Former Liberia Leader Faces More Corruption Charges," May 17, 2008; The Analyst, "Bryant Pities Country - He, Others Absolved of Sabotage Charges," via allAfrica.com, May 8, 2009; and information to CRS provided by the State Department February 2 and 3, 2009.

[11] These include several iron ore projects with China Union, $2.6 billion; BHP Billiton, $2 billion; Severstal, $2 billion; Elenilto; $2.2 billion; and ArcelorMittal, $1.5 billion. ArcelorMittal and BHP Billiton are also in talks to create a joint venture to export ore from BHP Billiton holdings in Guinea through an ArcelorMittal-controlled rail link to Liberia's coast and achieve other business synergies, and Liberia's government is in talks with Brazil's Vale, which also owns concessions in Guinea, regarding a possible iron ore deal. AmLib Holdings, a gold mining firm, owns a $200 million concession. Recent large agricultural contracts include an $800 million palm oil concession deal with Sime Darby, and a possible $1.6 billion palm oil with Golden Agri Resources; and two prospective rubber deals, with the Cavalla Rubber Corporation ($75 million) and the Liberia Agricultural Company ($25 million). Liberia has also recently entered into several oil exploration contracts worth a total of $60 million. Reuters, "Major Foreign and Local Investments in Liberia," May 4 2010; Boakai Fofana, "Liberia: Govt Secures Huge Investment in Palm Oil Production," December 1, 2009, AllAfrica.com; Eric Onstad and Philip Blenkinsop, "ArcelorMittal, BHP Discuss Africa Iron Ore JV," Reuters, January 19, 2010.

[12] For information on past U.S.-Liberian relations, see CRS Report RL32243, *Liberia: Transition to Peace*, by Nicolas Cook and CRS Report RL3 0933, *Liberia: 1989-1997 Civil War, Post-War Developments, and U.S. Relations*, by Nicolas Cook.

[13] This report focuses on current issues and recent events. CRS Report RL32243, *Liberia: Transition to Peace*, and CRS Report RL3 0933, *Liberia: 1989-1997 Civil War, Post-War Developments, and U.S. Relations*, both by Nicolas Cook, provide in-depth background on events in Liberia during recent decades, and on the presidential tenure of Charles Taylor.

[14] S/2007/151, March 15, 2007.

[15] On benchmarks, see S/2007/479, August 8, 2007; S/2008/183, March 19, 2008; and S/2009/86, February 10, 2009.

[16] See S/RES/1885, September 15, 2009; and S/2010/88, February 17, 2010.

[17] Text Box Sources: CIA *World Factbook 2009*; World Bank *World Development Indicators*; International Monetary Fund press release, April 2010; Liberian 2008 Census; Economist Intelligence Unit (EIU); Ethnologue.com; and *Liberia Demographic and Health Survey 2007*; IMF Country Report No. 09/332, December 2009; and UNAIDS.

[18] Between January 1, 2004 and June 8, 2006, 17 UNMIL military personnel were repatriated to their home countries for probable SEA crimes; two UNMIL civilians were dismissed or faced a non-renewal of their contract; three UNMIL civilians were suspended; and investigations cleared 13 UNMIL military personnel and three UNMIL civilian police. State Department compilation.

[19] See UNMIL, "Statement on the Departure from Liberia of Five Crew Members, Employees of a UN Contractor," March 14, 2006.

[20] It was not clear, based on information available to CRS as of the date of this report, how much overlap there may have been in the number of cases reported during these two overlapping periods. State Department compilation of U.N. Office of Internal Oversight Services data

covering the period January 1, 2009 through August 31, 2009; and UNSC, S/2010/88, February 17, 2010.

[21] CPA text available from U.S. Institute of Peace (USIP), http://www.usip.org/library/pa.html.

[22] Current junior senators, those who obtained the second highest number of votes in the 2005 elections, will serve a six-year term. Thereafter, all senators will serve nine year terms.

[23] Full election results are available online from the NEC at http://www.necliberia.org/results.

[24] See "**Error! Reference source not found.**" under section *Current Governance Issues*, below.

[25] Coalition for International Justice, *Following Taylor's Money: A Path of War and Destruction*, May 2005.

[26] Various periodic UNSG progress reports on UNMIL; State Department information, both published and provided to CRS; and NEC data. The author of this section served as an election observer. In the county where he monitored the voting process, the election was well-run. Poll workers appeared well trained; voting equipment and materials were distributed on time and in sufficient quantity; and voting was peaceful and voter turnout rates high.

[27] Various periodic UNSG progress reports on UNMIL; and information provided to CRS by USAID.

[28] For an assessment of these and subsequent USAID-administered elections and participatory democracy- strengthening work, see USAID/Liberia, *Liberia Elections and Political Processes Program Evaluation, Final Report,* November 2008.

[29] NEC, Statement by Hon. James M. Fromayan, Chairman of the National Elections Commission (NEC) on the Occasion of the Announcement of the Final Results of the Montserrado County Senatorial By-election Run-Off, November 26, 2009; IFES-Liberia, "Briefing Note on Liberia's Successful Senatorial By-election," December 4, 2009; and IFES, "IFES Returns to Work with Liberia's National Elections Commission," October 7, 2009.

[30] IFES's $17.5 million project, which runs through 2014, seeks to support the NEC's elections administration capabilities and will support its activities as they relate to the 2011 general election, a planned constitutional referendum, local elections, and any by-elections. Key activities center on boundary delimitation, voter registration processes, civic and voter education, notably at the community level, and making the NEC's capacity to undertake its mandate autonomously in the absence of donor assistance, notably through the provision of technical assistance and training. IFES, *Building Sustainable Elections Management in Liberia*, n.d. (current as of late April 2010).

[31] Post-war unemployment was often cited in U.N. documents and reports by diverse private research organizations as standing between 80% and 85%. In late 2007, President Sirleaf stated that previous reports that the unemployment rate stood at 85% were exaggerated. A 2007 study funded by the U.S. Agency for International Development (USAID), several U.N. donors, and the Liberian government and undertaken by several Liberian government agencies with with technical assistance from Macro International Inc. reported a national unemployment rate of 26.5%, 34.2% for women and 18.8% for men. See *Liberia Demographic and Health Survey 2007*, June 2008.

[32] President Sirleaf, *Inaugural Address of H.E. Ellen Johnson Sirleaf*, January 16, 2006.

[33] President Sirleaf, *Inaugural Address, op cit.*

[34] On China's diplomatic rivalry with Taiwan, see CRS Report RL33510, *Taiwan: Overall Developments and Policy Issues in the 109th Congress.*

[35] President Sirleaf, *Inaugural Address, op cit.* According to UNMIL media summaries, local Liberian media reported that a Liberian women's group demanded the establishment of a special expedited rape cases court during a late June 2006 public demonstration. See also Katharine Houreld, "Liberia's Women Fight Back," *Mail & Guardian*, June 2, 2006.

[36] Available online from PeaceAfrica, a project of the AllAfrica Foundation. See http://allafrica.com/peaceafrica/ resources/view/00010785.pdf.

[37] EIU, *Country Report/Liberia*, December 2007.

[38] Liberian Government, "Liberia: President Sirleaf Urges African Union to Denounce Zimbabwe Election Results," July 2, 2008. The MRU is a sub-regional body, originally an economic development entity that later became a forum for political crisis interventions and dialogue, made up of Liberia, Sierra Leone, and Guinea, which Cote d'Ivoire agreed to join in 2008 during a visit by President Johnson-Sirleaf.

[39] On Guinea, see CRS Report R41200, *Guinea's New Transitional Government: Emerging Issues for U.S. Policy*, by Alexis Arieff and CRS Report R40703, *Guinea: Background and Relations with the United States*, by Alexis Arieff and Nicolas Cook.

[40] Janneh was the transitional government's justice minister and is a former leading member of the LURD rebel group. Critics see Janneh as responsible, in part, for violence committed by LURD fighters against civilians during the Liberian war and view his nomination as counter to the goals and spirit of the TRC. Michael Kpayili, "Liberia: Liberian Senate Confirms Kabineh Jan'eh As Associate Supreme Court Justice," *The Liberian Times*, May 9, 2006.

[41] The Analyst, "Gov't Reconstitutes Human Rights Commission," August 18, 2009; Executive Mansion, "Commissioners of Independent Human Rights Commission Named," August 18, 2009; and International Center for Transitional Justice (ICTJ), "Liberia: Delay of Human Rights Commission Undermines Human Rights and Accountability," February 19, 2010.

[42] *The Analyst* (Monrovia), "Liberia: President Promises to Probe Manhandling of Journalists," June 19, 2006.

[43] James Butty, "Liberian Media Reports Government Harassment of Press," VOA, June 16, 2006; CPJ, "Liberia: Journalist Assaulted by Security Forces," May 24, 2006; and CPJ, "Liberia: Sports Editor Assaulted," March 10, 2006, among others.

[44] Ann Cooper, Exec. Dir, "Liberia: CPJ Urges President to Probe Attacks on Press [open letter]," CPJ, June 16, 2006.

[45] See Tristan McConnell, "Persistent Corruption Threatens Liberian stability," *Christian Science Monitor*, September 25, 2008; and FrontpageAfrica.com, "Liberian Govt. Responds to 'Persistent Corruption Threatens Stability'," January 10, 2008 [response to McConnell article published on third party website by Dr. Laurence Bropleh, Minister of Information, Culture & Tourism and Chief Spokesperson].

[46] *The Inquirer* (Monrovia), "Liberia: Ellen Signs Anti-Corruption Act, Commissions Several Officials," via AllAfrica.com, August 26, 2008; Nana Adu Ampofo, "Liberian President Signs Anti-Corruption Commission Act into Law," *Global Insight Daily Analysis*, August 27, 2008; Africa Confidential, Liberia: A Second Term for Sirleaf, May 14, 2010; and Liberian Presidency, "Cllr. Frances Johnson Morris Appointed Head of Anti-Corruption Commission," September 1, 2008.

[47] See "Liberia Shows Dramatic Improvement in Controlling Corruption," document posted on Liberian presidential website, no date (likely circa mid-2008).

[48] LISCR administers Liberia's widely used flag of convenience ship registry, which under the Taylor regime was alleged to have been a source of corruptly diverted funds. Prior to the allegations that led to the appointment of the Dunn Commission, the Sirleaf Administration had faced a sex scandal associated with the Acting State and Presidential Affairs Minister, Willis Knuckles, that was linked in the press to a corruption probe associated with the ouster of former Liberian House Speaker, Edwin Melvin Snowe (see below). See Nana Adu Ampofo, "President Appoints Special Corruption Commission in Liberia," *Global Insight Daily Analysis*, September 4, 2008; Liberian Presidency, "Executive Mansion Reacts to Purported Email Exchanges—Distances President Johnson Sirleaf," August 24, 2008; James Butty, "Under Pressure, Liberian Government Appoints Special Corruption Commission," VOA, September 3, 2008; and Ugochukwu Ejinkeonye, "The Willis Knuckles Saga," *SaharaReporters.Com*, March 7, 2007, among others.

[49] Its findings were complex, due to the alleged nature of the allegations. In some cases, it refuted the allegations, while in others it found partial or clear proof of wrong-doing. It found that there "were violations and breaches of Liberian laws and policies by some" government officials, private individuals, and private businesses investigated, but was not able to fully

investigate all matters under its purview because some of its subjects refused to cooperate with the Commission. See *Report of the Ad-Hoc Independent Commission on the E-Mail Saga*, January 7, 2009; and Liberian presidency, "ECOWAS Summit on Guinea and Dunn Commission Report Take Center Stage at Press Conference," January 12, 2009.

[50] Africa Confidential, "Liberia: A Second Term for Sirleaf, " May 14, 2010; and GAC, multiple documents available from GAC website, http://www.gacliberia.com/.

[51] Africa Confidential, "Liberia: A Second Term for Sirleaf, " May 14, 2010; Economist Intelligence Unit, Country Report Liberia, March 2010; Agence France Presse, "Liberia's Agriculture Minister Resigns Amid Caterpillar Crisis," April 5, 2009; and The Analyst, "Sirleaf Draws the Dagger," September 9, 2009.

[52] S/2010/88, February 17, 2010.

[53] S/2008/88, February 17, 2010.

[54] State Department/International Narcotics and Law Enforcement Affairs Bureau, *Fiscal Year 2010 Program and Budget Guide*.

[55] S/2008/8 8, February 17, 2010; S/2009/640, December 11, 2009; State Department, *Liberia Country Specific Information* [Travel Information], August 10, 2009; and Magnus Jörgel and Mats Utas, *The Mano River Basin Area: Formal and Informal Security Providers in Liberia, Guinea and Sierra Leone*, Swedish Defence Research Agency, 2007.

[56] In mid-2009, the U.N. Secretary-General reported that "many of the 14,000 deactivated Armed Forces of Liberia soldiers also maintain viable command and control structures, which are utilized to organize recurrent, sometimes violent, demonstrations to challenge the legality of their deactivation or demand benefit arrears owed by the Government." S/2009/299, June 10, 2009.

[57] "Heartmen" is a Liberian English term for killers whose purpose is to remove various body organs for uses, including consumption, in traditional occult ceremonies that participants believe bestow supernatural powers, allowing beneficiaries to increase their personal wealth, power over others, and achieve other ends. Such practices, known as *gboyo* in southeast Liberia, have been reported to increase during times of armed conflict, notably in situations in which combatants have harvested organs from dead enemies in order to increase their chances of further military victory. Analagous occult practices occur in some other African countries. New Dawn, "More Arrest in "Gbo-yo" Business," March 29, 2010; Christopher Melville, "Riots and Ritual Killings in South-Eastern Liberia Highlight Paradox of Improving Security," *WMRC Daily Analysis*, January 26, 2005; and Stephen Ellis, "Mystical Weapons: Some Evidence from the Liberian War," *Journal of Religion in Africa*, 31: 2, May, 2001, among others.

[58] Amos Sawyer, "Land Governance Challenges: The Case Of Liberia," World Bank presentation, n.d./circa 2008; and S/2009/640, December 11, 2009; Executive Mansion, "Special Land Commission Presents Report to Liberian President," May 24, 2009; The Analyst (Monrovia), "Liberia: Land Commission Act Approved," July 24, 2009; and UN-HABITAT, "A New Land Programme in Liberia, December 21, 2009.

[59] These sanctions were first imposed under U.N. Security Council Resolution 1521 (2003), which prohibited trade in arms and diamonds with Liberia, and the travel of certain designated individuals, mostly members or associates of the Taylor regime. Some of the listed individuals are also subject to financial asset freezes mandated by U.N. Security Council Resolution 1532 (2004).

[60] Liberia remains under an arms embargo, with an exception for government purposes, although all arms transfers to the government must occur under a Security Council notification and control regime; see Resolution 1903 (S/RES/1903, December 17, 2009). When the war ended in 2003, Liberia was subject to a general arms embargo, but the Security Council gradually amended it to allow certain vetted and trained police and security forces to be trained and armed, and for military training purposes. UNMIL regularly inspects government security force weapons armories; see S/2009/290, June 5, 2009.

[61] The accord is the Ouagadougou Political Agreement of March 2007, which lays out political and military disarmament processes leading to elections, which have repeatedly been delayed.

[62] For further information, see CRS Report R40703, *Guinea: Background and Relations with the United States*, by Alexis Arieff and Nicolas Cook.

[63] Navy News Stand, "Navy Tug Fights Fire Aboard Freighter in Liberia," August 11, 2006 and "Navy Tug Rescues Liberian Fishermen," August 16, 2006; U.S. Embassy-Monrovia, "U.S. Navy Tug Begins Repair Work in Liberian Harbor," August 10, 2006; and Karfa Jamanka, "Maritime Receives Assessment Team," *The Inquirer*, September 22, 2006.

[64] Marcus Malayea, "Gunmen Seize Cocopa, Claim Right of Inheritance," *The Analyst*, August 18, 2006, among others.

[65] Executive Mansion, "Liberian Leader Concludes Visit to Sinoe," May 5, 2009; Rebecca Murray , "Liberia: Wild West - the Sinoe Rubber Plantation," Inter Press Service, April 8, 2009; IRIN, "Liberia: Gov't Reclaims Rubber Plantation from Former Fighters," August 16, 2006; Alphonso Toweh, "Liberia takes rubber estate back from ex- rebels," Reuters, August 15, 2006; IRIN, "Liberia: UN Vows to Repossess another Troubled Rubber Plantation," 23 August 23, 2006; and D. Sonpon Weah II, "Ex-Combatants at SRC Ready to Leave," *The Analyst*, September, 27, 2006.

[66] UNMIL, *Human Rights in Liberia's Rubber Plantations: Tapping into the Future*, May 2006.

[67] S/2010/88, February 17, 2010.

[68] S/2010/88, February 17, 2010. Nine indicted grand jury defendants went on trial for the murder in February 2010. Marcus Zoleh, "Liberia: Keith Jubah Murder Trial to Resume Tomorrow," *The Informer* (Monrovia), February 16, 2010, *inter alia*.

[69] The size of the force reflects a compromise between the need to build a force that can be sustainably funded over the long-term, taking into account Liberia's high rate of poverty and relatively small national budget; field a force capable of defending against possible regional threats; start with a relatively moderately-sized force and potentially gradually enlarge it in response to emergent need; and create a force over which civilian control can be maintained, in part by limiting its size and rate of growth.

[70] In mid-February 2006, President Sirleaf, stating that "our country currently lacks the technical and tactical capacities and proficiency to provide for its own defense and national security," appointed Major-General Luka Yusuf, a Nigerian UNMIL officer, to be Liberia's military Chief of Staff heading the rebuilding of the armed forces. He was later replaced by another Nigerian, General Suraj Abdurrahman. The appointment of a Nigerian head of the army drew criticism from former Liberian military elements, who called it unconstitutional and an insult to Liberia's national pride. See *Agence France-Presse*, "Liberian Leader Names Nigerian to Head Military," February 13, 2006 and Alphonso Toweh, "Liberia Leader Gets Flak for Hiring Nigeria General," Reuters, February 14, 2006.

[71] Female recruitment reportedly faced substantial cultural and gender biases against the participation of women in the military. Jonathan Paye-Layleh, "Liberia Begins Recruiting Women Soldiers," Associated Press, June 5, 2006; International Crisis Group (ICG), *Liberia: Uneven Progress in Security Sector Reform*, January 13, 2009; and Mark Malan, *Security Sector Reform In Liberia: Mixed Results From Humble Beginnings*, U.S. Army Strategic Studies Institute, March 2008.

[72] CRS field visit, 2006; Dorina Bekoe and Christina Parajon, "Security Sector Reform in Liberia: Domestic Considerations and the Way Forward," Center for Conflict Analysis and Prevention/USIP, April 2007; and *The Inquirer* (Monrovia), "Liberia: Public Vetting for Army Recruits Begins Monday," June 23, 2006. For more detailed information on recruitment and vetting, see ICG, *Liberia: Uneven Progress*.

[73] S/2010/88, February 17, 2010; and President Sirleaf, annual message to the legislature, January 26, 2009.

[74] A number of officers and other personnel underwent training at Nigeria's Command Army Staff College. The United States, China, and Germany, among other donor governments,

have also provided specialist training to some personnel. See S/2008/553, August 15, 2008; and S/2008/183, March 19, 2008.

[75] Total demobilization costs totaled approximately $15 million, and the process was the subject of some local controversy. In late April 2006, 400-500 former AFL soldiers claiming nonpayment of salary arrears and retirement benefits conducted a violent protest outside the defense ministry and clashed with UNMIL peacekeepers sent to contain the unrest. Some of these soldiers reportedly later received some back pay, although some arrears remain. "President Authorizes Defense Ministry to Pay Salary Arrears to Former Soldiers," UNMIL media summary citing ELBS Radio and Star Radio, June 14, 2006; USIP, "A Discussion with Liberia's Defense Minister, Brownie J. Samukai, Jr.," May 11, 2007; Executive Mansion, "Leadership of Demobilized AFL Soldiers Assure President Sirleaf of Unwavering Support," February 24, 2010; periodic U.N. reports on the progress of UNMIL and developments in post-war Liberia; and State Department information (email communication April 2, 2010).

[76] Camp Sandee Ware was formerly known as VOA Camp, named for a nearby former Voice of America and U.S. government communcations transmission tower, now scrapped. Sorbor George, "VOA Military Camp renamed 'Camp Sandee Ware'," Star Radio, July 22, 2007.

[77] According to one observer, at one point, due to "U.S. Government funding shortfalls, the MOD Reform program was terminated following completion of civil servant training but prior to the implementation of a planned five-month mentoring and 'on the job' training phase. Consequently, new civil servants had no source of advice or assistance as they assumed their official duties in the newly restructured Ministry of National Defense. The failure to follow through with the mentoring component of MOD Reform missed a valuable opportunity to shape the operation of the new MOD as an institution." See Thomas Dempsey, "Security Sector Reform in Liberia Part I: An Assessment of Defense Reform," *Perspectives on Peace & Stability Operations* (Issue Paper No. 2008), Peacekeeping and Stability Operations Institute, U.S. Army War College, July 1, 2008. Liberian defense officials were sometimes critical about the manner in which U.S. SSR resources were used by contractors, notably with regard to subcontracting issues, and sometimes complained of a lack of information or consultation regarding assistance-related communications between U.S. SSR contractors and U.S. embassy officials in Monrovia. USIP, "A Discussion with Liberia's Defense Minister..."; Jake Sherman, *Strengthening Security Sector Governance in West Africa*, Center on International Cooperation, New York University, March 2009; Charles Crawford, "Samukai Destests Awarding of Feeding Contract of New Army to Foreigners," *The Inquirer*, August 22, 2006; *The Inquirer*, "Delay Over Army Training?," January 29, 2007; Michael M. Phillips, "In Liberia, an Army Unsullied by Past," *Wall Street Journal*, August 14, 2007; and *The Inquirer*, "Who's Responsible for Soldiers' Outburst," April 14, 2008

[78] The document signed is an Acquisition and Cross-Servicing Agreement (ACSA), one of at least 90 worldwide, which permits "the exchange of logistics, support, supplies and services," between the United States and Liberia. U.S. EUCOM, "U.S.-Liberia Agreement Meant to Ease Acquisition Process," Press Release, April 24, 2007.

[79] S/2010/88, February 17, 2010; and The Analyst, "Liberia: From the Cold - AFL Marches Gallantly," February 12, 2010.

[80] The work is being undertaken under a five-year, State Department PKO account-funded indefinite delivery/indefinite quantity [IDIQ]) defense services, support, and capacity-building contract called the Africa Peacekeeping Program (AFRICAP). Awardees under AFRICAP include DynCorp International, PAE Government Services, AECOM, and Protection Strategies Incorporated. See Business Wire, "DynCorp International Wins $20 Million AFRICAP Task Order in Liberia," January 28, 2010; and documents pertaining to State Department Africa Peacekeeping Program contract solicitation SAQMMA08R0237 ("AFRICAP Recompete") available from the Federal Business Opportunities (FBO) website, https://www.fbo.gov.

[81] The projected contract for this work would be worth between $.25 million and $.5 million. See Army Corps of Engineers, Ammunition/Arms Facility Design and Upgrade Liberia, Africa LI-B-HAB [Pre-Solicitation Synopsis], solicitation number W912GB10-R0029, March 11, 2010, available from the FBO website.

[82] S/2010/88, February 17, 2010; and S/2009/411, August 10, 2009.

[83] The U.S. mentoring team is complemented by a United Kingdom Ministry of Defense-level advisor. Lydia M. Davey, "ONWARD LIBERTY Provides U.S. Mentors to Armed Forces of Liberia," Marine Forces Africa press release, February 24, 2010; and AFRICOM, *US Africa Command Contribution to Defense Sector Reform in Liberia*, January 15, 2010.

[84] The 2009/10 fiscal year national budget totaled $371.9 million. S/2010/88, February 17, 2010.

[85] DIRI is a DoD-led program designed initiated in FY 2010 to help selected foreign governments to "develop accountable, professional, and transparent defense establishments that can manage, sustain, and employ their forces and the capabilities developed through U.S. security cooperation programs." While DoD-led, it "supports broad USG security sector reform objectives and whole-of-government approaches. The program primarily supports activities related to defense policy and strategy formulation, and planning, budgeting and resource management; civilian and military defense sector human resource development and training; logistics and infrastructure capacity-building; civil- military relations; and interagency coordination. Defense Security Cooperation Agency (DSCA), *Fiscal Year 2011 Budget Estimates*, February 2010; and DoD/Office of the Secretary of Defense, *Defense Institution Reform Initiative Fact Sheet*, September 1, 2009.

[86] Information from DIRI Liberia Program officer current as of April 13, 2010.

[87] S/2009/640, December 11, 2009

[88] USIP, "A Discussion with Liberia's Defense Minister, Brownie J. Samukai, Jr.," May 11, 2007.

[89] Defense Minister Samukai has suggested that in the long-term, public investments in the AFL are likely to contribute to non-defense related national development, as members of the AFL with specialized functional training enter the civilian sector upon retiring from the AFL. USIP, "A Discussion with Liberia's Defense Minister, Brownie J. Samukai, Jr.," May 11, 2007

[90] UNMIL reports that there have been continuing tensions between the AFL and civilian security agencies, including at least eight confrontations, some violent, since September 2008, and that there have been several "aggravated assaults" by AFL members on civilians, including at least two stabbings. See S/2010/88, February 17, 2010, along with Julius Kanubah, "AWOL Soldiers Begin Returning to Base," Star Radio, May 5, 2008; and Rebecca Murray, "Liberia: New Army Faces Greatest Challenge," Inter Press Service, December 26, 2009.

[91] S/2010/88, February 17, 2010.

[92] Louise Andersen, *Post-Conflict Security Sector Reform and the Challenge of Ownership - The Case of Liberia*, Danish Institute for International Studies, July 2006; Sean McFate, "Outsourcing the Making of Militaries: DynCorp International as Sovereign Agent," *Review of African Political Economy*, December 1, 2008; and Alan Bryden, Linkage between DDR and SSR, Second International Conference on DDR and Stability in Africa/U.N. Office of the Special Adviser on Africa (OSAA), June 12-14, 2007.

[93] David C. Gompert, Olga Oliker, Brooke Stearns, Keith Crane, and Kevin Jack Riley, *Making Liberia Safe: Transformation of the National Security Sector*, RAND, June 2006. RAND is a U.S. think tank and policy research organization that often carries out sensitive U.S. government contract work. Quotation from Adedeji Ebo, "Local Ownership and Emerging Trends in SSR: A Case Study of Outsourcing in Liberia," in Timothy Donais (Ed.), Local Ownership and Security Sector Reform, LIT Verlag, 2008. See also Alexander Loden, "Civil Society and Security Sector Reform in Post-conflict Liberia: Painting a Moving Train without Brushes," *The International Journal of Transitional Justice*, Vol. 1, 2007.

[94] The GRC, later called the Governance Commission (GC), was created under the 2003 peace accord to assess and reform public sector institutions with respect to such outcomes as operational effectiveness, transparency, accountability, and public participation and access.

[95] Quote from Ebo, "Local Ownership...," who discusses this process at length. On challenges associated with the GRC-led process, see also Malan, *Security Sector Reform in Liberia.* Notwithstanding the GRC's role, executive branch domination of the SSR process and lack of public access to it has been a central point of criticism; in early 2009, for instance, the International Crisis Group reported that "more than halfway through Johnson-Sirleaf's term, the official national security strategy has yet to be made public, though a supposedly final version is circulating among Liberian and international officials." See International Crisis Group, *Liberia: Uneven Progress in Security Sector Reform*, Africa Report 148, January 13, 2009, as well as Malan, *Security Sector Reform in Liberia* and Ebo, "Local Ownership..."

[96] This account is based on a 2008 U.S. Coast Guard assessment report, discussed below; a discussion with a representative of the Office of International Affairs, Security Cooperation Office, U.S. Coast Guard on March 31, 2010 and subsequent email communications; and CRS research.

[97] It dealt with issues including LCG legal authority; personnel and staffing; training (technical, leadership, and management); infrastructure needs; vessels, equipment, and supplies; technical assistance and mentoring; and planning and development.

[98] The maritime advisor is attached to the Office of Security Cooperation within the U.S. Embassy in Liberia.

[99] President Sirleaf, *Goodwill Message* [2010 Armed Forces Day speech], February 11, 2010.

[100] Jason Morris, "APS, Seabees Bolster Liberia's Coast Guard," Africa Partnership Station [APS] Public Affairs, U.S. Navy, October 20, 2009.

[101] Patrick McCollum, "National Guard Adds State Partnership in Liberia," National Guard Bureau, August 13, 2009; and National Guard (NG), written communication to CRS, April 5, 2010.

[102] According to the National Guard, the SPP mission is to "enhance combatant commanders' ability to build enduring civil-military relationships that improve long-term international security while building partnership capacity across all levels of society." SPP "states and their partners participate in a broad range of strategic security cooperation activities to include homeland defense/security, disaster response/mitigation, consequence/crisis management, interagency cooperation, border/port/aviation security, combat medical, fellowship-style internships, and bilateral familiarization events that lead to training and exercise opportunities. All activities are coordinated through the Combatant Commanders, U.S. Ambassadors' country teams, and other agencies as appropriate to ensure National Guard cooperation is tailored to meet U.S. and international partners' objectives." National Guard, written communication to CRS, April 7, 2010 [*NG to CRS* hereafter].

[103] *NG to CRS*, April 7, 2010.

[104] According to the NGB, the pairing followed "a comprehensive review and selection process, analyzing state port security operations, military development, agriculture development, engineer operations, medical services delivery, crisis management, and State Partnership Program events with previous partners and while considering geographical, economic, military, and political factors with respect to Liberia." McCollum, "*National Guard Adds*," *op cit.;* and *NG to CRS*, April 7, 2010.

[105] NG, written communication to CRS, April 8, 2010.

[106] Ellen Johnson Sirleaf, "AFRICOM can Help Governments Willing to Help Themselves," *AllAfrica.com*, June 25, 2007. Also see CRS Report RL34003, *Africa Command: U.S. Strategic Interests and the Role of the U.S. Military in Africa*, by Lauren Ploch.

[107] Jason Morris, "APS, Seabees Bolster Liberia's Coast Guard," APS/U.S. Navy, October 20, 2009; APS/U.S. Navy, "Liberian President Accepts Donation from HVS Swift," via DoD Live, September 8, 2009; Dan Meaney, "APS Swift Army veterinary team in Liberia," U.S. Army news release, September 16, 2009; Elsa Portillo, "U.S. Marines, Soldiers and Sailor Join With Liberian Soldiers, for AFL Rebuilding," Marine Forces Africa, March 2, 2009; Elsa Portillo, "Marines Partner With Liberian Soldiers to Deliver School Supplies," Marine Forces Africa, March 3, 2009; Marine Forces Africa, "Flagship Brings Musical Approach to

APS Mission," October 26, 2009; and Jason Morris, "Africa Partnership Station and Project Hope Team Up in Liberia," APS/U.S. Navy, March 27, 2008.

[108] J. D. Hood, *Enhancing Maritime Safety and Security in Africa/Africa Partnership Station*, U.S. Navy, November 2009.

[109] The goal of the APS program, a component of the Navy's larger Global Maritime Partnership (GMP) and the Global Fleet Stations security cooperation efforts, is to bolster U.S. security relations and coastal security and related maritime capabilities in African countries. APS cooperation, which began in West Africa and now is being undertaken in East Africa; is responsive to U.S. and African-identified training and capacity needs, and incorporates contributions by selected foreign donor nations. Training is tailored to specific country needs and takes place over repeated port calls by APS vessels, which are capable of housing and deploying multiple training teams, platforms, and mechanisms. Training is diverse, pertaining to such areas of activity as port management and security capacity building; law and regulatory enforcement; engineering and logistics; maritime skills and professionalization education; search and rescue; and disaster response. APS personnel also provide humanitarian and limited development assistance, sometimes inland. Hood, *Enhancing Maritime Safety*, op cit; Gene Porter, "Global Maritime Partnerships - GMP," Office of Global Maritime Situational Awareness Wiki, January 4, 2010; David B. Waidelich, *A New Twist to an Age Old Naval Tradition: the Maritime Strategy and its Impact on Humanitarian Assistance and Maritime Security Operations* [Master of Military Studies thesis], Marine Corps University, 2008/9; U.S. Marine Corps, *Global Fleet Stations Concept*, July 30, 2007; and Ploch, *Africa Command* (CRS Report RL34003, *Africa Command: U.S. Strategic Interests and the Role of the U.S. Military in Africa*), *op cit.*

[110] Such agreements allow boarding by security officials of each signatory country and certain third countries of a ship flagged and registered under the other signatory country's laws, if the vessel is suspected of engaging in illicit proliferation activities. See State Department, "Proliferation Security Initiative Ship Boarding Agreement with Liberia," signed and provisionally applied as of February 11, 2004; entered into force December 9, 2004; and State Department, "The Proliferation Security Initiative (PSI)," Fact Sheet, May 26, 2008.

[111] S/2009/4 11, August 10, 2009.

[112] See periodic reports on UNMIL and Liberia by the U.N. Secretary-General; and Andreas Mehler, *The Production of Insecurity by African Security Forces: Insights from Liberia and the Central African Republic*, GIGA Working Paper 114, November 2009, among others.

[113] S/2008/553, August 15, 2008; see also S/2008/183, *op cit.*

[114] S/2008/553, August 15, 2008, *op cit.*

[115] S/2010/88, February 17, 2010.

[116] The SSS is also armed. UNSC Resolution 1903 (S/RES/1903, December 17, 2009) allows the controlled shipment of arms and related materiel to the Liberian government.

[117] S/2010/88, February 17, 2010; and President Sirleaf, annual message to the legislature, January 26, 2009.

[118] There were 10 U.S. UNMIL CIVPOL officers in February 2010, according to the United Nations.

[119] INL, FY 2010 Program and Budget Guide.

[120] See S/2007/15 1, March 15, 2007; other Secretary-General's reports on Liberia; and INL *Program and Budget Guides* for FY 2008, FY 2009, and FY 2010.

[121] In 2006, DSS planned to continue to assist the SSS on an interim basis, and proposed provision of a more structured two-year-long assistance package. The proposal called for DSS to provide five U.S. contract-based presidential security advisors who would help run SSS operations on an interim basis and at the same time help the SSS to enhance its operational and administrative capacities. It also called for some equipment and training to be provided under the package, projected to cost about $3 million per year.

[122] War-related psycho-social trauma is also seen as widespread. The preliminary findings of a September 2005 WHO/Liberian government sexual and gender-based violence survey

found that 9 1.7% of women and girls interviewed had been the victims of multiple violent acts during Liberia's war (Security Council, S/2005/764, December 7, 2005). The transitional legislature made all rape illegal in December 2005 (only gang rape had previously been illegal) and laid out punishments for rape-relation violations, but activists say increased sexual violence-related law enforcement is needed. See U.N. Integrated Regional Information Networks (IRIN hereafter), "Liberia: Sexual Abuse of Children Still Rampant, Report Says," February 22, 2006, *inter alia.*

[123] UNAIDS, *AIDS Epidemic Update*, December 2007.

[124] IRIN PLUSNEWS, "Youth Not Putting HIV Prevention Lessons into Practice," October 27, 2005 and USAID, Health Profile: West Africa-HIV/AIDS, n.d.

[125] For background on the Global Fund, see CRS Report RL3 1712, *The Global Fund to Fight AIDS, Tuberculosis, and Malaria: Background*, by Tiaji Salaam-Blyther.

[126] See, for instance, *The Analyst*, "NTGL's Past Haunts Bryant, Others," March 9, 2006, regarding Liberian parliamentary investigations into the transitional government's budget and EU audits of key Liberian parastatals, available online through FrontPage Africa http://www.frontpageafrica.com.

[127] Discussion with U.S. embassy official.

[128] See U.S. Embassy-Monrovia, "U.S. Embassy Shocked and Disappointed at Abuse Of Public Trust," Press Release, November 18, 2005, and Integrated Regional Information Networks (IRIN), "Liberia: Scramble for Goodies Ahead of Political Handover," November 21 2005. IRIN is an editorially independent component of the U.N. Office for the Coordination of Humanitarian Affairs. It provides news and analysis about sub-Saharan Africa and other selected global regions. It seeks to inform decision makers in host and donor governments, non-governmental and international humanitarian and advocacy organizations, academic institutions, and the media about developments in the regions it covers.

[129] See Proclamation by the President, *To Suspend Entry as Immigrants or Non-immigrants of Persons Engaged in or Benefitting From Corruption*, January 12, 2004.

[130] Two of the other LPRC accused include the former speaker of the incumbent Liberian House of Representatives, Edwin Swone, Jr., and Senator Richard Devine. C. Emmanuel Johnson, "Court Continues Jurors Selection," *The News* (Monrovia) via AllAfrica.com January 6, 2009; and Agence France Presse (AFP), "Former Liberia Leader Faces More Corruption Charges," May 17, 2008.

[131] The agreement is between the government of Liberia and Firestone Natural Rubber Company, a U.S. limited liability firm that is an affiliate of Bridgestone-Firestone North American Tire, and its Liberian subsidiary, Firestone Plantations Company.

[132] A coalition of Liberian human rights groups unsuccessfully petitioned the Liberian Supreme Court to halt execution of the two contracts on such grounds and contended that the deals had been made without public input. The complainants reportedly may seek to re-file their case after the formation of the new elected government. See Morrison O.G. Sayon, "Supreme Court Places 'Stay Order', Firestone, Mittal Steel Agreements," *The Inquirer* (Monrovia), November 7, 2005; John Walsh, "Supreme Court Issues Stay Order On NTGL; Ja'neh Appears Today," FrontPageAfrica, November 7, 2005; George Bardue, "Supreme Court Stops Budget Execution and Summons NTGL Officials," *The News* (Monrovia), November 7, 2005.

[133] Ben Garside, "Police probe Mittal Steel's Liberian Iron Ore Deal," Metal Bulletin News Alert Service, July 13, 2006.

[134] Alphonso Toweh, "Liberia Minister Wants Mittal Iron Ore Deal Revised," Reuters, September 14, 2005; D. Moses Wantu, "Mittal Steel Hearing Backfires," *The Analyst* (Monrovia), September 6, 2005; Economist Intelligence Unit, "Liberia: A steel?," *Country Monitor*, August 29, 2005; Steve Swindells, "Mittal Steel Defends Pursuit of Liberian Iron Ore Concession," June 14, 2005 *Metal Bulletin News Alert Service*; *The Analyst* (Monrovia), "Bryant, Mittal Steel Flout Law," June 13, 2005; *The Analyst* (Monrovia), "NTGL Sued in U.S. District Court - Over LIMINCO Bidding," June 13, 2005, *inter alia.*

[135] A smaller former mine railroad between Monrovia and Bong County has been rehabilitated by AmLib, a mineral exploration firm, and put into use as a multi-use transport line. It has reportedly contributed to a several-fold drop in charcoal prices in Monrovia, and is increasing the supply of other farm products to the capital. Charcoal is the main cooking fuel in Liberia.

[136] Pollutants that reportedly may potentially be released into rivers or streams in the Firestone concession area as a result of agricultural or rubber processing include chemical residues such as ammonium nitrates, sulfuric acid, formaldehyde, and pesticides like dieldrin. *The Analyst* (Monrovia), "EPA Wants Tough Measures Against Firestone," April 5, 2005; George Bardue, "Firestone Discharges Waste Without Permit, Management Admits," *The News*, March 18, 2005; Gibson W. Jerue, "Threat to Life," The Analyst (Monrovia), March 14, 2005; and Syrulwa Somah, "Liberia is At a Brink of Irreversible Environmental/Ecological Impotency," *Liberian Observer*, March 21, 2005; and *The Analyst* (Monrovia), "Firestone Refutes Allegations, Says It Has Acted In Line With The Laws, But," March 17, 2005.

[137] The Firestone spokesperson reportedly stated that such effluent "is comparable to if not lower than the effluent standards in other rubber-producing countries such as India Malaysia and Indonesia." See BBC News, "Liberia Rubber Pollution Denied," May 2, 2007.

[138] Femi Oke, "Is Bridgestone/Firestone Exploiting Liberian Workers?," *Inside Africa*, CNN International, November 12, 2005; Joe Bavier, "Firestone Lease an Issue in Liberia Election Campaign," VOA News, September 14, 2005; Gary Gentile, "Firestone Accused of Using Slave Labor," Associated Press, November 17, 2005; and Reuters, "Labor Group Sues Bridgestone on Liberia Plantation," November 17, 2005, *inter alia.*

[139] See U.S. District Court, Southern District of Indiana, Indianapolis Division, John Roe I, et al., Plaintiffs v. Bridgestone Corporation, et al., Defendants, Case No. 1 :06-cv-0627-DFH-JMS, http://www.insd.uscourts.gov/ Opinions/AP6270O1 .pdf.

[140] Reportedly at issue in strike was an internal union split dividing, including between workers supportive of leaders favorable to accommodation with Firestone and a group seen as sympathetic to the views of the Minister of Labor, a long time human rights and labor activist. Tim Urquhart, "Strikes Hit Production at Bridgestone's Liberian Factory," Global Insight Daily Analysis, April 30, 2007; James Butty, "Liberia Begins Reviewing Firestone Agreements," VOA News, April 5 2007; and information provided by the State Department.

[141] See "Summary of the Main Changes Brought About by the Review of the Mittal Mineral Development Agreement," http://www.emansion.gov.lr/doc/MittalAgreementFinalMitrix.pdf.

[142] See Global Witness, "Mittal Steel Did the Right Thing—Will Firestone?," April 4, 2007.

[143] See Global Witness, "Mittal Steel Did the Right Thing...".

[144] President Sirleaf, annual message to the legislature, January 28, 2008.

[145] Liberia's Solicitor-General, the former human rights lawyer Tiawan Gongloe, reportedly stated that the Liberian government will seek to extradite from the United States the former Maritime Commissioner, J.D. Slangar, to face charges of alleged public funds embezzlement. "Accused Former Official to Be Extradited," UNMIL Media Summary June 19, 2006 citing the *Daily Observer* and *New Democrat* newspapers.

[146] Katharine Houreld, "Liberian Leader Says to Review Govt Contracts," Reuters, February 20, 2006.

[147] "Global Witness Welcomes President Sirleaf's Decision to Cancel All Forest Concession Agreements," February 9, 2006.

[148] Information on the LFI is available online. See http://www.fao.org/forestry/site/lfi.

[149] See *Liberia, Forest Sector Reform* (Executive Order #1), February 7, 2006, available online at http://www.elaw.org/ resources/text.asp?id=305 1.

[150] See Global Witness, "United Nations Security Council Lifts Liberia Timber Sanctions Despite Insufficient Reform of the Industry [press release]," June 22, 2006, and Global Witness's *Cautiously Optimistic: The Case for Maintaining Sanctions in Liberia*, June 2006.

[151] E.g., remarks at "Conflict Timber, Sustainable Management, and the Rule of Law: Forest Sector Reform in Liberia," Woodrow Wilson Center panel presentation, June 8, 2006.

[152] "Liberian Leader to Ratify Forest Concession Pact to Ensure End of Un Timber Ban," Liberian Star Radio via BBC Monitoring Africa, October 4, 2006; UN News, "Country Enacts New Forest Policy With UN Help to Ensure Benefits for All," October, 5, 2006; IRIN, "Government Lays Foundation for Legal Logging," December 15, 2006; and Environmental Law Institute, "Liberian President Ellen Johnson-Sirleaf Signs National Forestry Reform Law of 2006," October 5, 2006.

[153] See United Nations, Report of the Secretary-General in Pursuance of Paragraph 19 of Resolution 1478 (2003) Concerning Liberia, S/2003/793, August 5, 2003.

[154] See *Taylor-Made: The Pivotal Role of Liberia's Forests and Flag of Convenience in Regional Conflict*, Global Witness and the International Transport Workers Federation, September 2001, *inter alia.* The environmental activist Silas Siakor, who ran the Save My Future Foundation (SAMFU) of Liberia from 2000 to 2003, is credited by many with carrying out then-politically risky documentary work that eventually led to the imposition of U.N. forestry sanctions on Liberia. Siakor, a 2006 Goldman Environmental Prize winner, now heads the Sustainable Development Institute (SDI), an NGO that helps to coordinate Liberian civil society participation in national forest sector reform efforts. See SAMFU, *Living Dangerously: An Assessment of Multinationals in Liberia Logging Industry*, February 20, 2001.

[155] The Kimberley Process Certification Scheme (KPCS) is a voluntary international trade regime that regulates the global trade in rough diamonds in order to prevent the sale of "conflict diamonds," i.e., rough diamonds used to fund armed conflict.

[156] The Kimberley Process decision followed a March 2007 Kimberley Process Review Mission to Liberia that had concluded that Liberia met the conditions for admission. European Community, "Kimberley Process: Liberia Enters the Diamond Trade," (press release IP/07/612) May 4, 2007.

[157] The diamond ban had been left in place when the Security Council lifted timber sanctions on Liberia (Resolution 1689) in June 2006. It had last been renewed in December 2006. A diamond embargo was initially imposed on Liberia in 2001 after the Security Council found that the Taylor government was "actively supporting" the RUF, the rebel group then fighting the government of Liberia's neighbor, Sierra Leone, including by illicitly trading in Sierra Leonean diamonds. See U.N. Security Council, Resolution 1343, March 7, 2001. The diamond sanctions under Resolution 1343 were terminated by Security Council Resolution 1521 (December 22, 2003), which imposed a new ban on diamond exports from Liberia. Resolution 1521 asserted that there existed a "linkage between the illegal exploitation of natural resources such as diamonds and timber, illicit trade in such resources, and the proliferation and trafficking of illegal arms as a major source of fueling and exacerbating conflicts, in West Africa, [and] particularly in Liberia."

[158] State Department/Monrovia Embassy, "U.S. Contributions to the Kimberley Process Certification Program," Embassy News, [n.d.].

[159] See DFI, "Diamond Fields Announces the Discovery of Kimberlite in Liberia and Progress with Gold Exploration," January 9, 2006. Several other firms are involved in diamond explorations in various counties of Liberia. DFI is also involved in gold exploration in Liberia.

[160] The GEMAP agreement and a wide range of GEMAP reports, bulletins, and other documents are online at http://www.gemapliberia.org/. On the goals of GEMAP, see GEMAP-Liberia, "What are the components of GEMAP?/Frequently Asked Questions (FAQ) Regarding GEMAP," n.d.

[161] The program appears to have resulted in some rapid early gains; Sirleaf administration officials reported that 2006 first quarter revenues collections were reportedly 34% higher than those for the same period in 2005, and similar revenue gains continued. *The Analyst* (Monrovia), "Liberia: Govt. is 34 Percent Richer!," June 8, 2006; and USAID/Liberia, "Governance and Economic Management (GEMAP)," current as of May 11, 2010.

[162] The external management and financial monitoring role components of GEMAP was initially opposed by some in Liberia as an intrusion on national sovereignty, but donor governments, including the United States, pushed for strict conditionality for future assistance to Liberia. IRIN, "Liberia: Foreign Nationals Step into Government Positions to Combat Graft," March 3, 2006; IRIN, "Liberia: Foreign Corruption Spotters Now in Place," May 24, 2006; and S/2006/159, *op. cit.*, among others.

[163] USAID/Liberia, *Overview of USAID* Programs in Liberia, March 2010; and State Department, Background Note: Liberia, April 19, 2010.

[164] GEMAP is overseen by an Economic Governance Steering Committee (EGSC) chaired by President Sirleaf, assisted by representatives of the United States, the European Union, the African Union, ECOWAS, and the International Monetary, World Bank, and U.N. agencies.

[165] On the U.S. role, see USAID/Liberia, "GEMAP International Controllers End Terms at Four Government Enterprises-Technical Assistance and Training to Continue," October 7, 2009; and USAID/Liberia, "Governance and Economic Management (GEMAP)," current as of May 11, 2010.

[166] LEITI documents available online (http://www.leiti.org.lr); GOL, *LEITI Act of 2009: An Act Establishing the Liberia Extractive Industries Transparency Initiative (LEITI)*, July 10, 2009; and EITI, "Liberia," September 30, 2009.

[167] See section entitled "Governance: Background."

[168] The following account draws from the author's observations; John Johnson and Robert Nakamura, Liberia Legislative Needs Assessment, Univ. at Albany, State Univ. of New York for U.N. Development Program-Liberia, February 2006; parliamentary information by European Commission/Konrad Adenauer Foundation, SUNY; and news accounts. In July 2006, the author participated in a U.S. government mission to assess the needs and status of the Liberian legislature; the assessment team met with numerous Members of the Liberian legislature.

[169] Konrad Adenauer Foundation, *Background information on the National Legislature Senior Staff Workshop*, March 13, 2006.

[170] Although some legislators later explained that they had removed personal property prior to the rehabilitation project, press reports suggested that what was removed in many cases included physical fixtures, such as doors and windows, and publicly funded office equipment and furnishings.

[171] An audit of the NTGL performed by ECOWAS reportedly "points to a lot of criminal activities, criminal charges, malpractices, inefficiencies, [and] corruption of former officials in the Gyude Bryant administration, including chairman Bryant himself," according to the current information minister, Lawrence Bropleh. Bropleh's comments came in the wake of the detainment of two former NTGL officials, finance minister Lusinee Kamara and his deputy, Tugbeh Doe, in a $9 million public funds corruption probe. See James Butty, "Liberia - Government Says Former Leader Could Face Charges," VOA News, December 5, 2006; *The Analyst*, "Police Clutches Lusinee Kamara, Tugbeh Doe," December 5, 2006; and Jonathan Paye-Layleh, "Liberia Charges Former Finance Minister with Stealing from Government," Associated Press, December 4, 2006, among others.

[172] USAID political institution strengthening, starting with support for the 2005 elections, was supported through FY 2008 under a USAID-backed contracting coordination mechanism known as the Consortium for Elections Political Process Strengthening (CEPPS). See Democracy International/USAID, *Liberia Elections and Political Processes Program Evaluation, Final Report*, November 2008; IFES, *IFES Final Report - Liberia Election*

Administration Program, November 1, 2004-January 31, 2009; and information from NDI, IRI, and IFES.

[173] NDI, "Liberia," http://www.ndi.org/liberia. Much of the work takes the form of workshops, technical assistance, mentoring and overseas study visits. According to USAID, the program also seeks to codify standing rules and orders; develop ethics rules; improving legislative research and information resource capacities; institutionalizing a lawmaking training program; and professionalize legislative staff. The radio program element centers on production of Legislative Spotlight, a current legislative events program aimed at expanding democratic participation in legislative processes. USAID/Liberia, "Support to the Legislature," current as of May 11, 2010.

[174] HDAC fact sheet, November 2006.

[175] HDAC, *House Democracy Assistance Commission – At a Glance*, n.d.; also see annual HDAC reports.

[176] The original indictment, dated March 3, 2003, approved on March 7, 2003, and unsealed on June 4, 2003 during Liberian peace talks in Ghana, charged Taylor with 17 counts of war crimes, crimes against humanity, and other serious violations of international humanitarian law. The indictment was amended on March 16, 2006, to 11 counts to "ensure a more focused trial," according to a statement by the prosecutor. The SCSL Prosecutor's indictment is online; see http://www.sc-sl.org/Taylor.html.

[177] The trial was transferred to the Hague from the SCSL premises in Freetown, Sierra Leone for reasons of security and to prevent possible instability in Sierra Leone and Liberia arising from the trial. Trial documents and recordings are available at the SCSL website: http://www.sc-sl.org/taylor.html. A non-governmental group has also created a Taylor trial tracking website: http ://charlestaylortrial. org.

[178] Taylor's trial, which began and then recessed in mid-2007, had resumed on January 7, 2008. See SCSL/Office of the Prosecutor, "Testimony for the Prosecution Concluded in Taylor Trial," February 2, 2009, and other SCSL documents (see http://www.sc-sl.org Cases >> The Prosecutor vs. Charles Ghankay Taylor); and Open Society Institute, "Trial Proceedings," http://www.charlestaylortrial.org.

[179] The arraignment hearing judge, however, reminded Taylor that the SCSL Appeals Chamber had in May 2004 decided that heads of state could be prosecuted before the SCSL. It had ruled in response to a motion by an attorney, acting on behalf of then-president Taylor, who requested that the court quash Taylor's indictment on the grounds that the court lacked jurisdiction to indict Taylor because he was a head of state at the time he was indicted. At Taylor's April arraignment, a court-appointed defense attorney for Taylor also requested that he be tried in Sierra Leone, to facilitate the logistics of bringing defense witnesses resident in the sub-region before the SCSL and to prevent their possible denial of visas to travel to a venue held in Europe. See IRIN, "Transcript of Charles Taylor's Plea on First Court Appearance," April 4, 2006.

[180] On the day that Taylor was taken into SCSL custody, the SCSL made a request to the Dutch government and to the ICC asking that the SCSL be permitted to use the Hague premises of the ICC while hearing Taylor's trial. See SCSL Press and Public Affairs Office, "Special Court President Requests Charles Taylor be Tried in The Hague," March 30, 2006. The U.N. Security Council subsequently endorsed an agreement later reached between the Dutch government and the SCSL, after a memorandum of understanding was agreed between the SCSL and the ICC.

[181] The Netherlands agreed to accept Taylor's transfer onto its territory on the condition that, prior to the transfer, provisions be put in place to ensure that Taylor depart Dutch soil following his trial. It is not clear where Taylor might go if he is acquitted, but Dutch authorities will not, at present, permit him to remain in the Netherlands after he is tried. Britain's offer to imprison Taylor is subject to approval by its parliament, but prior to its proffer, the UK government reportedly consulted the political opposition, which agreed to support the proposal. Sweden's parliament had earlier passed legislation, "specifically

because of the Charles Taylor case," that amended Swedish laws to enable it to imprison an SCSL convict. The Swedish government, however, had not formally offered to imprison Taylor if he were convicted, though it had reportedly considered doing do.

[182] Once the decision to transfer Taylor out of Sierra Leone had been made, the SCSL Prosecutor stated that the transfer of the Taylor trial to the Hague was "the only option" because the courts of the International Criminal Tribunal for the Former Yugoslavia or the International Criminal Tribunal for Rwanda (ICTR)—two institutional venues to which the transfer of the Taylor case was reportedly considered—are "too full." The ICTR is based in Arusha, Tanzania. The Prosecutor also stated that President Sirleaf had requested that Taylor's case be heard outside of Sierra Leone and the local Mano River sub-region. See SCSL, Office of the Prosecutor, "The Prosecutor's Meeting with Civil Society of Sierra Leone: The Prosecutor's Statement," April 12, 2006, as well as U.N. Security Council resolution 1688 (S/RES/1688, June 16, 2006).

[183] Human Rights Watch (HRW) has reviewed many of the arguments for and against transferring Taylor's case to the Hague and has made a number of related recommendations. See HRW, *Trying Charles Taylor in The Hague: Making Justice Accessible to Those Most Affected*, HRW Briefing No. 2, June 2006, as well as Howard Lesser, "In Sierra Leone, Mixed Reaction to Taylor's Trial Transfer," VOA, June 21, 2006, among other press analyses of the transfer.

[184] The potentially higher costs of conducting a trial in the Netherlands may pose a particularly significant funding challenge to the SCSL. See IRIN, "Sierra Leone: New War Crimes Court President Pleads for Extra Funds," May 25, 2006.

[185] Marlise Simons, "Liberian Ex-Leader's War Crimes Trial Is Stalled," *New York Times*, August 25, 2007.

[186] The assets of such persons are subject to a U.N. assets freeze imposed in 2004 under U.N. Security Council Resolution 1532. For information and documents pertaining to the assets seizure and related matters and a list of affected individuals, see the website of the U.N. Liberia sanctions committee: http://www.un.org/sc/committees/1521/ index.shtml.

[187] BBC News, "Liberia 'to Seize Taylor Assets'," July 2007; and Jonathan Paye-Layleh, "Liberian lawmakers reject bill to freeze Taylor's assets," Associated Press, September 23, 2007, *inter alia.* See also the May 2007 report by the Security Council Panel of Experts on Liberia (S/2007/340, published June 7, 2007) and *Following Taylor's Money*, *op cit.*

[188] Simons, "Liberian Ex-Leader's War Crimes Trial is Stalled," *op cit.*

[189] See, for instance, Amnesty International, Liberia: Time for Truth, Justice and Reparation for Liberia's Victims, 2007.

[190] See Catherine Maddux, "Hague Trial Could Mean Justice for More West African War Victims," VOA News, April 10, 2006 and IRIN, "Liberia: Youths Petition for War Crimes Court," April 11, 2006; Jeremy I. Levitt and J. Peter Pham, "Liberia Must Confront its Past If It Wants a Brighter Future," *The Baltimore Sun*, December 8, 2005; IRIN, "Liberia: Post-war justice stirs division," July 6, 2006; and Sebo Daniels, "Liberia: War Crime Advocate Arrested," The Inquirer (Monrovia), February 14, 2007.

[191] The TRC website http://www.trcofliberia.org contains documents about the mandate and current activities of the Commission.

[192] The Advocates for Human Rights, "Liberian Truth and Reconciliation Commission Diaspora Project," http://liberiatrc.mnadvocates.org; and VOA, "Liberia's Truth and Reconciliation Commission to Get Boost From Northwestern University in Chicago," March 8, 2007.

[193] TRC, "Liberia's TRC Presents Final Report," June 29, 2009.

[194] TRC, *Consolidated Final Report* (unedited), Volume II, June 29, 2009.

[195] TRC press release, December 11, 2009 and other TRC documents.

[196] TRC, *Consolidated Final Report* (unedited), Volume II, June 29, 2009; TRC, "Liberia's TRC Presents Final Report," June 29, 2009; The Analyst, "TRC Members Threatened," via AllAfrica, July 9, 2009; IRIN, "TRC Furore Overshadows Peace Building Proposals," July

9, 2009; Boakai Fofana, "Sirleaf Testifies to Truth Commission," AllAfrica.com, February 13, 2009.

[197] President Sirleaf, annual message to the legislature, January 25, 2010.

[198] Jay Weaver, "Son of Liberia's Taylor sentenced to 11 months," *Miami Herald*, December 7, 2006; Curt Anderson, "Son of Ex-Liberian President Admits Passport Fraud," Associated Press, September 15, 2006; verbal communication from U.S. Attorney's office, November 28, 2006; Dept. of Justice press release, Sept 15, 2006; Curt Anderson, "Activists Want Charles Taylor's Son Tried for War Crimes, Torture," Associated Press, August 6, 2006; and HRW, "U.S.: Investigate Taylor's Son for Torture, War Crimes," May 26, 2006, *inter alia.*

[199] The main charges were brought under 18 USC § 2340, which was first passed under P.L. 103-236, later amended, to implement U.S. commitments as a signatory of the U.N. Convention Against Torture and Other Cruel, Inhuman, or Degrading Treatment or Punishment. For background, see Human Rights Watch, "Charles 'Chuckie' Taylor, Jr.'s Trial in the United States for Torture Committed in Liberia/Questions and Answers," September 23, 2008 and CRS Report RL32438, *U.N. Convention Against Torture (CAT): Overview and Application to Interrogation Techniques*, by Michael John Garcia.

[200] Department of Justice (DOJ), "Roy Belfast Jr. AKA Chuckie Taylor Indicted on Torture Charges/First-Ever Torture Charges," December 6, 2006; and R. Jeffrey Smith, "Anti-Torture Statute Used to Indict Son of Liberia's Ex-Leader," *Washington Post*, December 7, 2006; and IRIN, "Liberia: Speaking Out About Taylor's Son," December 13, 2006; Jay Weaver, "Liberian ex-official faces more torture charges," Miami Herald, September 7, 2007; and DOJ, "Chuckie Taylor Charged with Additional Acts of Torture in Superseding Indictment," September 6, 2007; and Elise Keppler, Shirley Jean, and J. Paxton Marshall, "First Prosecution in the United States for Torture Committed Abroad: The Trial of Charles 'Chuckie' Taylor, Jr.," Human Rights Brief, 15:3, Spring/Summer 2008, *inter alia.*

[201] Commenting on the sentence, Acting Assistant Attorney General Matthew Friedrich of the Criminal Division stated that "Our message to human rights violators, no matter where they are, remains the same: We will use the full reach of U.S. law [...] to hold you fully accountable for your crimes." FBI Executive Assistant Director Arthur M. Cummings, II, similarly, stated that the sentence "sends a resounding message that torture will not be tolerated here at home or by U.S. nationals abroad" and that such acts would be investigated "wherever they occur." See Department of Justice, "Roy Belfast Jr., AKA Chuckie Taylor, Convicted On Torture Charges," October 30, 2008; and Department of Justice, "Roy Belfast Jr., A/K/A Chuckie Taylor, Sentenced On Torture Charges," January 9, 2009.

[202] World Organization for Human Rights USA, "Final Judgment Issued in Civil Case Against Charles Taylor, Jr. – Plaintiffs Awarded $22.4 Million," February 5, 2010; Curt Anderson, "Liberians Look For Justice In Miami Court Torture Victims Seek Damages From Ex-President's Son, Associated Press/*South Florida Sun-Sentinel*," December 15, 2009; and Associated Press via *Boston Globe*, "$22m Awarded in Liberia Torture Case," February 6, 2010.

[203] See James Rupert, "Diamond Hunters Fuel Africa's Brutal Wars; In Sierra Leone, Mining Firms Trade Weapons and Money for Access to Gems," *Washington Post*, October 16, 1999; U.S. Treasury, Office of Foreign Assets Control (OFAC), *Liberia Sanctions*, http://www.treas.gov/offices/enforcement and U.N., *Security Council Committee Established Pursuant to Resolution 1521 (2003) Concerning Liberia*, http://www.un.org/Docs/sc/committees/Liberia3Template.htm.

[204] See section entitled "Background: Historical U.S.-Liberian Ties" in CRS Report RL30933, *Liberia: 1989-1997 Civil War, Post-War Developments, and U.S. Relations*, by Nicolas Cook, among other sources.

[205] Their presence, Sirleaf stated in her inaugural speech, was welcome because it manifested "a renewal and strengthening of the long-standing historic special relations which bind our two countries and peoples." She also stated that it "reflects a new partnership with the United

States based on shared values" and that Liberians are "confident that we can continue to count on the assistance of the United States [...] in the urgent task of rebuilding of our nation."

206 See CRS Report RL32243, *Liberia: Transition to Peace*, by Nicolas Cook.

207 She was cited for her efforts as the first elected female African president to "heal a country torn apart by conflict" and "to expand freedom and improve the lives of people in Liberia and across Africa." White House, "Citations Recipients of the Presidential Medal of Freedom," November 5, 2007.

208 State Department, "Remarks With Liberian President Ellen Johnson Sirleaf After Their Meeting," April 21, 2009.

209 William J. Burns, "Under Secretary Burns Travels to Liberia," April 26, 2010 [State Department blog]. According to a May 14, 2010 State Department response to a CRS inquiry; the $19.75 million is made up of $9 million in FY 2010 INCLE account funds and $6.25 million in combined FY 2005 and FY 2009 ESF funding implemented by INL; and $4.5 million in FY 2010 ESF funding for work implemented by USAID.

210 State Department, "Address to Joint Session of Liberian National Legislature," August 13, 2009.

211 A proposed threshold bill would guide a constitutionally-required legislative boundary delimitation and reapportionment process following Liberia's 2008 population census. It has been controversial due to its potential impact on the national budget and political representation patterns, in part given that nearly 1/2 of the population is centered in and around Monrovia, as well as issues of constitutionality, and President Sirleaf has vetoed two versions of legislature-passed bills. At the heart of the matter is a constitutional conundrum: The Constitution requires that House of Representatives electoral constituencies be delimitated after any national census and prior to the next election. It also requires nearly equally-sized constituencies made up of 20,000 persons or a number prescribed by the legislature, but also requires that there be no more than 100 constituencies in total. Based on the 2008 census of 3.48 million, constituencies of 20,000 persons would produce a constitutionally-barred total of 174 seats, while ones made up of 35,000 persons would yield 99 seats, the maximum constitutionally-permitted number of seats. If the current 64-seat system was to be maintained, the size of constituencies would rise to 54,000. *The Analyst*, "Liberia: Threshold Quagmire -Constitutional Hypocrisy, Power Play Or Democratic Doom?," April 19, 2010; *The Informer* (Monrovia), "Liberia: Referendum Before 2011 Poll Impossible - as Lawmakers Sit Over Election Bills," December 9, 2009; and internal IFES working report by consultant Dr. Lisa Handley, March 2010.

212 State Department, "Remarks at Liberian National Police Academy," August 13, 2009.

213 Secretary Condoleezza Rice, Statement at Liberia Partners' Forum, Washington, DC, February 13, 2007.

214 *Congressional Record* (House), pp. H996-H998, March 15, 2006.

215 Reed Kramer, "Showered With Enthusiasm, Liberia's President-Elect Receives High-Level Reception in Washington," *AllAfrica.com*, December 11, 2005, *inter alia.* During a March 20 appearance with Sirleaf, World Bank President Paul Wolfowitz reportedly announced that the World Bank would provide $25 million for a road-building fund for Liberia and stated that he was seeking debt forgiveness for Liberia by the World Bank, the IMF, and the African Development Bank. See VOA, "World Bank Commits $25 Million to Liberian Infrastructure Fund," March 21, 2006.

216 In addition to allocating funds to specific countries and programs, the Congress annually allocates appropriations foreign operations to broad functional accounts. The President, for the most part via the State Department, then notifies the Congress of the manner in which he intends to allocate these funds by category of assistance or program and by beneficiary foreign country or international organization. Formally, this process — defined under Section 653(a) of the Foreign Assistance Act of 1961, as amended — only requires notification. In practice, the Administration seeks congressional sign-off on these

allocations, which in some cases is only provided following protracted executive- legislative branch negotiations. Allocations of appriopriations may also be subject to other applicable reporting or notification requirements.

[217] Under Section 5 of P.L. 111-8, the House Explanatory Statement has the same effect as would a Joint Explanatory Statement.

[218] See H.Rept. 111-366, the conference report which accompanied P.L. 111-117, which contains a Joint Explanatory Statement; it has the force of law, in accordance with conditions set out in section 7019 of P.L. 111-117.

[219] See U.S. Citizenship and Immigration Services (USCIS), "Deferred Enforced Departure," current as of March 10, 2010; Administration of Barack H. Obama, 2009, "Memorandum on Deferred Enforced Departure for Liberians," March 20, 2009; Department of Homeland Security, "Fact Sheet: Liberians Provided Deferred Enforced Departure (DED)," September 12, 2007; and CRS Report RS20844, *Temporary Protected Status: Current Immigration Policy and Issues*, by Ruth Ellen Wasem and Karma Ester, *inter alia.*

[220] Honorable Donald M. Payne, "Dear Colleague: Conference on Liberian Immigration," March 8, 2010

[221] The Honorable Patrick J. Kennedy, "Dear Colleague: Support Liberia's Refugees," February 23, 2010

[222] These restrict certain kinds of assistance to Liberia owing to its arrears on national debt repayments to the United States. See USAID, *Audit of USAID/Liberia 's Compliance with the Brooke Amendment and Sections 620(q) and 61 7 of the Foreign Assistance Act of 1961*, (Audit Report No. 7-669-02-001-P), March 7, 2002, provides background on the Brooke Amendment.

[223] Funding breakouts are specified in **Table 3**, below. Specific allocations for some accounts were not finalized until August 2007, and funding for some accounts, such as food aid, is allocated from centralized accounts in response to changing needs, and is subject to change.

[224] The Liberia-related provisions of S. 396, S. 554, and S. 1508 would have designated Liberia as a "tax-haven country," allowing the Internal Revenue Code to treat certain foreign corporations created or organized under Liberian law as U.S. domestic corporations for tax purposes.

[225] President Bush had previously extended DED, but did not act in response to the Congressional request. The Obama Administration has not, to date, stated if and how it may intend to act regarding this matter. Representative Patrick J. Kennedy and Representative Keith Ellison, "Support Liberia's Recovery: Request Deferred Enforced Departure for Liberians in the United States," ["Dear Colleague" letter soliciting co-signatories for a letter to former President Bush], December 16, 2008; and oral information from office of Representative Kennedy, February 6, 2009.

[226] State Department, "Liberia," Congressional Budget Justification - Foreign Operations, Annex: Regional Perspectives, FY 2011 [FY 2011 CBJ].

[227] In addition to the sources noted below, this section draws from USAID/Liberia, *Overview of USAID* Programs in Liberia, March 2010; FY 2011 CBJ; and multiple USAID/Liberia program descriptions found online at http://liberia.usaid.gov/.

[228] See discussion of IFES's work on elections administration and NDI's legislature strengthening activities in previous sections of this report.

[229] State Department/U.S. Embassy-Monrovia, "LIPA/USAID Training Program Graduation," March 3, 2010.

[230] These goals are being pursued, in part, through a five-year, $11 million USAID civil society and media support program run by the International Research and Exchanges Board (IREX) and a five-year, $6 million USAID human rights capacity-building and legal training program run by Freedom House and the American Bar Association. USAID response to CRS inquiry, April 28, 2010.

[231] For background, see CRS Report R40945, *The U.S. Global Food Security Initiative: Issues for Congress*, by Charles E. Hanrahan and Melissa D. Ho.

[232] MCC, "Liberia Program Status," Threshold Quarterly Status Report, October 2009; and USAID, "Millennium Challenge Corporation Threshold Country Program," April 9, 2010

[233] Peace Corps, "Liberia," December 17, 2009; Peace Corps press releases "Peace Corps Reopens Program in Liberia," August 20, 2008; "Peace Corps Response Volunteers Will Serve in Education and Health," October 22, 2008; communication to CRS from Peace Corps, May 12, 2010; and Peace Corps, *Congressional Budget Justification*, FY 2011.

[234] USTR, "U.S. Reinstates Trade Preference Benefits for Liberia," February 22, 2006.

[235] See CRS Report RL3 1772, *U.S. Trade and Investment Relationship with Sub-Saharan Africa: The African Growth and Opportunity Act*, by Vivian C. Jones.

[236] Trade and Investment Framework Agreement between the United States of America and the Republic of Liberia, February 15, 2007, *http://www.ustr.gov/Trade_Agreements/TIFA /Section_Index.html.*

[237] USTDA, "USTDA Supports Development of the Power Sector in Liberia During President Ellen Johnson-Sirleaf's Visit," February 15, 2007; and USTDA, *Pipeline* [Bi-Weekly E-Mail Update], May 12, 2006.

[238] See Export-Import Bank, "EX-IM Bank Renews, Expands Africa Short-Term Insurance Initiative," February 10, 2006. The STIPP helps businesses in eligible countries buy U.S.-made goods and services by insuring short-term export credit transactions involving various payment terms in countries where Ex-Im Bank is otherwise not open.

[239] OPIC, "OPIC Reopens Programs In Liberia," March 21, 2006. OPIC provides political risk insurance and financing aimed at helping U.S. businesses invest in emerging markets and developing nations.

[240] See CHF International, "Liberia Economic Development Fund Launched by CHF, RLJ, OPIC & ADF," February 14, 2007, http://www.chfhq.org/content/general/detail/4614.

[241] The purpose of the agreement is to "significantly modernize U.S.-Liberia aviation relations by allowing airlines from the two countries to make commercial decisions with minimal government intervention" and "provide for open routes, capacity, frequencies, designations, and pricing, as well as cooperative marketing arrangements, including code- sharing." See State Department, "U.S. Signs Open Skies Aviation Agreement with Liberia" [Media Note], February 16, 2007; and State Department, "Open Skies Agreement Highlights," June 1, 2006.

[242] The Delta route is planned between Atlanta, GA and Monrovia, with a stop-over in Cape Verde.

[243] Harry R. Weber, "Delta Air Lines Making Changes to International Schedule; Some Additions Coming," Associated Press, October 20, 2009; and President Sirleaf, annual message to the legislature, January 25, 2010.

[244] Delta reportedly had held Department of Transportation to authority to serve Liberia since April 2007. Weber, "Delta Air Lines..."; Kelly Yamanouchi and Jeffrey Scott, "Delta flights to Nairobi put on hold: Homeland Security postpones approval," *The Atlanta Journal - Constitution*, June 3, 2009; Kerry Lynch, "TSA Cites Threat In Blocking Delta's Atlanta-Nairobi Service," *The Weekly of Business Aviation*, June 8, 2009; Dow Jones News Service , "TSA Blocks Delta Flights To 2 African Cities On Security," June 3, 2009; and Liberian Government, "Delta Postpones New Service to Liberia And Kenya," June 3, 2009 via All Africa.

[245] Andrew Compart, "TSA Holds Up Two Africa Routes, Citing 'Credible Threat' To Aviation," *Aviation Daily*, June 3, 2009; TSA, "TSA and Liberia Partner to Enhance Aviation Security," April 7, 2009.

[246] The cost of the entire ASSIST technical assistance is currently estimated at $.34 million in FY 2009 and FY20 10 funds. TSA/DHS written response to CRS inquiry, March 19, 2010; African Press Agency, "Lockheed Martin Global Services Takes Over Liberia's Roberts International Airport," August 21, 2009 via Net News Publisher; AirportTechnology.Com, "American Firm Gains Control of Roberts International Airport," August 27, 2009; Lennart Dodoo, "RIA Will Be 'Hub for Aviation in Sub-region'," *Liberian Observer*, August 26,

2009; and Sidiki Trawally, "Roberts International Airport Meetings International Standards," Ministry of Planning & Economic Affairs - Liberia Reconstruction and Development Committee (LRDC), n.d.

[247] Agência Lusa, "Cabo Verde: Delta Airlines Começa a Voar Para o Sal No Primeiro Trimestre de 2010," October 23, 2009.

[248] Derek Repp, "Liberians Soon May Be Getting More Mail, with U.S. Help," *America.gov*, April 7, 2008.

[249] Items reviewed included the status of peace consolidation, Liberia's transition to democracy, and the rule of law; public financial management, civil service, and anti-corruption reforms; the status of public financial management reform efforts, including with respect to budgeting, revenue administration, and auditing and procurement; requirements for clearing local and national public debt; private sector-driven economic revitalization and job creation, and the status of basic services and infrastructure provision; and planning and international backing for reconstruction and development, including the status of Liberia's international financial institution-backed Interim Poverty Reduction Strategy (iPRS).

[250] Secretary Condoleezza Rice, "Liberia Partners' Forum" [statement], Washington, DC, February 13, 2007; and U.S. Treasury, "Treasury Working with Congress to Relieve Liberia's Debt Burden," press release HP-262, February 14, 2007.

[251] State Department, "U.S. Joins Paris Club in Forgiving Liberia's Debt" [press statement], April 18, 2008; and information provided by Treasury Department officials, June 2008 and March 2010.

[252] World Bank, "Liberia Slashes Debt with $1.2 billion Buyback at Steep Discount," 2009/3 10/AFR, April 16, 2009; IMF, "Liberia: Enhanced Initiative for Heavily Indebted Poor Countries Initiative—Request for Additional Interim Assistance; and Press Release," IMF Country Report No. 10/9 1, April 2010; Ansu Konneh, "Liberia Government 'Unable' to Repay Debt Owed to Vulture Funds," Bloomberg News, November 27, 2009 .

In: Liberia: Development and Resources
Editor: Anya M. Micallef
ISBN: 978-1-61209-396-3
© 2011 Nova Science Publishers, Inc.

Chapter 2

BACKGROUND NOTE: LIBERIA

United States State Department

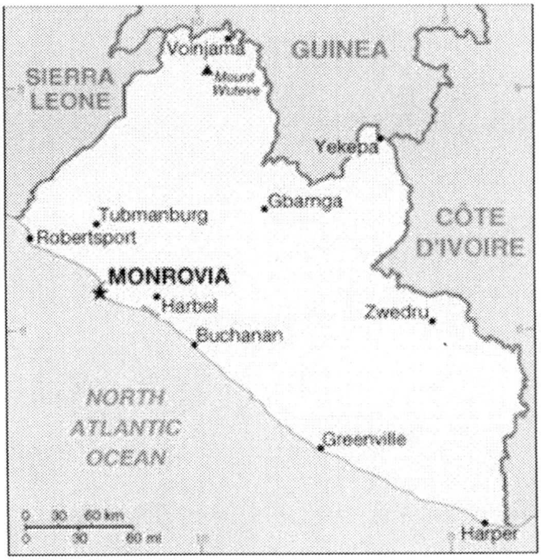

Profile

Official Name: Republic of Liberia

Geography

Area: 111,369 sq. km. (43,000 sq. mi.). Slightly larger than Ohio. Cities: *Capital*--Monrovia (pop. 1,010,970). *Principal towns*--Ganta (pop. 41,000), Buchanan (pop. 34,000), Gbarnga (pop. 34,000), Kakata (pop. 33,000), Voinjama (pop. 26,000). Terrain: *Three areas*--Mangrove swamps and beaches along the coast, wooded hills and semideciduous shrub lands along the immediate interior, and dense tropical forests and plateaus in the interior. Liberia has 40% of West Africa's rain forest.

People

Nationality: *Noun and adjective*--Liberian(s).

Population (2008): 3.49 million.

Annual growth rate (2008): 2.1%.

Ethnic groups: Kpelle 20%, Bassa 16%, Gio 8%, Kru 7%, 49% spread over 12 other ethnic groups.

Religions: Christian 40%, Muslim 20%, animist 40%.

Languages: English is the official language. There are 16 indigenous languages.

Education: *Literacy* (2003)--20%.

Health: *Life expectancy* (2005)--42.5 years.

Work force: *Agriculture*--70%; *industry*--15%; *services*--2%. Employment in the formal sector is estimated at 15%.

Government

Type: Republic.

Independence: From American Colonization Society July 26, 1847.

Constitution: January 6, 1986.

Political parties: 30 registered political parties.

Economy

GDP (IMF 2007 est.): $473.9 million.

Real GDP growth rate (2008, projected): 9.6%.

Per capita GDP (2006): $185.50.

Average annual inflation (2008, projected): 9.0%.

Natural resources: Iron ore, rubber, timber, diamonds, gold, and tin. The Government of Liberia believes there may be sizable deposits of crude oil along its Atlantic Coast.

Agriculture: *Products*--coffee, cocoa, sugarcane, rice, cassava, palm oil, bananas, plantains, citrus, pineapple, sweet potatoes, corn, and vegetables.

Industry: *Types*--agriculture, iron ore, rubber, forestry, diamonds, gold, beverages, construction. Trade (2007, provisional): *Exports*--$184.1 million (of which rubber $170.9 million). *Major markets*--Germany, Poland, U.S., Greece. *Imports*--$498.7 million (petroleum $125 million; rice $65.3 million).

People

There are 16 ethnic groups that make up Liberia's indigenous population. The Kpelle in central and western Liberia is the largest ethnic group. Americo-Liberians who are descendants of freed slaves that arrived in Liberia early in 1821 make up an estimated 5% of the population.

There also are sizable numbers of Lebanese, Indians, and other West African nationals who comprise part of Liberia's business community. The Liberian constitution restricts citizenship to only people of Negro descent, and land ownership is restricted to citizens.

Liberia was traditionally noted for its academic institutions, iron-mining, and rubber. Political upheavals beginning in the 1980s and a 14-year civil war (1989-2003) largely destroyed Liberia's economy and brought a steep decline in living standards.

History

Portuguese explorers established contacts with Liberia as early as 1461 and named the area Grain Coast because of the abundance of "grains of paradise" (Malegueta pepper seeds). In 1663 the British installed trading posts on the Grain Coast, but the Dutch destroyed these posts a year later. There were no further reports of European settlements along the Grain Coast until the arrival of freed slaves in the early 1800s.

Liberia, "land of the free," was founded by free African-Americans and freed slaves from the United States in 1820. An initial group of 86 immigrants, who came to be called Americo-Liberians, established a settlement in Christopolis (now Monrovia, named after U.S. President James Monroe) on February 6, 1820.

Thousands of freed American slaves and free African-Americans arrived during the following years, leading to the formation of more settlements and culminating in a declaration of independence of the Republic of Liberia on July 26, 1847. The drive to resettle freed slaves in Africa was promoted by the American Colonization Society (ACS), an organization of white clergymen, abolitionists, and slave owners founded in 1816 by Robert Finley, a Presbyterian minister. Between 1821 and 1867 the ACS resettled some 10,000 African-Americans and several thousand Africans from interdicted slave ships; it governed the Commonwealth of Liberia until independence in 1847.

In Liberia's early years, the Americo-Liberian settlers periodically encountered stiff and sometimes violent opposition from indigenous Africans, who were excluded from citizenship in the new Republic until 1904. At the same time, British and French colonial expansionists encroached upon Liberia, taking over much of its territory. Politically, the country was a one-party state ruled by the True Whig Party (TWP). Joseph Jenkins Roberts, who was born and raised in America, was Liberia's first President. The style of government and constitution was fashioned on that of the United States, and the Americo-Liberian elite monopolized political power and restricted the voting rights of the indigenous population. The True Whig Party dominated all sectors of Liberia from independence in 1847 until April 12, 1980, when indigenous Liberian Master Sergeant Samuel K. Doe (from the Krahn ethnic group) seized power in a coup d'etat. Doe's forces executed President William R. Tolbert and several officials of his government, mostly of Americo-Liberian descent. One hundred and thirty-three years of Americo-Liberian political domination ended with the formation of the People's Redemption Council (PRC).

Over time, the Doe government began promoting members of Doe's Krahn ethnic group, who soon dominated political and military life in Liberia. This raised ethnic tension and caused frequent hostilities between the politically and militarily dominant Krahns and other ethnic groups in the country.

After the October 1985 elections, characterized by widespread fraud, Doe solidified his control. The period after the elections saw increased human rights abuses, corruption, and ethnic tensions. The standard of living further deteriorated. On November 12, 1985, former Army Commanding Gen. Thomas Quiwonkpa almost succeeded in toppling Doe's government. The Armed Forces of Liberia repelled Quiwonkpa's attack and executed him in Monrovia. Doe's Krahn-dominated forces carried out reprisals against Mano and Gio civilians suspected of supporting Quiwonkpa.

Despite Doe's poor human rights record and questionable democratic credentials, he retained close relations with Washington. A staunch U.S. ally, Doe met twice with President Ronald Reagan and enjoyed considerable U.S. financial support.

On December 24, 1989, a small band of rebels led by Doe's former procurement chief, Charles Taylor, invaded Liberia from Cote d'Ivoire. Taylor and his National Patriotic Front rebels rapidly gained the support of many Liberians and reached the outskirts of Monrovia within six months.

From 1989 to 1996 one of Africa's bloodiest civil wars ensued, claiming the lives of more than 200,000 Liberians and displacing a million others into refugee camps in neighboring countries. The Economic Community of West African States (ECOWAS) intervened in 1990 and succeeded in preventing Charles Taylor from capturing Monrovia. Prince Johnson--formerly a member of Taylor's National Patriotic Front of Liberia (NPFL)--formed the break-away Independent National Patriotic Front of Liberia (INPFL). Johnson's forces captured and killed Doe on September 9, 1990. Taking refuge in Sierra Leone and other neighboring countries, former AFL soldiers founded the new insurgent United Liberation Movement of Liberia for Democracy (ULIMO), fighting back Taylor's NPFL.

An Interim Government of National Unity (IGNU) was formed in Gambia under the auspices of ECOWAS in October 1990, headed by Dr. Amos C. Sawyer. Taylor (along with other Liberian factions) refused to work with the interim government and continued fighting. After more than a dozen peace accords and declining military power, Taylor finally agreed to the formation of a five-man transitional government. A hasty disarmament and demobilization of warring factions was followed by special elections on July 19, 1997. Charles Taylor and his National Patriotic Party emerged victorious. Taylor won the election by a large majority, primarily because Liberians feared a return to war had Taylor lost.

For the next six years, the Taylor government did not improve the lives of Liberians. Unemployment and illiteracy stood above 75%, and little investment was made in the country's infrastructure. Liberia is still recovering from the ravages of war; pipe-borne water and electricity are generally unavailable to most of the population, especially outside Monrovia, and schools, hospitals, roads, and infrastructure remain derelict. Rather than work to improve the lives of Liberians, Taylor supported the Revolutionary United Front in Sierra Leone (see *Sierra Leone Country Background Note*). Taylor's misrule led to the resumption of armed rebellion from among Taylor's former adversaries. By 2003, armed groups called "Liberians United for Reconciliation and Democracy" (LURD) and "Movement for Democracy in Liberia" (MODEL), largely representing elements of the former ULIMO-K and ULIMO-J factions that fought Taylor during Liberia's previous civil war (1989-1996), were challenging Taylor and his increasingly fragmented supporters on the outskirts of Monrovia.

On June 4, 2003 in Accra, Ghana, ECOWAS facilitated peace talks among the Government of Liberia, civil society, and the LURD and MODEL rebel groups. On the same day, the Chief Prosecutor of the Special Court for Sierra Leone issued a press statement announcing the opening of a sealed March 7, 2003 indictment of Liberian President Charles Taylor for "bearing the greatest responsibility" for atrocities in Sierra Leone since November 1996. In July 2003 the Government of Liberia, LURD, and MODEL signed a cease-fire that all sides failed to respect; bitter fighting reached downtown Monrovia in July and August 2003, creating a massive humanitarian disaster.

On August 11, 2003, under intense U.S. and international pressure, President Taylor resigned office and departed into exile in Nigeria. This move paved the way for the deployment by ECOWAS of what became a 3,600-strong peacekeeping mission in Liberia (ECOMIL). On August 18, leaders from the Liberian Government, the rebels, political parties, and civil society signed a comprehensive peace agreement that laid the framework for constructing a 2-year National Transitional Government of Liberia (NTGL), headed by businessman Gyude Bryant. The UN took over security in Liberia in October 2003, subsuming ECOMIL into the United Nations Mission in Liberia (UNMIL), a force that grew to over 12,000 troops and 1,148 police officers.

The October 11, 2005 presidential and legislative elections and the subsequent November 8, 2005 presidential run-off were the most free, fair, and peaceful elections in Liberia's history. Ellen Johnson Sirleaf defeated international soccer star George Weah 59.4% to 40.6% to become Africa's first democratically elected female president. She was inaugurated in January 2006 and formed a government of technocrats drawn from among Liberia's ethnic groups and including members of the Liberian diaspora who had returned to the country to rebuild government institutions. The president's party, the Unity Party, does not control the legislature, in which 12 of the 30 registered political parties are represented.

The political situation has remained stable since the 2005 elections. The Government of Liberia has made positive strides aimed at political stability and economic recovery. President Sirleaf has taken a public stance against corruption and has dismissed several government officials. The President is supported by highly experienced and technically competent senior officials, and the public has more confidence in her administration than in any of its recent predecessors. President Sirleaf enjoys good relations with international organizations and donor governments, with whom she is working closely on Liberia's development. The national legislature has enacted several key reforms.

In order to maintain stability through the post-conflict period, Liberia's security sector reform efforts have led to the disarmament of more than 100,000 ex-combatants, the wholesale U.S.-led reconstruction of the Armed Forces of Liberia, and a UN-led effort to overhaul the Liberian National Police. The mandate of UNMIL was extended to September 2009, and a gradual drawdown was to commence in 2008, to last several years. During this period the Government of Liberia and its development partners will focus on creating jobs, attracting investment, and providing education and other essential services to Liberia's communities. The Government of Liberia won substantial donor support for its new Poverty Reduction Strategy at the June 2008 Liberia Poverty Reduction Forum in Berlin, Germany.

Government and Political Conditions

Liberia has a bicameral legislature consisting of 64 representatives and 30 senators. The 2005 election placed a spectrum of political personalities in the legislature, most for six-year terms. Senior senators were elected for nine-year terms. Party structures remain weak, and politics continues to be personality-driven. Historically, the executive branch heavily influenced the legislature and judicial system.

The judiciary is divided into four levels, including justices of the peace, courts of record (magistrate courts), courts of first instance (circuit and specialty courts), and the Supreme Court. Traditional courts and lay courts exist in rural areas of the country. Trial by ordeal, though officially outlawed, is practiced in various parts of Liberia. The formal judicial system remains hampered by severe shortages of qualified judges and other judicial officials. Locally, political power emanates from traditional chiefs (town, clan, or paramount chiefs), mayors, and district commissioners. Mayors are elected in principal cities in Liberia. Superintendents appointed by the president govern the counties. There are 15 counties in Liberia.

Liberia maintains an *embassy* in the United States at 5201 16th Street, NW, Washington DC, 202-723-0437.

Economy

The Liberian economy relied heavily on the mining of iron ore and on the export of natural rubber prior to the civil war. Liberia was a major exporter of iron ore on the world market. In the 1970s and 1980s, iron mining accounted for more than half of Liberia's export earnings. Following the coup d'etat of 1980, the country's economic growth rate slowed down because of a decline in the demand for iron ore on the world market and political upheavals in Liberia.

The 1989-2003 civil war had a devastating effect on the country's economy. Most major businesses were destroyed or heavily damaged, and most foreign investors and businesses left the country. Iron ore production stopped completely, and the United Nations banned timber and diamond exports from Liberia. UN sanctions on Liberian timber were removed in 2006; activity in the timber sector is expected to resume on a large scale during the October 2008-May 2009 dry season. Diamond sanctions were terminated by the UN Security Council in April 2007, and Liberian diamond exports have resumed through the *Kimberley Process Certification Scheme*. Gold deposits, some of which are currently nearing production, should soon begin to contribute to government revenues and provide additional employment.

Currently, Liberia's revenues come primarily from rubber exports and revenues from its maritime registry program. Liberia has the second-largest maritime registry in the world; there are 2,724 vessels totaling 83.3 million gross tons registered under its flag, earning some $16 million in maritime revenue in Liberian FY 2007/2008 (July 1-June 30). There is increasing interest in the possibility of commercially exploitable offshore crude oil deposits along Liberia's Atlantic Coast.

With a democratically elected government in place since January 2006, Liberia seeks to reconstruct its shattered economy. The Governance and Economic Management Assistance Program (GEMAP), which started under the 2003-2006 transitional government, is designed to help the Liberian Government raise and spend revenues in an efficient, transparent way. In addition, the Liberian Government is working to improve the business climate, has formed a commission to deal with land tenure issues, and is reviewing tax and tariff regimes to harmonize them with neighbors in the Economic Community of West African States (ECOWAS). The Liberian National Investment Commission reported $97 million in new investment in 2007 and has set a target of $100 million a year for future years. Investors are finding opportunities in mining, rubber, agro-forestry, light industry, and other sectors. Arcelor Mittal Steel has negotiated an agreement to invest over $1.5 billion in the mining sector, and the Liberian Government is engaged in negotiations with several other large foreign investors.

Years of conflict and mismanagement also left Liberia with a large debt burden of $3.4 billion, owed to multilateral development banks, bilateral creditors, and commercial creditors. On June 12, 2008, the United States became the first bilateral creditor to sign a bilateral agreement implementing the Paris Club's April 2008 debt treatment for Liberia. Several other bilateral creditors have pledged debt relief, and the International Monetary Fund (IMF), World Bank, and African Development Bank have approved a formal program to clear Liberia's $1.5 billion in arrears to international financial institutions. With this support, and with technical assistance provided by Liberia's international partners, the Liberian Government seeks to make key economic reforms to attract investment and qualify for eventual debt relief under the Heavily Indebted Poor Countries (HIPC) initiative.

Foreign Relations

Liberia has maintained traditionally cordial relations with the West. Liberia currently also maintains diplomatic relations with Libya, Cuba, and China.

Liberia is a founding member of the United Nations and its specialized agencies and is a member of the African Union (AU), the Economic Community of West African States (ECOWAS), the African Development Bank (ADB), the Mano River Union (MRU), and the Non-Aligned Movement.

During the administration of Charles Taylor, relations between Liberia and its West African neighbors became seriously strained. West African countries backed by the African Union and the United Nations negotiated a peace agreement in Accra, Ghana that subsequently led to the exile of Charles

Taylor to Nigeria in August 2003. With the election of Ellen Johnson Sirleaf, Liberia has seen significant improvements in relations with its West African neighbors and the wider world. Relations between Liberia and its immediate neighbors in the Mano River region are back on track, and efforts are underway to strengthen relations with other countries. Liberia currently holds the chairmanship of the reinvigorated Mano River Union. Liberia signed a non-aggression pact with Sierra Leone when newly elected President Ernest Bai Koroma visited in September 2007. Liberia is a major proponent of regional integration.

Liberia has taken steps to forge closer ties with Western countries, especially the United States. President Ellen Johnson Sirleaf has visited several Western countries, including the United Kingdom, Sweden, Norway, Spain, France, and Germany. President Sirleaf has also visited China and Libya, with whom Liberia maintains close ties.

U.S.-Liberia Relations

Congress appropriated $100,000 in 1819 for the establishment of Liberia (and resettlement of freemen and freed slaves from North America) by the American Colonization Society, led by prominent Americans such as Francis Scott Key, George Washington's nephew Bushrod, Henry Clay, Daniel Webster, and Presidents Monroe, Adams, and Jackson. The first group of settlers arrived in Liberia from the United States in the 1820s. The United States, which officially recognized Liberia in 1862, shared particularly close relations with Liberia during the Cold War.

The outbreak of civil war in Liberia and the long dominance of Charles Taylor soured bilateral relations. However, Liberia now counts the United States as its strongest supporter in its democratization and reconstruction efforts. Since the end of Liberia's civil war in 2003, the United States has contributed over $750 million in bilateral assistance and more than $750 million in assessed contributions to the UN Mission in Liberia (UNMIL). In FY 2008, the U.S. was to commit another $162 million bilaterally and $179 million through UNMIL. In February 2008, President Bush visited Liberia, where he held his fourth one-on-one meeting with President Sirleaf since Sirleaf's inauguration in January 2006. Peace Corps volunteers returned to Liberia in 2008 for the first time since 1990.

The U.S. Agency for International Development (USAID) implements the U.S. Government's development assistance program in Liberia, the second-largest USAID development program in Africa. USAID's post-conflict rebuilding strategy focuses on reintegration and is increasingly moving towards a longer-term development focus. Rehabilitation efforts include national and community infrastructure projects, such as expanding access to electricity, building roads, refurbishing government buildings, training Liberians in vocational skills, promoting business development, and improving livelihoods while protecting Liberia's forests. USAID also funds basic education programs, improving education for children, focusing on girls, and training teachers. In the health area, USAID programs include primary health care clinics, HIV/AIDS prevention, and a large malaria program. USAID supports rule of law programs, establishing legal aid clinics and victim abuse centers, training judges and lawyers, community peace building and reconciliation efforts, and anti-corruption projects to promote transparency and accountability in public sector entities. USAID is also providing support to strengthen the legislature and other political processes. USAID is strengthening civil society's role in delivering services and advocating good governance. Total USAID funding in FY 2008 was $105 million.

In: Liberia: Development and Resources
Editor: Anya M. Micallef
ISBN: 978-1-61209-396-3
© 2011 Nova Science Publishers, Inc.

Chapter 3

ASSESSMENT OF BIOMASS RESOURCES IN LIBERIA

Anelia Milbrandt

ACKNOWLEDGMENTS

The author would like to thank the International Resources Group (IRG) staff for managing this project on behalf of the U.S. Agency for International Development USAID, and particularly Mr. Simba Mangwengwende, the project overseer, for his review and feedback. Thanks to Dr. Ralph Overend, retired NREL Research Fellow, for his review and valuable recommendations.

A special thanks to Kristin Stroup from the Energy and Security Group (ESG) for her invaluable contributions in the data gathering process.

ABBREVIATIONS AND ACRONYMS

DFID	United Kingdom Department for International Development
EPA	Environmental Protection Agency
FAO	Food and Agriculture Organization
FAOSTAT	The FAO Statistical Database

FDA	Forestry Development Authority
GDP	Gross domestic product
GIS	Geographic information system
GHG	Greenhouse gas
LHV	Low heating value
MOA	Liberia's Ministry of Agriculture
MSW	Municipal solid waste
UNDP	United Nations Development Programme
UNEP	United Nations Environmental Programme
UNICEF	The United Nations Children's Fund

UNITS OF MEASURE

dam^3 – cubic decameter or 1,000 m^3 or 10^6 L, described in some sources as a ML (Megaliter)

GWh – Gigawatt hour (10^9 Wh)

ha – hectare

hm^3 – cubic hectometer or 1,000,000 m^3 or 10^9 L, described in some sources as a GL (Gigaliter)

kg – kilogram kWh – kilowatt hour (10^3 Wh)

L – liter (decimeter or dm^3)

m^3 – cubic meter

Mt – Megatonne (10^6 tonnes)

MWh – Megawatt hour (10^6 Wh)

TJ – Terajoule (10^{12} J)

Tonne - metric ton

Glossary of Plant Names

African walnut (*Lovoa klaineana*)

Banana (*Musa* sp.)

Cacao (Theobroma cacao)

Cassava (*Manihot esculenta*)

Coconut Palm (*Cocos nucifera*)

Cocoyam (*Colocasia esculenta*)

Coffee (*Rubiaceae family*)

Jatropha (*Jatropha Curcas*)
Kola tree (*Malvaceae sp.)*
Mahogany (Swietenia mahagoni)
Maize (*Zea mays*)
Oil Palm (*Elaeis guineensis)*
Pineapple (*Ananas comosus*)
Plantain (*Musa sp.*)
Rubber Tree (*Hevea brasiliensis)*
Sugarcane *(Poaceae sp.*)
Yam (*Dioscorea sp.*)

EXECUTIVE SUMMARY

Biomass resources meet about 99.5% of the Liberian population's energy needs so they are vital to basic welfare and economic activity. Already, traditional biomass products like firewood and charcoal are the primary energy source used for domestic cooking and heating. However, other more efficient biomass technologies are available that could open opportunities for agriculture and rural development, and provide other socio-economic and environmental benefits.

The main objective of this study is to estimate the biomass resources currently and potentially available in the country and evaluate their contribution for power generation and the production of transportation fuels. It intends to inform policy makers and industry developers of the biomass resource availability in Liberia, identify areas with high potential, and serve as a base for further, more detailed site-specific assessments.

A variety of biomass resources exist in the country in large quantities and with opportunities for expansion. The study found that these resources are more than enough to cover the country's annual electricity consumption of 297 GWh and oil consumption of 206 dam^3. While the contribution of food crop residues, animal manure, and municipal solid waste is small in comparison to other resources at a national level, they could play a valuable role in stand-alone electricity applications and be particularly effective for households in remote rural areas. On the other hand, cash crop and forest residues, resulting mainly from medium and large enterprises, provide opportunities for large-scale centralized power generation.

The study considers potential biomass resources and the expansion of key existing resources, such as oil palm, coconut, and sugarcane, to evaluate their fuel and power production potential on available cropland. It is unrealistic to assume that all of this land would be used for cash crop cultivation. A portion of it may go under afforestation to maintain forest ecosystems and their unique biodiversity, or be used for food crops production and other agricultural activities, or be converted to urban land. Therefore, the study evaluates the fuel and power production potential of biomass resources under three scenarios: using 10%, 25%, and 50% of the available cropland for cash crop expansion.

The local production and use of biomass resources as substitute for fossil-based fuels offers many socio-economic and environmental benefits for Liberia including energy security, investment opportunities, job creation, rural development, decreased greenhouse gas (GHG) emissions, waste utilization, and erosion control. However, if not managed properly, biomass resource development could have negative impacts, particularly to the environment. These include deforestation, increased GHG emissions, loss of biodiversity, and soil erosion. The socio-economic and environmental implications briefly described in this paper should form the basis of a more detailed study on the impact of biomass resources development in order to guide appropriate national policies and measures.

INTRODUCTION

Biomass energy is derived from plant-based material and residues where solar energy has been converted into organic matter. Biomass resources can be broadly classified into the following categories:

- Agricultural crops and residues;
- Dedicated energy crops (herbaceous and tree species);
- Forestry products and residues;
- Residues and byproducts from food, feed, fiber, wood, and materials processing plants [sawdust from sawmills, black liquor (a byproduct of paper making), cheese whey (a byproduct of cheese-making processes), and animal manure];

- Post-consumer residues and wastes, such as fats, greases, oils, construction and demolition wood debris and other urban wood wastes, municipal solid wastes and wastewater, and landfill gases.

There are competing uses for biomass resources because of their economic and environmental value. Biomass can be used to generate power, heat, steam, and for producing transportation fuels. Biomass is also used by the food processing industries, animal feed industry, and the wood products industry, which includes construction and fiber products (paper and derivatives); along with chemical products made by these industries that have diverse applications including detergents, fertilizers, and erosion control products.

In Liberia, as in nearly all of Sub-Sahara African countries, biomass (firewood, charcoal, and crop residues) is the primary energy source used for domestic cooking and heating. Up to 99.5% of the population relies on biomass-based fuels according to the United Nations Development Programme (UNDP). Such an overwhelming and persistent dependence on biomass fuels is associated with severe environmental, health, and social implications, such as the destruction of forests, loss of biodiversity, soil erosion, indoor air pollution, and increased travel distances for resource collection. Liberia's economic recovery and population growth will lead to higher energy demand; therefore, managing and improving the production and consumption efficiency of biomass resources are key to sustainable development. Furthermore, introducing other alternative renewable energy sources like wind and solar, as well as further development of hydroelectricity would relieve the pressure on biomass resources in Liberia.

Project Objectives and Approach

This study intends to inform policy makers and industry developers of the biomass resource availability in Liberia, identify areas with high potential, and serve as a base for further, more detailed and site-specific assessments.

The project's objective is to estimate the biomass resources currently and potentially available in the country and evaluate their potential contribution for power generation and transportation fuels production. To accomplish this objective, agricultural, environmental, and socio-economic data are analyzed both statistically and graphically using geographic information systems (GIS). A GIS is a computer-based information system used to create, manipulate, and analyze geographic information. The results are presented in a tabular and geospatial format (maps) at a national, sub-national (county), and site-specific level.

The biomass resource estimates are based on numerous assumptions and factors that relate agricultural, industrial, and demographic statistics to the amount of residue generated. A detailed description of the methodology is provided throughout the document. For several plantation crops (cacao, rubber, coconut, and oil palm), for example, the study evaluates the contribution of a small portion (10%) of all residues available after replanting, and suggests that only 30% of cacao pods and rubber leaves are collected as biomass (the rest should be left on the field to maintain soil quality and control erosion). Although these numbers are conservative and somewhat arbitrary, the users have all the information necessary to adjust assumptions and conversion factors for further evaluation of the biomass resource availability.

Detailed on-site analysis is recommended before developing any facilities; however, this analysis should be useful in refining the prospecting process of site identification.

AGRICULTURAL RESOURCES

Overview of Agricultural Sector

Liberia has immense agricultural potential with an estimated 3.7 million hectares of arable land (38% of the total land area), of which about 6% is currently cultivated (FRM 2004). About 60% of the country, situated in the moist belt along the coast of West Africa, is covered by forest and woodland. The rain forest soils, while well drained, are highly leached, making Liberia better adapted to tree crop agriculture than to annual field crop production.

The climate and terrain conditions in Liberia are very favorable for agricultural development. Due to abundant water resources in the country, irrigation infrastructure is virtually non-existent. The rainy season lasts from April to October with a very high annual rainfall, ranging from 1,600 mm inland to 4,600 mm on the coast. The terrain is mostly made up of flat to rolling coastal plains, running into some interior plateaus and low mountains in the northeast. The country is divided into four agro-ecological zones: coastal plains (up to 100 m above sea level), interior hills (100–300 m), interior plateaus (300-600 m), and mountainous areas (in excess of 600 m).

Agriculture is the backbone of Liberia's economy, providing informal employment for more than 70% of the workforce (mostly in rural areas) and contributing an estimated 53% to the gross domestic product (GDP) in 2006 (MOA 2007 and ITTAS 2008). The agricultural sector was left in ruin after Liberia's 14-year civil war (which ended in 2003), and it is slowly starting to revive itself. The damage to the agricultural sector is manifested in low productivity of agricultural systems; disruption of production due to the displacement of farming communities; erosion of marketing systems due to road, transport, and processing infrastructure degradation; physical insecurity; lack of farming opportunities (including seeds and tools) in the areas of displacement; and socio-economic dislocation (FAO 2006).

The Ministry of Agriculture defines three agricultural production systems, differentiated by the scale of production (MOA 2007):

- *Large plantations* (between 800 and 40,000 ha) produce export crops from perennials such as rubber, oil palm, and to a lesser degree, coffee and cacao. This system can be sub-divided into the large commercial plantations that are owned and managed by the private sector (found particularly in the rubber and palm oil sectors) and the state-owned plantations run by the Liberian Palm Products Corporation and the Liberian Cocoa and Coffee Corporation. Production in this second group is limited, although they remain in existence.
- Domestically owned, *medium-sized commercial farms* (between 5 and 200 ha) produce industrial crops for export and the local market (although these farms are extremely small in number).
- *Small household farms* (average size of 1.2 ha), the livelihood of the rural population, make up the majority of all farming. They use traditional production techniques with extremely limited use of modern inputs. Household farms are based on family labor and concentrate on growing food crops like rice and cassava, with some growing cash crops like rubber, coffee, cacao, and oil palm.

Food Crop Residues

Liberia produces a variety of basic food crops, including rice (the staple food of the country), cassava, other roots and tubers (sweet potato, yam, and cocoyam), maize, vegetables, groundnuts, and pulses. After these crops have been harvested and processed, various residues and byproducts remain, such as stalks, straw, husks, and shells. No data have been published on the quantities of crop residues and agro-industrial byproducts produced in Liberia. However, based on crop production statistics, and using appropriate crop to residue ratios, it is estimated that some 125,000 tonnes of food crop residues are produced each year (Table 1). The corresponding energy content is about 2,100 TJ, equivalent to 188 GWh of electricity.[1] Leading counties include Nimba, Montserrado, and Bong (Table 2). The methodology for estimating the food crop residues by county is presented in Appendix A.

Table 1. Food Crop Residues in Liberia

Commodity	Production (tonnes)	Residue Type	Crop to Residue Ratio	Moisture Content (%)	Residue (dry tonnes)	LHV (MJ/kg)	Total Energy (TJ/yr)	GWh
Rice	110,000	straw	0.45	12.71	43,209	16	691	65
		husk	0.27	12.37	26,026	19	494	39
Cassava	490,000	stalk	0.06	15	24,990	17.5	437	37
Other root and tuber crops	64,500	stalk	0.06	15	3,290	17.5	58	5
Groundnut	4,800	shells	0.48	6.2	2,115	16	34	3
		straw	2.30	12	9,715	18	175	15
Maize	15,000	stalk	1.00	15.5	12,675	15	190	19
		cob	0.25	8	3,450	15	52	5
Total	684,300				125,469		2,131	188

Source: FAOSTAT 2005; Koopmans and Koppejan 1997; other root and tuber crops include sweet potatoes, coco yams, and yams; GWh calculation assumes that a tonne of dry biomass generates on average 1.5 MWhe with the efficiency in the range of 20 – 40%.

Table 2. Food Crop Residues in Liberia by County

County	Annual production (tonnes)					
	Rice Straw & Husk	Cassava Stalk	Other Roots & Tubers Stalk	Groundnuts Shell & Straw	Maize Stalk & Cob	Total
Bomi	521	216	19	77	88	921
Bong	11,128	2,360	586	4,572	3,080	21,727
Grand Bassa	3,790	1,655	34	0	0	5,479
Grand Cape Mount	812	231	38	0	20	1,100
Grand Gedeh	3,589	407	32	0	247	4,274
Grand Kru	809	244	27	0	0	1,080
Lofa	10,021	540	173	953	946	12,633
Margibi	2,667	1,922	22	0	1,243	5,854
Maryland	3,686	1,170	136	0	894	5,885
Montserrado	5,810	9,840	792	0	7,447	23,890
Nimba	16,852	4,947	1,264	5,713	1,620	30,396
River Cess	967	267	16	104	15	1,369
Sinoe	2,335	610	107	0	361	3,413
River Gee	2,387	125	7	0	62	2,581
Gbarpolu	3,825	458	38	417	177	4,915

Unlike other regions in the world, such as Southeast Asia, where food crops are produced commercially and generate large concentrations of residues, much of Liberia's production is run by small households for self-consumption or local markets. Additionally, food crops cultivation in the country is widely scattered. Figure 1 illustrates the food crop residues by county and the location of populated places as an indicator of where these residues are generated within a county. The lack of large-scale food crops production, and their dispersion, increases collection and transportation costs, which would restrain the use of these residues for centralized electricity generation. Moreover, many crop residues and byproducts are seasonal and become available all at once at the same time of the year. Therefore, treatment and storage facilities will be required if they are to be made available as a bio-power feedstock throughout the year.

Caveats

It is difficult to estimate the amount of food crop residues that is actually available in Liberia for power generation or alternative transportation fuels. Considering Liberian households' lifestyle, it is very likely that a significant portion of the residues identified here are already in use as animal feed, on farm applications, or for cooking and water heating. These resources are site specific and require detailed analyses for any proposed project.

Cash Crop Residues

Cash crops grown in Liberia include rubber, coffee, cacao, coconut, sugarcane, plantain/banana (also serving as food crops), oil palm, pineapple, and kola nut (Table 3). Rubber, cacao, and coffee make very important contributions to the Liberian economy, accounting for 22% of GDP in 2005. In addition, these crops are a significant element of export earnings. Rubber currently accounts for almost 90% of total exports because timber exports, which made up 50–60% of the total exports until the early 2000s, have been eliminated due to sanctions (MOA 2007). These sanctions were lifted in 2006.

Currently, cash crops in Liberia are grown predominately on small household farms, except rubber and oil palm, grown on a range of small-, medium-, and large-scale production systems. Opportunities for growing cash crops on mid-size, commercial farms exist and it is expected that the share of this production system will grow as the agricultural sector in Liberia revives itself.

Rubber has been Liberia's principle cash crop since the 1920s. The country ranks third in Africa's production of natural latex after Nigeria and Ivory Coast, with about 117,000 tonnes in 2005 (FAOSTAT). Below is a list of the large-scale rubber plantations established in Liberia over the years and Figure 2 illustrates their locations:

- Firestone near Harbel, Margibi County
- Liberia Agricultural Company (LAC) near Buchanan, Grand Bassa County
- Guthrie (also known as Goodrich plantation) near Baha, Bomi County
- Liberia Company (LIBCO) near Cocopa, Nimba County
- Salala Rubber Corporation near Nienka, Margibi County
- Cavalla (initially part of the Firestone concession) near Harper, Maryland County
- Sinoe Rubber Corporation (SRC) near Greenville, Sinoe County

Some of these plantations were abandoned or taken over by rebel forces during the civil war. As a result, many suffered years of poor or indifferent management and would need significant investment to put them back in production. During this time, few plantations changed hands, such as Firestone, which sold its interests to the Japanese-owned Bridgestone in 1988, or ceased operation (the government suspended the agreement with LIBCO in December 2007, citing poor management). The two largest plantations, Firestone and LAC, remained in good condition after the war, and are currently producing significant quantities of rubber. As of July 2007, the Firestone factory was producing 3,000-4,000 tonnes of rubber per month, while LAC was producing about 2,000 tonnes per month (PAC 2007). Two other plantations, Guthrie and Cavalla, reported production of about 4,000 tonnes each in 2006 (MOA 2007). Because of these companies' operation, many household farmers in Liberia note that rubber is their current most important cash crop. They sell raw rubber to the companies, making the industry a big employment generator as well as a major income earner for the country (FAO 2006).

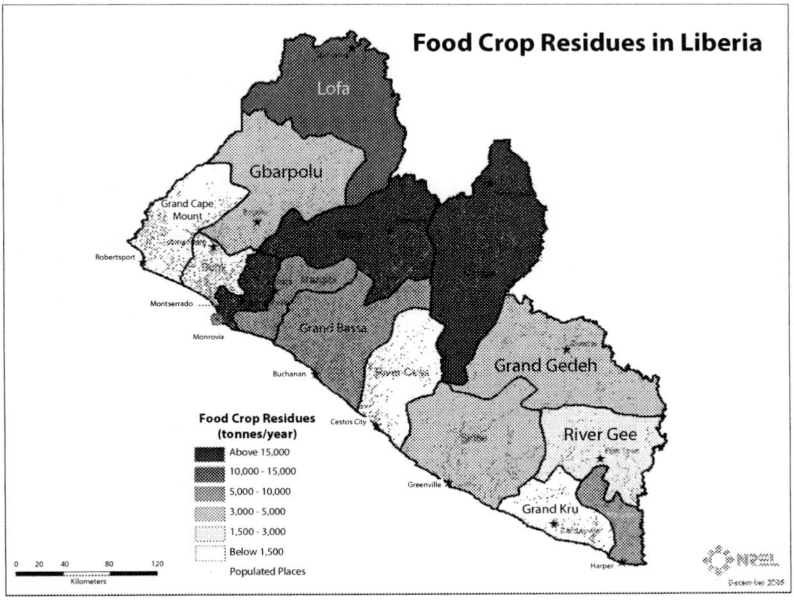

Figure 1. Food Crop Residues in Liberia by County.

The study estimates that large-scale rubber plantations in Liberia today cover an area of approximately 58,000 hectares (Appendix B). This type of plantation generates considerable amounts of wood residues from pruning and replanting activities. According to MOA, the tree stock in these plantations is still productive; however, UNEP indicates they are nearing the end of their productive lifespan. The rotation period, when the trees are cut down for replanting, is 25-30 years. Tree trunks and branches become available during replanting and approximately 81 dry tonnes of wood could be obtained per hectare (about 180 m^3 of green wood). Tree trunks are usually used as timber and the small branches (54% of total biomass) are left in the field. If only 10% of the current rubber tree stock (about 5,800 ha) is replanted, it would result in roughly 254,000 dry tonnes of wood branches. The corresponding energy content is about 4,600 TJ, equivalent to 381 GWh of electricity. Additional biomass resources from rubber trees that could be tapped as an energy source are the leaves. Rubber trees are deciduous—they shed their leaves during the dry season, resulting in a residue resource of about 1.4 tonnes per hectare. The leaves are often disposed of by burning at the end of the dry period. However, if collected, it would result in approximately 69,000 dry tonnes of biomass. Some of the leaves should be left on the field to maintain soil quality and control erosion; however, even if only 30% of this biomass resource is collected (~21,000 dry tonnes), about 31.5 GWh of electricity would be generated.

This analysis doesn't evaluate the residues generated from rubber trees grown on household farms because it is assumed that these residues are already in use as firewood or on farm applications. Additionally, MOA reports that more than 75% of the smallholder farms are newly planted, therefore no significant residue generation is expected in the next 15-20 years.

Another cash crop grown in Liberia is the **cacao** tree, whose seeds are the source of cocoa, cocoa butter, and chocolate. The Food and Agriculture Organization (FAO) estimates about 3,000 tonnes of cacao beans are produced annually in Liberia. Cacao trees need shade and are not very suitable for large-scale monoculture plantations, making intercropping with other cash or food crops a common practice in the small household farms. There were, however, a few industrial-scale plantations operated by the Liberia Coffee and Cocoa Corporation (LCCC) in the 1970s, one in Lofa County (15,000 ha) and another in Nimba County (13,000 ha). As with other industries, these plantations are currently under rehabilitation. Cacao is most commonly grown in interior counties with slightly higher altitudes, such as Grand Gedeh, River Gee, Lofa, and Gbarpolu.

Cacao trees of the unimproved variety become viable after six years and have a productive lifespan of 20-25 years, during which they have to be pruned regularly. Prunings are either left in the field or used as firewood by households. Pruning activities in Liberia would yield about 5,340 dry tonnes of biomass per year with a corresponding energy content of 96 TJ/year (8 GWh). Additionally, replacing old, non-productive trees after 20-25 years results in about 48 kg of dry organic matter per tree (about 5,760 kg per hectare), assuming there are 1,200 trees per hectare (Koopmans and Koppejan 1997). The FAO estimates that there are about 17,000 ha currently planted with cacao. According to MOA, the vast majority of cacao trees in Liberia are more than 20 years old. If only 10% of the current cacao tree stock (1,700 ha) is replanted over the next year, it would generate about 10,000 dry tonnes of biomass, equivalent to 176 TJ (15 GWh). Some of this resource is already in use as cacao trees are being cut and burned as charcoal in some areas of Liberia. Besides wood, residues in the form of cacao pods are generated and it is estimated that about 5,220 dry tonnes of pods were produced in 2005. A portion of this material should be left on the field as a source of valuable potassium fertilizer; however, if only 30% of this biomass resource is collected (1,566 dry tonnes), about 2.3 GWh of electricity would be generated.

Coffee is another cash crop grown in Liberia with about 3,200 tonnes of green coffee produced each year. Coffee dominates in the central and northern counties, particularly in Lofa County, where about 82% of the farming families are growing the crop (UN 2006).

The coffee tree grows fruit after 3-5 years, for about 50-60 years. Farmers prune coffee trees once per year, in a sequential rotation pattern (it takes 18 or more months for the coffee plants to grow back). The pruned material is left on the field to act as organic fertilizer and provide soil protection. No information is available on the amount of residues generated during coffee pruning activities; therefore, this biomass resource is not considered in this study.

The two main coffee processing by-products are husk and pulp. Coffee husk is produced by processing harvested coffee through the dry method; coffee pulp is produced by the wet method.[2] Liberia grows mainly Robusta, usually processed by the dry method, making coffee husks available after processing. Some of the husk is used as organic fertilizer, but if compressed into pellets, it can be used for power generation. The study estimates that about 500 dry tonnes of husk are generated per year, with a corresponding energy content of 8 TJ and electricity generation potential of less than one GWh.

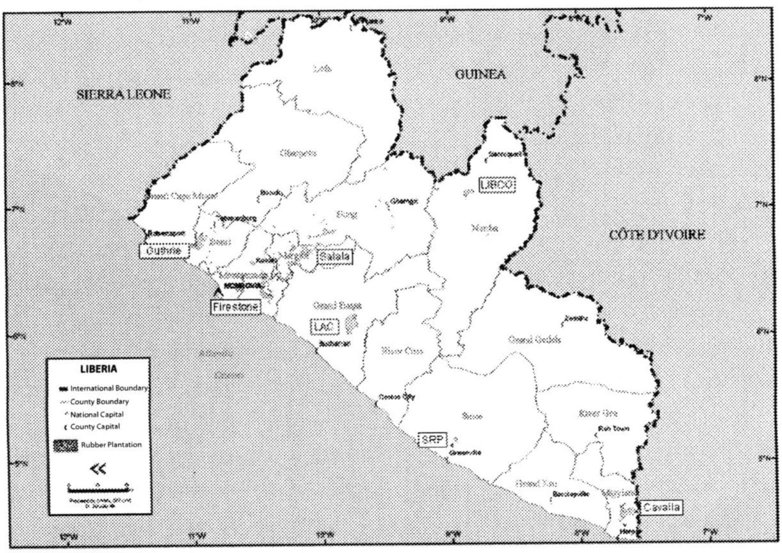

Source: UN 2006

Figure 2. Rubber Plantations in Liberia

Banana and plantains are major products in Liberia, serving as both cash and food crops. They are very important to food security during the hunger season (the period of time when all the food from the previous harvest has been consumed, and the next harvest hasn't begun) because they produce fruit year-round. Bananas and plantains are cultivated by small-scale farmers in every county for household consumption and market supply. Annual production is about 110,000 tonnes for bananas and 42,000 tonnes for plantains.

The life span of individual plants is about 1-1.5 years. Where plants receive care, the mat's lifespan is virtually unlimited because it continually regenerates new plants. Stems and leaves are available as part of the plantations' maintenance activities and it is estimated that about 89 dry tonnes of biomass could be collected per hectare per year (Sheikh 1989). There are about 29,000 ha under banana and plantain cultivation in Liberia; therefore, about 2.6 million tonnes of residues are collected annually. This amount corresponds to 41,000 TJ/year, equivalent to 3,872 GWh. Banana and plantain residues have many competing uses, so it is difficult to estimate the amount that could be available for power generation. The stems and leaves are a source of mulch and fertilizer (upon composting), animal fodder, wrapping, eating utensils, and roofing. They are also a source of fiber and can be processed into textiles or used for papermaking. Banana and plantain peels are another type of residue, used as animal feed or left to decompose on the field. They can also be used to produce briquettes or biogas for cooking, heating, and electricity production. The study estimates that about 32,000 dry tonnes of peels are generated annually in Liberia, equivalent to 549 TJ/year or 48 GWh.

Oil palm grows throughout Liberia but is particularly abundant in the coastal areas. It can yield cooking oil, animal food, and raw material for the manufacture of cosmetics, detergents, and pharmaceuticals. Palm oil can be used to produce biodiesel or used directly to run low-rpm diesel generators. In addition, the palm residues can be a feedstock for heat and power generation.

Oil palm is different from the other tree crops in that a large part of the final product (palm oil) is obtained from wild groves. FAO estimates that about 35,000 tonnes of palm oil was produced in Liberia in 2007, with perhaps half of that production coming from wild trees. Cultivation is done on small household farms and medium- to large-scale state-owned plantations. Small-scale farms growing oil palm are dominant in Cape Mount County (49% of all farming families), Gbarpolu (19%), Nimba (19%), Sinoe (17%), and Bomi (17%). The state-owned plantations were largely abandoned during the war, some partly taken over by the local population for its own use. There has been no maintenance or replanting for about 20 years and the trees are at the end of their productive life. Moreover, all processing facilities were destroyed. A number of these plantations are available for rehabilitation and privatization, covering an area of about 30,000 hectares. Recently, the government granted a management contract to Equatorial Biofuels Plc (EBF), a United Kingdom public company, for Butaw and LIBINCO oil palm plantations. No additional contracts have been awarded and the remaining plantations lie largely abandoned. Figure 3 illustrates the location of oil palm plantations in Liberia and their planted areas.

Oil palm residues generated during processing include fiber, shells, and empty fruit bunches (EFB). Liberia produced 183,000 tonnes of fruits in 2005 and the estimated residues amount to about 104,000 dry tonnes, or 1,680 TJ. Fronds become available on a regular basis during harvesting, and the study estimates that about 247,000 dry tonnes were generated in 2005 (1,980 TJ). All of these residues can be used for power generation and the study estimates that their potential is about 528 GWh (Table 3). However, there are other uses for these residues. For example, EFB are rich in potassium so they are used as fertilizer and the fronds are used for mulching. The productive life of the oil palm tree is about 25-30 years, and during replanting tree trunks and fronds become available. As mentioned earlier, trees on the state-owned plantations are at the end of their productive life, therefore a significant amount of residues could be available in the next few years as part of the rehabilitation process. The average yield per hectare is about 80 dry tonnes of biomass. If only 10% of the area planted with oil palm trees in Liberia (about 3,000 ha) is replanted, it would yield 240,000 tonnes of biomass, equivalent to 4,320 TJ (360 GWh).

Sugarcane grows very well in Liberia and production in 2005 was estimated at 255,000 tonnes. It is cultivated by small household farms mainly in the coastal south and central counties— Maryland, Nimba, Grand Kru, and Grand Bassa. There is a sugarcane plantation (about 2,428 hectares) with a factory in Maryland County, owned by the Liberia Sugar Corporation (LIBSUCO), which was destroyed during the Liberian civil conflict like many other industries in the country. A small quantity of sugar is produced for local consumption and the molasses and syrup are sold locally. In addition to sugar and syrup, alcohol for beverage and medicinal purposes is also produced for domestic and export consumption. The cane-juice liquor ("gin") is traded across the border to the Ivory Coast and is an important source of income.

The sugarcane residues - tops and leaves available during harvesting and the bagasse remaining after crushing - can be used to provide heat and power.

These residues are currently used as animal feed, fertilizer (tops and leaves), and for cooking by households. The study estimates that about 76,000 tonnes of sugarcane residues were generated in Liberia in 2005, equivalent to 1,300 TJ or 114 GWh (Table 3).

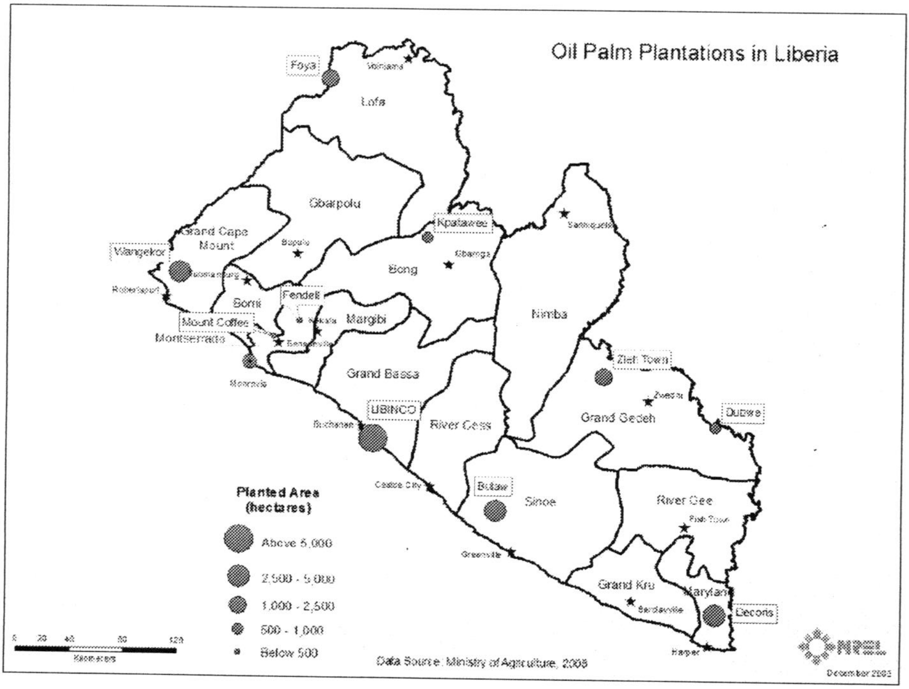

Figure 3. Oil Palm Plantations in Liberia

Coconut in Liberia is grown on small- to mid-size household farms, mainly along the coastline. The only large coconut plantation (8,000 ha) is owned by the Liberia Palm and Produce Corporation (LPPC) in Greenville, Sinoe County. It was operated in the 1980s and is currently under rehabilitation. The coconut tree is a source of edible oil and many other products: copra meal provides a highly nutritional animal feed; roots are used in traditional medicine; trunks provide timber; leaves are used as material for roofing, fences, and baskets; waste coconut husks provide fiber and peat; and coconut shells are used to create household products and fashion accessories. The lignocellulosic biomass from coconut trees (trunks, fronds, husks, and shells) are also used as direct fuel for cooking and can be used to provide electricity. The husks themselves can be a good source of charcoal. In addition, the oil can be used to produce biodiesel or used directly to run low-rpm diesel generators.

A study by the Sustainable Rural Enterprise (SRE) estimates that there are more than 81,000 hectares planted with coconut trees in Liberia (Manapol 2007). The average production per hectare per year of a coconut plantation is one tonne, thus about 81,000 tonnes of coconuts are produced annually in Liberia. Applying the appropriate crop to residue ratios, it is estimated that about 80,000 tonnes of processing residues (husks and shells) and 194,000 tonnes of harvesting residues (fronds) are generated. If only 10% of the area planted with coconut trees in Liberia is replanted, it would yield 7,800 tonnes of biomass equivalent to 125 TJ (12 GWh) (Table 3).

Table 3. Cash Crop Residues in Liberia

Commodity	Production (tonnes)	Residue Type	Crop to Residue Ratio	Moisture Content (%)	Residue (dry tonnes)	LHV (MJ/kg)	Total Energy (TJ/yr)	GWh
Coffee (green)	3,200	husk	0.18	13	501	17	8.52	0.75
Cacao (beans)	3,000	pods	2	13	5,220	18	94	7.63
		prunings	2	11	5,340	18	96	8.01
	17,000ha	wood (replanting)**	5.76 dry tonnes/ha	N/A	9,792	18	176	14.69
Oil Palm (fruit)	183,000	empty fruit bunches	0.43	9	71,757	16	1,148	107.64
		fibre	0.15	10	24,705	16	395	37.06
		kernel shells	0.05	13	7,961	17	135	11.94
		fronds	2.6	48	247,416	8	1,979	371.12
	30,000ha*	wood (replanting)**	80 dry tonnes/ha	N/A	240,000	18	4,320	360.00
Coconuts	81,000	husk	0.42	10	30,618	19	582	45.93
		shells	0.7	13	49,329	16	886	73.99
		fronds	2.4 dry tonnes/ha/yr	N/A	194,400	18	3,499	291.60
	81,000ha*	wood (replanting)**	0.96 tonnes/ha	11	7,776	18	125	11.66
Bananas and plantains	152,000	peels	0.25	15	32,300	17	549	48.45
	29,000 ha	stems/leaves	89 dry tonnes/ha/yr	N/A	2,581,000	16	41,296	3,871.60
Rubber	58,000ha*	branches (replanting)**	44 dry tonnes/ha	N/A	254,000	18	4,572	381.00
		leaves	1.4 tonnes/ha	15	68,663	18	1,236	102.99
Sugarcane	255,000	bagasse	0.29	49	37,715	16	679	56.57
		tops/leaves	0.3	50	38,250	16	612	57.36
Pineapple	1,200ha	leaves	80 tonnes/ha/yr	60	19,200	14	265	28.60
Total					3,925,943		62,655	5,889

Source: FAOSTAT (production in 2005); Koopmans and Koppejan 1997; Sajjakulnukit, B., et al 2005; SRE 2007 N/A – Not applicable

* Includes large-scale plantations only;

** Residues are calculated for 10% of current cacao, rubber, coconut, and oil palm tree stock; GWh calculation assumes that a tonne of dry biomass generates on average 1.5 MWhe with the efficiency in the range of 20 – 40%.

Other cash crops include pineapple and kola nut, grown in every county, and are usually intercropped with other plants. Leading counties for pineapple include Bomi and Grand Bassa, where 29% of all households are growing the plant, and Cape Mount (21% of all households). Kola nut is grown in Bomi (28% of all households), Gbarpolu (17% of all households), and Montserrado (16% of all households) (UN 2006).

Annual production of pineapple is estimated at 7,200 tonnes (FAOSTAT). Plants bear for 3-5 years after which they are usually replanted. Up to 80 tonnes of leaves per hectare are available annually after harvesting the fruits (moisture content is very high, 80-85%). There are about 1,200 hectares planted with pineapple in Liberia (FAOSTAT), so 19,200 tonnes of dry biomass can be collected annually (265 TJ). The leaves are used as animal feed and are a source of fiber. In some cases they are left on the field. No information is available on the amount of residues generated during harvesting, processing, and replanting of kola tree; therefore, this crop is not considered in the study.

Table 3 summarizes cash crop residues generated annually in Liberia and their relative energy content. The total amount is estimated at 3.9 million tonnes of biomass, equivalent to about 63,000 TJ per year (5,890 GWh of electricity). Residues from banana and plantains have the largest contribution (67%), followed by biomass material from oil palm (15%), and rubber (8%). The distribution of these resources by county is illustrated in Table 4 and Figure 3. Counties generating the largest amount of residues include Nimba, Montserrado, Margibi, and Bong.

Table 4. Cash Crop Residues in Liberia by County

County	Annual production (tonnes)							
	Cacao Pods & Prunings	Coffee Husks	Oil Palm EFB, Fiber, Shells & Fronds	Coconut Husks & Shells	Banana & Plantain Peels	Sugarcane Tops, Leaves & Bagasse	Rubber Leaves*	Total
Bomi	43	1	3,766	179	299	564	11,900	16,750
Bong	1,177	33	55,704	881	2,208	10,300	N/A	70,303
Grand Bassa	407	4	13,094	4,840	2,248	6,860	16,660	44,114
Grand Cape Mount	99	7	19,453	1,921	185	0	N/A	21,665
Grand Gedeh	995	15	4,000	538	985	0	N/A	6,531
Grand Kru	71	0	1,279	825	431	1,033	N/A	3,639
Lofa	2,001	250	27,332	0	860	818	N/A	31,252
Margibi	289	0	29,318	7,882	1,845	4,388	32,725	76,448
Maryland	339	3	5,163	3,123	1,673	6,375	4,760	21,435
Montserrado	650	32	47,049	48,063	11,950	15,493	N/A	123,237
Nimba	2,790	110	103,711	1,467	6,366	27,779	N/A	142,224
River Cess	78	1	3,580	1,283	387	313	N/A	5,643
Sinoe	292	7	12,394	4,116	1,115	873	2,618	21,414
River Gee	471	3	3,155	3,224	1,047	94	N/A	7,994
Gbarpolu	868	37	22,690	1,605	712	1,073	N/A	26,975

* Large-scale plantations only; N/A – Not applicable; these estimates don't include residues from replanting activities, coconut fronds, banana/plantain stems and leaves, and pineapple residues; EFB – Empty Fruit Bunches.

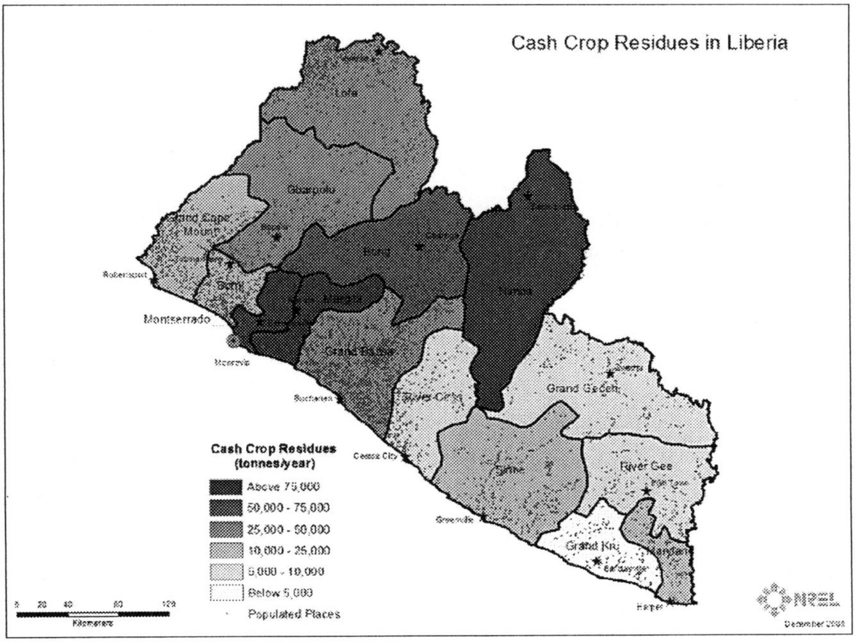

Figure 4. Cash Crop Residues in Liberia by County

Animal Manure

The livestock sector has never been a major feature of the agriculture in Liberia but it is an important activity to traditional farmers. There are an estimated 2 million hectares of pastureland in the country, yet the livestock sector accounts for only 14% of agricultural GDP, far below its potential (MOA 2007). According to the United Nations, the main livestock for rural and semi- urban Liberians today is poultry (about 47% of households). About 8% of farming families own ducks, and 5% own pigs and goats. Sheep and cattle are hardly present. Before the war, there were seven large cattle farms in Maryland, Grand Kru, and Sinoe counties, covering an area of 2,000 ha. Today they are only slowly being rehabilitated, mainly in Maryland. These three counties are characterized by vast areas of grassland which are less suitable for agricultural production but are ideal for raising livestock (UN 2006).

Livestock manure is used as an organic fertilizer, building material, and energy source. It can be used as fuel in two ways: either burned directly or anaerobically digested to produce biogas[3], which is then burned. Biogas is a more efficient source of energy than raw manure, and the residue from the bio-digesters (spent slurry) can be used as a valuable fertilizer. Under controlled and optimized conditions, a bio-digester can convert feedstock into biogas in a few days. Small- and medium-scale digesters (up to $6m^3$) can provide biogas for single-household cooking and lighting in rural communities. Large-scale digesters can supply biogas in large volumes for electricity generation, heat, steam, and transportation fuel production.

The study evaluates the animal manure generation in Liberia and estimates the potential biogas production at about 36 hm^3 per year, equivalent to 219 GWh (Table 5). An estimate of the biogas potential from animal husbandry on the sub-national level was possible for select counties where data on animal population was available. A project completed by the FAO (Smith 2002) assessed the livestock population in 8 counties: Montserrado, Margibi, Bong, Nimba, Grand Gedeh, Sinoe, River Cess, and Grand Bassa. Among these counties, Nimba had the highest population of livestock in 2001 (more than 21,500 cattle, sheep/goats, pigs, and poultry), followed by Montserrado (2,180), and Grand Gedeh (1,752). Considering the factors outlined in Table 5—animal type, manure generation, and biogas production—Nimba County has the highest potential for electricity generation from biogas (2,856 MWh), followed by Bong (97 MWh), Grand Bassa (80 MWh), Grand Gedeh (59 MWh), Montserrado (42 MWh), Margibi (36 MWh), River Cess (28 MWh), and Sinoe (15 MWh).

Table 5. Animal Manure and Biogas Potential in Liberia

Livestock Type	Population in 2005 (heads)	Manure (kg/head/day)	Biogas Yield (m3/kg)	Annual Biogas Production (hm3)	GWh
Cattle	25,000	10	0.04	3.65	22
Sheep/goats	435,000	2	0.05	15.88	95
Pigs	131,000	1.5	0.07	5.02	30
Poultry	5,428,000	0.1	0.06	11.89	71
Total	6,019,000			36.44	219

Source: MOA 2007; Manure generation per day considers medium size animals; The calorific value of biogas is about 6 kWh/m3, which corresponds to about 0.5 liter of diesel oil. The net calorific value depends on the efficiency of the burners or appliances. hm3 – cubic hectometer or 1,000,000 m^3

FOREST RESOURCES

Overview of Forestry Sector

Liberia possesses substantial forest resources covering about 5.7 million hectares, equivalent to 60% of the total area (FRM 2004). The country is situated in the Upper Guinean Forest, stretching from Cameroon to Guinea, which is believed to shelter a large number of diverse plant and animal species. Liberian forests are characterized by evergreen trees and shrubs along the more humid coastal regions where mangroves are also located; deciduous and mountain species, located in the hills of Northwest Liberia and Mount Nimba; and rainforest in the inland hills and plains. These forests are home to some 250 species of timber, including the highly valued mahoganies and African walnut. Figure 5 illustrates the spatial distribution of forests in Liberia, as well as the 11 designated National Forests in the country (under very limited protection), and the two legally protected areas, Sapo National Park (approximately 149,000 ha) and East Nimba (about 15,000 ha).

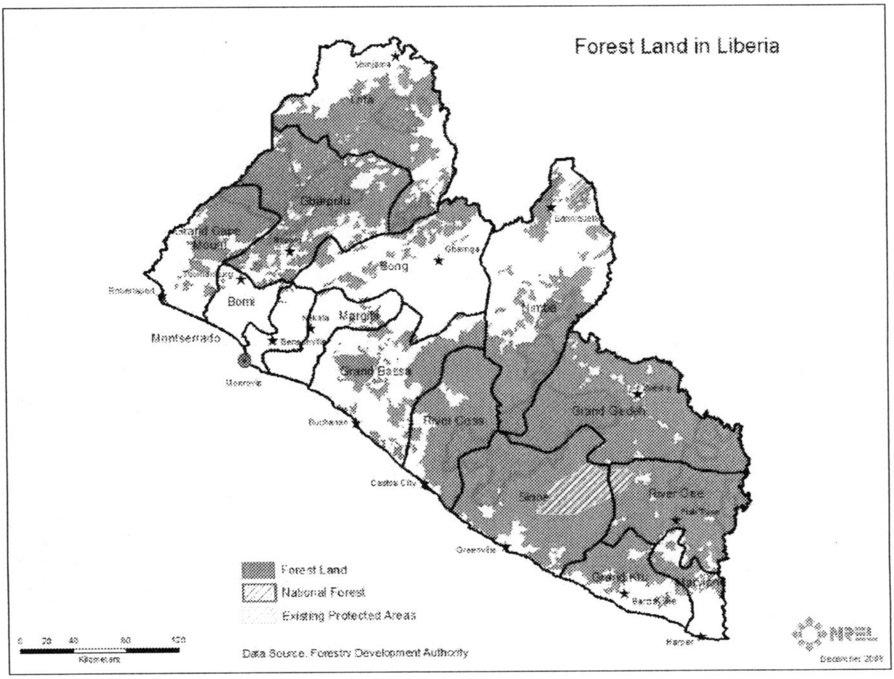

Figure 5. Forest Land in Liberia.

Liberia's forests are of special importance to the economy because they provide employment in the rural areas, fuel sources (charcoal and firewood), and export products (logs and timber). However, forest resources were mismanaged and the revenue generated from the sector was misappropriated during Liberia's civil conflict. As a result, the United Nations Security Council imposed sanctions on Liberia's timber exports in 2003 (FDA 2007). In 2004, the Liberian government, assisted by the international community, examined all 70 logging companies in Liberia. In addition to the lack of legality, the concession review found that these companies had violated many environmental, labor, and forestry laws and regulations (Woods et al. 2008). Following the concession review, President Sirleaf's administration cancelled all concessions by executive order in February 2006, put in place a moratorium on all logging activities, and passed a new National Forestry Reform Law. In June 2006, the U.N. Security Council acknowledged the reforms of the new government and lifted the sanctions on timber.

The Forestry Development Authority (FDA) is the sole government agency responsible for managing forest resources in Liberia. As a part of the forestry reform program, the FDA identifies areas suitable for logging and awards the harvesting contracts through competitive bidding. The new agreements are focused on responsible logging, which considers the environment and the needs of local communities. According to the National Forestry Strategy, there are two distinct types of logging contracts meant to achieve different objectives (Woods et al 2008):

- **Forest Management Contracts (FMC):** Long-term contracts for large areas of up to 400,000 hectares (akin to the traditional concessions). Small FMCs (50,000-100,000 hectares) are reserved for majority-owned (51%) Liberian companies, although they represent an opportunity for joint ventures between domestic and foreign partners. There are no restrictions on company ownership for larger FMCs.
- **Timber Sale Contracts (TSC):** Short-term contracts (less than 3 years) for smaller areas (less than 5,000 hectares). TSCs are focused on areas that will likely be cleared for plantations or farming, therefore the management requirements for harvesting the timber is less onerous. This means that TSCs require less planning and can be awarded more easily than FMCs. TSCs are also reserved for majority-owned Liberian companies.

In 2008, through the FDA, the government awarded three FMCs and six TSCs to pre-qualified companies in various counties. Additionally, the FDA announced that four more FMCs were available for purchase as of December 5, 2008. Table 6 illustrates the location, ownership, and size of the existing and pending logging contracts in Liberia.

Table 6. Logging Contracts in Liberia

County	Contract Category	Ownership	Area (hectares)
Gbarpolu and Lofa	FMC "A"	Alpha Logging and Wood Processing Inc.	119,240
River Cess	FMC "B"	EJ and J Investment Corporation	57,262
River Cess	FMC "C"	Liberia Tree and Trade Company	59,374
Grand Gedeh and River Gee	FMC "F"	Pending	253,670
Grand Gedeh and Sinoe	FMC "I"	Pending	131,466
Nimba, Grand Gedeh and River Cess	FMC "K"	Pending	266,910
Grand Kru, Maryland and River Gee	FMC "P"	Pending	119,344
Grand Bassa	TSC "A2"	Tarpeh Timber Corporation Inc.	5,000
Grand Bassa	TSC "A3"	Tarpeh Timber Corporation Inc.	5,000
Bong and Gbarpolu	TSC "A6"	B & V Timber Company Inc.	5,000
Gbarpolu	TSC "A7"	Bargor & Bargor Enterprise Inc.	5,000
Grand Cape Mount	TSC "A9"	B & V Timber Company Inc.	5,000
Grand Cape Mount	TSC "A10"	B & V Timber Company Inc.	5,000
Total			**1,037,266**

Source: FDA 2008

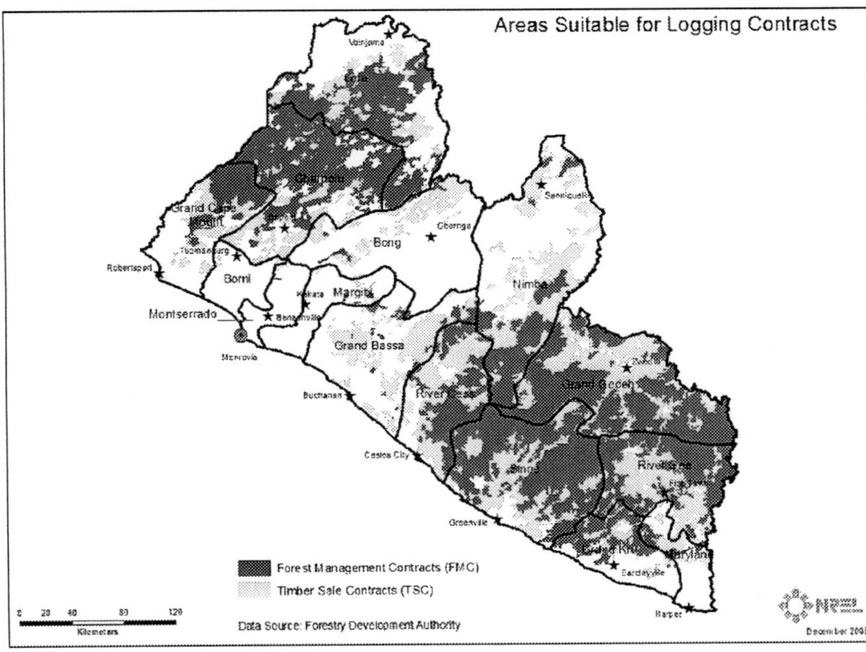

Figure 6. Areas Suitable for Logging Contracts in Liberia

Forest Residues include wood residues from logging and wood-processing activities. Logging residues are the unused portions of trees cut during logging operations and left in the woods. These include stumps, branches, leaves, off-cuts, and sawdust. Wood-processing residues, or primary mill residues, are composed of wood materials (such as discarded logs, bark, sawdust, and shavings) generated at manufacturing plants—sawmill, veneer mill, plywood mill, or pulp mill—when round-wood products are processed into primary wood products. Forest residues can be used to generate heat, electricity, liquid fuels, and solid fuels (compressed wood such as pellets, briquettes, or charcoal briquettes).

As mentioned above, due to the forestry reform program, the government cancelled all concession agreements across Liberia in early 2006. Consequently, there are no formal forestry activities in the country, though small-scale pit sawing is evident in many areas. This study evaluates the forest residues that could potentially be available in the country after logging concessions resume operation. It estimates that about 19.6 hm^3 of forest residues could be collected, equivalent to 162,645 TJ per year, or 15,248 GWh of electricity (Table 7). The analysis methodology is described below.

Table 7. Forest Residues in Liberia

Forest Residues	Volume (hm3)	Weight (Mt)	Total energy (TJ/yr)	GWh
Logging	8.71	6,898	110,373	10,347
Saw-milling	10.89	3,267	52,272	4,901
Total	19.6	10,165	162,645	15,248

hm^3 - cubic hectometer (1 hm3 = 1,000,000 m^3); Mt – Megatonne (106 tonnes); conversion of volume to mass is based on average density of 792 kg/m^3 for logging residues and 300 kg/m^3 for saw-milling residues with a moisture content of 20%. GWh calculation assumes that a tonne of dry biomass generates on average 1.5 MWhe with the efficiency in the range of 20 – 40%; Air-dry wood (20% moisture content) has an energy value of about 16 MJ/kg.

The current logging contracts in Liberia cover an area of about 1 million hectares (Table 6). According to Mano Properties & Investment, Inc., a company registered with the FDA and pre-qualified for TSCs, the average forest yield in the country is about 21 m^3 per hectare (MPI 2008). Therefore, approximately 21.78 hm^3 of wood could be available from forest lands. Residue generation varies considerably depending on species and local practices. For the purpose of this study, an average recovery factor of 40% for logging residues and 50% (38% solid wood waste and 12% sawdust) for saw-milling residues was used. This corresponds to roughly 9 hm^3 of logging residues and 11 hm^3 of saw-milling residues (Table 7). Table 8 and Figure 7 illustrate the distribution of these resources by county and the analysis methodology is presented in Appendix C.

Table 8. Forest Residues in Liberia by County

County	Area (ha)	Yield (dam3)	Logging Residues (dam3)	Saw-milling Residues (dam3)	Total (dam3)
Bomi	0	0	0	0	0
Bong	2,700	57	23	28	51
Grand Bassa	10,000	210	84	105	189
Grand Cape Mount	10,000	210	84	105	189
Grand Gedeh	263,643	5,537	2,215	2,768	4,983
Grand Kru	78,344	1,645	658	823	1,481
Lofa	59,620	1,252	501	626	1,127
Margibi	0	0	0	0	0
Maryland	16,000	336	134	168	302
Montserrado	0	0	0	0	0
Nimba	120,000	2,520	1,008	1,260	2,268
River Cess	195,636	4,108	1,643	2,054	3,698
Sinoe	65,733	1,380	552	690	1,242
River Gee	148,670	3,122	1,249	1,561	2,810
Gbarpolu	66,920	1,405	562	703	1,265

dam^3 – cubic decameter or 1,000 m^3

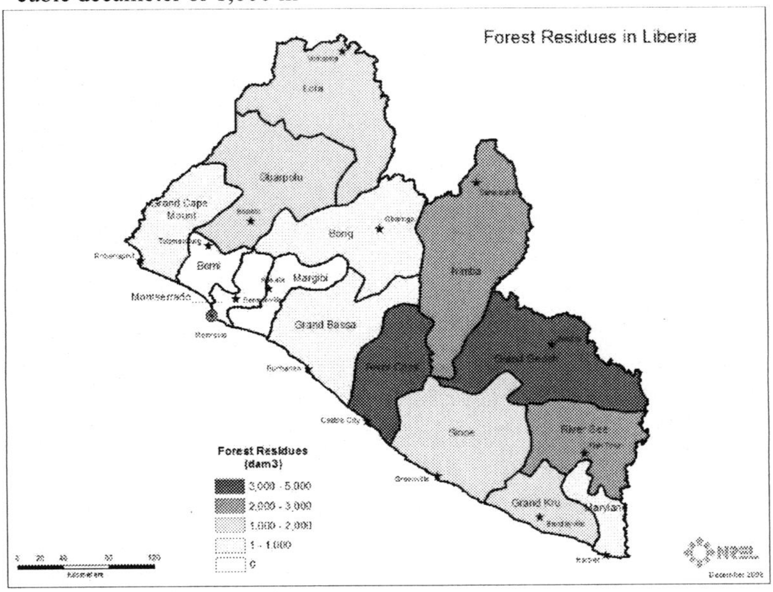

Figure 7. Forest Residues in Liberia by County

URBAN RESOURCES

The concentration of population and activities in urban areas is responsible for the generation of waste. This waste, referred to as municipal solid waste (MSW), is generated by households and the commercial and industrial sectors. The waste takes many forms, including plastics, paper, textiles, glass, metal, wood, food, and other organic wastes. MSW, particularly the biogenic fraction, is a resource that can be converted to electricity, heat, gaseous and liquid fuels through thermo-chemical (incineration, pyrolysis, and gasification), and bio-chemical (anaerobic digestion and fermentation) conversion processes.

The use of waste as an energy source provides two important benefits of environmentally safe waste management and disposal, as well as the generation of clean electric power. Waste-toenergy combustion reduces the volume of trash by about 90%, resulting in a 90% decrease in the amount of land required for garbage disposal. The amount of ash on a weight basis is as high as 25% of the input. Using biogas emitted from landfill sites, also called "landfill gas", can capture roughly 60-90% of the methane, depending on system design and effectiveness. Given that all landfills generate methane, it is logical to use the gas for energy generation rather than emitting this highly potent greenhouse gas to the atmosphere (U.S. EPA).

The waste disposal method practiced in Liberia is open dumping and swampland reclamation. There is a complete absence of engineered landfills, though one is under development in Wehnn Town, Montserrado County; instead, there are many dumpsites available in proximity to major communities posing threat to humans' health, wetland ecosystems, and water resources. Despite the fact that there are no landfill sites in Liberia, the study evaluates the MSW resource to illustrate its electricity generation potential. Waste-to-energy and landfill gas-to-energy facilities tend to be built at the landfills of large urban centers, although small-scale projects could be developed in rural areas. Therefore, the study estimates the generation potential of waste-to-power in major populated places in Liberia with more than 5,000 people.

Table 9. Municipal Solid Waste Generation and Electricity Potential in Major Urban Areas in Liberia

Urban Area	Population	MSW Generation (tonnes/yr)	Biogenic MSW Generation (dry tonnes/yr)	Electrical Energy via Thermo-Chemical Pathway (MWh/yr)
Saclepea	12,117	2,399	834	459
Monrovia	1,010,970	200,172	69,580	38,269
Tubmanburg	13,114	2,597	903	496
Foya	19,522	3,865	1,344	739
Zorzor	5,131	1,016	353	194
Voinjama	26,594	5,266	1,830	1,007
Ganta	41,106	8,139	2,829	1,556
Harper	17,837	3,532	1,228	675
Karnplay	7,664	1,517	527	290
Pleebo	22,963	4,547	1,580	869
River Gbeh	7,313	1,448	503	277
Sanniquellie	11,415	2,260	786	432
Zwedru	23,903	4,733	1,645	905
Buchanan	34,270	6,785	2,359	1,297
Gbarnga	34,046	6,741	2,343	1,289
Greenville	16,434	3,254	1,131	622
Harbel	23,402	4,634	1,611	886
Kakata	33,945	6,721	2,336	1,285
Total	1,361,746	269,626	93,722	51,547

Population numbers are for 2008; waste generation rate: 0.6 kg/day/person; the study considers 330 annual operating days; Biogenic materials are 64% of total MSW with moisture content as follow: paper – 6%, wood/straw – 40%, textiles – 10%, vegetable/putrescibles – 60%;Thermo-Chemical pathway considers incineration technology.

Estimations for MSW generated in Liberia's major urban areas use 2008 population numbers derived from the National Population and Housing Census (LISGIS 2008) and a factor that relates population to the amount of post-consumer residue generation. A waste generation rate of 0.6kg/day/person was used in this study adopted from the World Bank Technical Paper No. 426 (World Bank 1999), which includes 0.5kg/day/person for domestic waste generation, plus a further 0.1kg/day/cap for commercial and industrial waste. Figure 8 illustrates the results of this analysis.

The amount of MSW generated annually in Liberia's major urban areas is estimated at 270,000 tonnes (Table 9). The biogenic materials (paper, wood, textiles, and vegetable/putrescibles) are 64% of total MSW or about 172,000 tonnes, based on the waste composition in Liberia (Table 10). A typical waste-to-energy plant generates about 550 kWh per tonne of waste combusted. Modern waste incineration plants have efficiencies for power generation of 20%-25%, and new designs could exceed 30%. The electrical energy from the biogenic portion of the MSW in Liberia's major urban areas, via thermo-chemical conversion, is estimated at 52 GWh per year.

An alternative treatment of the biogenic waste fraction is anaerobic digestion. Approximately 50 to 200 m^3 of landfill gas is produced per tonne of MSW collected and dumped in landfills. The volume of gas produced depends on several factors: the amount, type, and age of waste; moisture content; temperature; pH; and site conditions. Without a particular site in mind, it is difficult to estimate the energy potential of MSW via bio-chemical conversion in Liberia. Also, it is difficult to put a timeframe on landfill gas recovery. As opposed to bio-digesters where waste feedstock is converted to biogas in controlled, optimized conditions, anaerobic decomposition in a landfill is uncontrolled and very slow. It may take several years before the level of production is sufficient to fuel an electricity generator, although an advanced technology exists to accelerate the digestion process within a few months.

Table 10. Waste Composition in Monrovia

Waste composition in Monrovia	
Component	**% by weight**
Paper	10.0
Glass, Ceramics	1.2
Metals	2.0
Plastics	13.0
Leather, Rubber	0.2
Wood, Bones, Straw	4.6
Textiles	6.0
Vegetable /Putrescible	43.0
Miscellaneous Items	20.0
Total	**100**
Density	**250 kg/m3**

Source: UNEP 2007; adopted from the Waste Management Plan for Monrovia, 2004

Note: Miscellaneous items include sand, ash, and small grained and wet food waste that could not be sorted.

Table 11. Biofuels Potential in Liberia

County	Total Area (ha)	Cropland (ha)	Cropland Under Cultivation (ha)			Available Cropland (ha)	Biodiesel from palm oil (dam3/yr)			Biodiesel from coconut oil (dam3/yr)			Ethanol from sugarcane (dam3/yr)		
			Area Planted by Small Household Farms	Area Planted by Large Plantations*	Total		10% of Available Cropand	25% of Available Cropland	50% of Available Cropland	10% of Available Cropland	25% of Available Cropland	50% of Available Cropland	10% of Available Cropland	25% of Available Cropland	50% of Available Cropland
Bomi	212,188	206,064	1,858	10,000	11,858	188,206	113	282	565	40	99	198	94	235	471
Bong	838,360	678,361	53,451	607	54,058	615,303	370	924	1,849	129	324	647	308	770	1,541
Grand Bassa	747,785	449,696	28,989	27,759	56,748	392,948	236	589	1,179	83	206	413	196	491	982
Grand Cape Mount	496,254	189,867	5,181	2,833	8,014	181,853	109	273	546	38	95	191	91	227	455
Grand Gedeh	1,028,201	41,482	13,048	2,186	15,234	26,248	16	39	79	6	14	28	13	33	66
Grand Kru	369,908	117,036	2,264	0	2,264	114,772	69	172	344	24	60	121	57	143	287
Lofa	1,031,743	440,149	68,789	17,428	86,217	353,931	212	531	1,062	74	186	372	177	442	885
Margibi	281,222	239,856	29,280	27,500	56,780	183,076	110	275	549	38	96	192	92	229	458
Maryland	218,819	117,641	16,843	10,880	27,723	89,917	54	135	270	19	47	94	45	112	225
Montserrado	181,113	167,077	166,652	425	167,077	0	0	0	0	0	0	0	0	0	0
Nimba	1,191,121	652,135	66,145	13,000	79,145	572,990	344	859	1,719	120	301	602	286	716	1,432
River Cess	528,199	76,132	5,840	0	5,840	70,291	42	105	211	15	37	74	35	88	176
Since	938,783	55,757	9,174	13,518	22,692	33,065	20	50	99	7	17	35	17	41	83
River Gee	619,854	35,153	5,589	0	5,589	29,564	18	44	89	6	16	31	15	37	74
Gbarpolu	923,776	212,837	12,801	0	12,801	200,036	120	300	600	42	105	210	100	250	500
Total	9,605,327	3,665,243	485,906	126,136	612,042	3,053,202	1,832	4,580	9,160	641	1,603	3,206	1,527	3,817	7,633

* Cash crops only; total area and cropland data provided by FRM; Note: Crop yields, and biofuels yield respectively, can vary widely. This analysis uses the following yields: biodiesel from palm oil – 6,000 L/ha, biodiesel from coconut oil – 2,100 L/ha, ethanol from sugarcane – 5,000 L/ha; the energy content of ethanol is about 67% that of gasoline. The energy content of biodiesel is about 90% that of petroleum diesel.

Table 12. Bio-Power Potential in Liberia

County	Total Area (ha)	Cropland (ha)	Cropland Under Cultivation (ha)			Available Cropland (ha)	Electricity from oil palm residues (GWh/yr)			Electricity from coconut residues (GWh/yr)			Electrici
			Area Planted by Small Household Farms	Area Planted by Large Plantations*	Total		10% of Available Cropland	25% of Available Cropland	50% of Available Cropland	10% of Available Cropland	25% of Available Cropland	50% of Available Cropland	10% Availa Cropl
Bomi	212,188	200,064	1,858	10,000	11,853	188,206	1,085	2,713	5,425	28	70	139	
Bong	838,360	670,361	53,451	607	54,053	616,303	3,553	8,883	17,766	91	228	456	
Grand Bassa	747,785	449,696	28,989	27,759	56,743	392,948	2,266	5,664	11,328	56	145	291	
Grand Cape Mount	496,254	189,867	5,181	2,833	8,014	161,853	1,348	2,621	5,242	27	67	135	
Grand Gedeh	1,028,201	41,482	13,048	2,186	15,234	26,248	151	378	757	4	10	19	
Grand Kru	369,909	117,036	2,264	0	2,264	114,772	562	1,654	3,309	17	42	85	
Lofa	1,031,743	440,149	68,789	17,428	86,217	353,931	2,341	5,101	10,203	52	131	262	
Margibi	281,222	239,856	29,280	27,500	56,780	183,076	1,056	2,639	5,278	27	68	136	
Maryland	218,619	117,641	16,843	10,880	27,723	89,917	518	1,296	2,592	13	33	67	
Montserrado	181,113	167,077	166,652	425	167,077	0	0	0	0	0	0	0	
Nimba	1,191,121	652,135	66,145	13,000	79,145	572,990	3,304	8,259	16,518	85	212	424	
River Cess	528,199	76,132	5,840	0	5,840	70,291	405	1,013	2,026	10	26	52	
Sinoe	936,783	55,757	9,174	13,518	22,692	33,065	191	477	953	5	12	24	
River Gee	619,654	35,153	5,589	0	5,589	29,564	170	426	852	4	11	22	
Gbarpolu	923,776	212,837	12,801	0	12,801	200,036	1,153	2,883	5,766	30	74	148	
Total	9,605,327	3,665,243	485,906	126,136	612,042	3,053,202	17,503	44,007	88,015	452	1,130	2,260	

* Cash crops only; total area and cropland data provided by FRM; Note: Crop yields can vary widely. This analysis uses the following yields: oil palm – 20 tonnes of fresh fruit bunches per hectare, coconut – 1 tonne of nuts/ha, sugarcane - 65 tonnes/ha. The residues generated by each crop are estimated using the methodology described earlier in the paper; one dry tonne of biomass can generate 1-2 MWh of electricity (20-40% efficiency) - this analysis uses an average of 1.5 MWh per dry tonne.

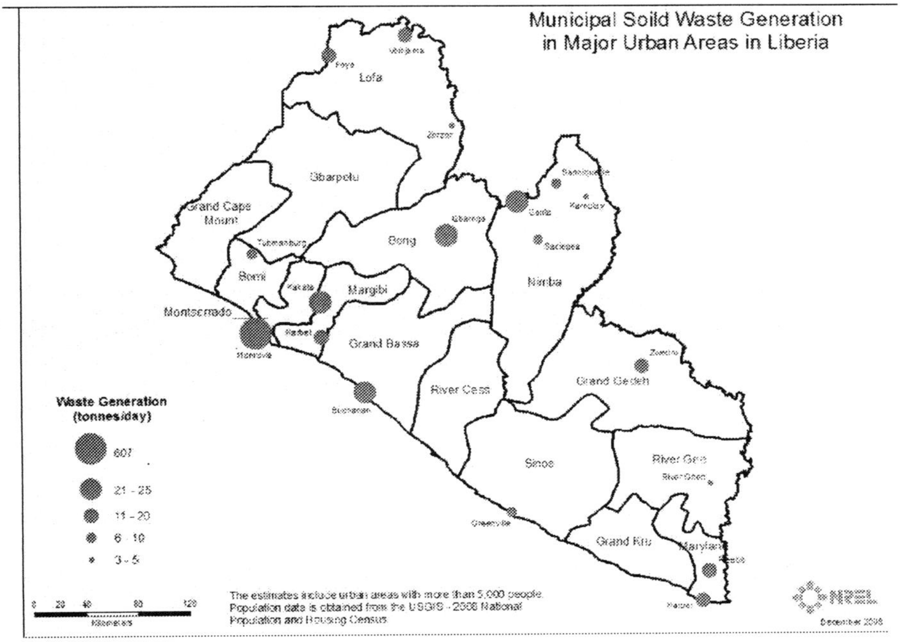

Figure 8. Municipal Solid Waste Generation in Major Urban Areas in Liberia.

Potential Biomass Resources

Real opportunities for biomass resource expansion exist in Liberia considering the favorable agro-climatic conditions. As mentioned earlier, the Liberian soils are better adapted to tree-crop agriculture than annual field-crop production. Even if food-crop production increases, it will predominantly be used to secure food supply rather than as a biomass resource. Therefore, the study evaluates the potential expansion of tree crops in the country, particularly oil palm and coconut. These two crops have diverse applications as an energy source—they can be used in parallel as feedstock for the production of transportation fuels and power generation. Sugarcane is also evaluated for the same reason. The study does not evaluate the potential forest resources in Liberia due to the reforms that are taking place in this sector and the uncertainty of their outcome. Additionally, all of the proposed protected areas fall within the forest lands (see Appendix C); therefore, the extent of the areas that are designated as protected would determine the forest land available for logging, and respectively, the residues that could be collected as biomass. The same applies to the rubber, coffee, and cacao industries which are going through a rehabilitation process.

The study estimates that of the total cropland in Liberia, only 6% is currently cultivated. The remaining cropland amounts to some 3 million hectares. It is unrealistic to assume that all of this land would go under tree-crop cultivation. A portion of it may go under afforestation to maintain forest ecosystems and their unique biodiversity, or be used for food crops production and other agricultural activities, or be converted to urban land. Therefore, the study evaluates the fuel and power production potential of biomass resources grown on the available cropland under three scenarios: using 10%, 25%, and 50% of the available cropland for cash crop expansion. The results of this analysis are presented in Table 11 and Table 12.

Liberia, situated in the tropical biome, has the advantage of growing the most desirable feedstocks for biofuels production—with the highest yield per land unit—compared to those in the temperate biome. Liberian feedstocks include oil palm, coconut, and sugarcane. Biodiesel yielded from oil palm is about 6,000 L/ha. Rapeseed supplies on average 1,200 L/ha and soybeans about 500 L/ha. Ethanol yielded from sugarcane is between 5,000-6,500 L/ha while corn supplies about 3,100 L/ha. If only 10% of the available cropland is used to expand oil palm or coconut cultivation, it would yield about 1,800 dam^3 and 641 dam^3 of biodiesel per year, respectively. If 10% of the available cropland is used for expansion of sugarcane production, it would yield about 1,500 dam^3 of ethanol annually. This volume of biofuels would be more than enough to cover the country's transportation needs of about 206 dam^3 per year (Index Mundi 2005). In addition to vegetable oil, used cooking oil and animal fat could also be used as feedstocks for biodiesel production. Moreover, as one liter of vegetable oil provides about 2 kWh of electricity with conversion efficiency at 21%, these oils and fats could be used directly in stand-alone diesel generators to provide electricity for rural communities.

As mentioned earlier, the residues generated during the harvesting and processing of the tree and herbaceous crops can be used to generate electricity or to produce charcoal, thereby reducing deforestation and improving public health. In the case of sugarcane, bagasse can be used to provide heat and electricity for use in the mill, making the industrial process self- sufficient and even generating a surplus. If 10% of the available cropland is used to expand the cultivation of oil palm, coconut, or sugarcane, it would generate about 18,000 GWh, 452 GWh, and 9,000 GWh of electricity per year, respectively. This production would be more than enough to meet Liberia's current electricity consumption of 297 GWh (CIA 2005). In addition to power generation, the crop residues could be used to produce transportation fuels via advanced conversion technologies: ethanol production via enzymatic fermentation and Fischer Tropsch hydrocarbons via gasification to syngas (a mixture of carbon monoxide and hydrogen). Significant research and development efforts are underway in many developed countries to improve and commercialize these technologies.

Another multipurpose plant receiving a lot of attention recently is *Jatropha Curcas*. This tropical perennial shrub is already used as a live fence and to control erosion; the oil extracted from the seeds is used for medicinal purposes and soap making; and the seedcake is used as organic fertilizer and animal feed. As of late, the plant's oil has been targeted as a feedstock for biodiesel production or a direct substitute for petroleum diesel in power generators. In addition, the processing residues (shells and husks) can be used as solid biofuels in power plants.

Although Jatropha holds considerable potential as a diesel substitute, there are many uncertainties surrounding its cultivation, primarily because while it grows abundantly in the wild, it has never been domesticated. The establishment, management, and productivity of the plant are not well understood and documented. Until this knowledge is improved, it is perhaps best to think of Jatropha as a secondary crop (as an intercrop or hedge), as part of rural livelihoods and local energy projects, and not as a monoculture. If used as an intercrop, Jatropha can provide an additional source of income for small farmers. For example, in Peru there are plans for intercropping the plant with coffee; in the Philippines with coconut trees. The United States has a trial orange farm intercropped with Jatropha. In Madagascar, farmers traditionally use it to support the climbing stem of vanilla. Jatropha can also be intercropped with banana/plantains and used for attracting scarring beetles so they don't scratch the fruits and lower their selling value. The range of oil yield per land unit varies widely in the literature—between 500 and 1,500 liters per hectare (some sources even suggest 2,000 liters/ha). If planted as a fence, its yield is approximately equal to one-tenth the yield of the area enclosed by the fence (Krypton Systems 2008). For example, if 5 ha farm is fenced with Jatropha, the collected oil would be about 500 L, assuming a yield of 1,000 L/ha. The oil-to-biodiesel ratio is almost 1:1, therefore about 500 L of biodiesel could be produced on a 5 ha farm.

Caveats

To calculate the forest and cropland area in Liberia, the project relies exclusively on the 2004 GIS data provided by Liberia's Environmental Protection Agency. The data was created by the French firm Forest Resources Management (FRM). However, the spatial distribution of the land cover types in this dataset (Figure 9) is different than those illustrated by Google's latest satellite imagery (Figure 10). Therefore, additional work is needed to ensure accurate and up-to-date information on the land cover distribution in Liberia for a more precise analysis of the land availability and biomass resource potential.

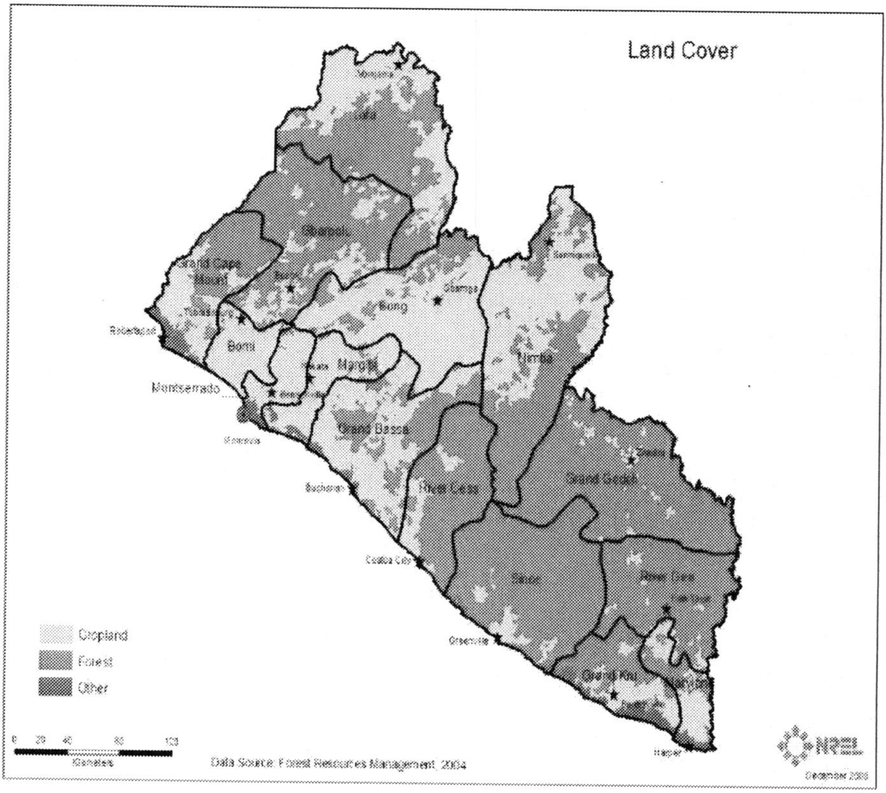

Figure 9. Land Cover.

Figure 10. Satellite Imagery.

SOCIO-ECONOM IC AND ENVIRONMENTAL IMPLICATIONS OF BIOMASS RESOURCE DEVELOPMENT IN LIBERIA

The local production and use of biomass resources as substitute for fossil-based fuels offers many attractive benefits for Liberia; however, they could also have negative effects if not managed properly. The following socio-economic and environmental implications should form the basis of a more detailed study on the impact of biomass resource development to guide appropriate national policies and measures.

Socio-Economic Implications

The global quest for alternative sources of energy, especially in the area of transportation fuels, presents an opportunity for local and foreign investments in Liberia, as well as increased export earnings. Pursuing Liberia's biomass potential would have a domino effect: it would boost agricultural development, boost technological advancement, and bring job opportunities, thereby improving quality of life. Also, because biomass resources can be converted to liquid and gaseous fuels electricity, and process heat, they can increase access to modern forms of energy for the Liberian population. Moreover, producing biomass resources domestically reduces the country's dependence on foreign energy sources and vulnerability to supply disruptions.

Biomass resource cultivation, harvesting, and processing could have a direct impact on rural development and poverty reduction. It could improve rural livelihoods by providing new income opportunities to families and communities growing biomass, or through direct employment. Using biomass resources in stand-alone power generation units could insulate poor rural households from energy price fluctuations, allowing for an independent electricity source.

Although there are numerous benefits, the expansion of biomass resource development could also have some negative socio-economic effects on rural communities. A study by the Worldwatch Institute points out that in the biofuels industry, most jobs are found at plantations where wages and working conditions can be very poor (Worldwatch 2008). Also, companies can make false promises about jobs for local communities. The study found that small farms could be more effective in job development than large scale plantations, stating that small farming systems in Indonesia provide livelihoods for 260 times as many people per hectare of land as oil palm plantations. Depopulation of regions could also be associated with large-scale monoculture plantations due to depletion of traditional wood and food resources.

Environmental Implications

The local production and use of biomass resources offers many benefits to the environment, including offsetting greenhouse gas (GHG) emissions associated with burning fossil fuels, waste utilization, and erosion control among others. Clearly biomass technology directly benefits the environment while helping solve pressing environmental problems.

Using biomass to produce energy is carbon neutral because it releases roughly as much carbon dioxide (CO_2) as it takes in. For every MWh of biomass power, approximately 1.6 tonnes of CO_2 are avoided (Morris 2008). This figure includes 0.8 tons/MWh from avoided fossil fuel use and 0.8 tons/MWh avoided from biomass decomposition or open burning. Carbon dioxide is the principal GHG that causes global warming, and the increasing levels of its concentration in the atmosphere are of great concern. The use of biomass resources, managed in a sustainable way, would reduce CO_2 emissions and help tackle global warming.

While CO_2 is the principal GHG, methane is a close second. According to the Intergovernmental Panel on Climate Change, methane is about 21 times as effective as CO_2 at trapping heat in the atmosphere. Therefore, reducing 1 tonne of methane has the same positive effect as reducing 21 tonnes of CO_2. Methane is the principal component in biogas, and as described earlier, it is produced by anaerobic digestion or fermentation of biodegradable materials such as manure, sewage, and MSW. Biogas capture and utilization presents an attractive opportunity for waste management in Liberia because it is a valuable renewable energy source that can be used to provide electricity while reducing methane emissions. This technology could be particularly effective in handling rubber wastewater, which is otherwise dumped in rivers, creating serious pollution problems. The green byproduct from biogas digesters are rich in nutrients and could be reapplied to rubber plantations. As Liberia plans to further develop the palm oil industry, biogasto-electricity technology could be used to handle the industry's waste. Another waste management problem with environmental and human health implications in Liberia that could be tackled with biomass technology is the disposal of MSW. The use of waste as an energy source provides two important benefits: environmentally safe waste management and disposal, as well as clean electric power generation. Waste-to-energy combustion reduces the volume of trash by about 90%, decreasing the amount of land required for garbage disposal by 90%.

Biomass resource development, under proper management, could be very beneficial in managing soil erosion. Afforestation and reforestation activities could prevent the soils from being washed or blown away, and residues from production and harvesting could provide additional soil protection as well as other benefits such as nutrient supply and moisture retention.

Some of the negative environmental impacts associated with the production and use of biomass resources include deforestation, increased GHG emissions, loss of biodiversity, and soil erosion. Deforestation is caused primarily by shifting cultivation (land clearing for crop production) and excessive logging. This could have reverse GHG effects: first, clearing is often done by burning, which releases CO_2; and second, once removed, the trees no longer contribute to carbon storage. Liberia's population relies almost entirely on biomass resources (firewood and charcoal) for its energy needs; therefore, using alternative sources is critical to forest sustainability. Charcoal, for example, is produced mainly from trees, so using alternative sources like coconut husks and banana peels would relieve the pressure on native forests.

Deforestation also leads to soil erosion and decline in biodiversity. Additionally, loss of biodiversity could result from an increase in monoculture crops and plantations. A study by the Integrated Framework in 2008 stated that where forest has been replaced by oil palm or rubber trees, up to 80% of reptile, mammal, and bird species previously found cannot be supported by the new environment. The use of pesticides and herbicides also devastates fauna and flora. The study also points out that the palm oil and rubber industries are rife with unsustainable environmental practices. As Liberia plans to revive and expand these industries, proper planning and management will be required to ensure protection of its rich biodiversity.

CONCLUSIONS

This study estimates the biomass resources currently and potentially available in Liberia and evaluates their power generation and transportation fuels production potential. A variety of biomass resources exist in the country with large quantities and opportunities for expansion. As illustrated in Table 13, these resources are more than enough to cover the country's annual electricity consumption of 297 GWh (CIA 2005) and oil consumption of 206 dam^3 (Index Mundi 2005). While the contribution of food crop residues, animal manure, and MSW is small in comparison to other resources at a national level, they could play a valuable role in stand-alone electricity applications and be particularly effective for households in remote rural areas. On the other hand, cash crop and forest residues, resulting mainly from medium and large enterprises, provide opportunities for large-scale centralized power generation.

Considering the potential biomass resources or the expansion of key existing resources such as oil palm, coconut, and sugarcane, the study evaluates their fuel and power production potential on available cropland. The study estimates that of the total cropland in Liberia, only 6% is currently cultivated and that the remaining cropland amounts to some 3 million hectares. It is unrealistic to assume that all of this land would go under cash crop cultivation—a portion of it may go under afforestation to maintain forest ecosystems and their unique biodiversity, or be used for food crops production and other agricultural activities, or be converted to urban land. Therefore, the study evaluates the fuel and power production potential of biomass resources under three scenarios: using 10%, 25%, and 50% of the available cropland for cash crops expansion. Table 13 illustrates the conservative results of this analysis—using up to 30% of the available cropland for expanded cash crops production. If this percentage increases, it would double or triple the bio-power and biofuels production potential as shown by the different analysis scenarios in the previous chapter.

The contribution of each county to the total amount of bio-power and biofuels from existing and potential biomass resources is presented in Table 14. With regard to existing resources, Nimba County ranks first with the highest amount, thus the highest electricity potential, followed by Montserrado, Bong, Margibi, Grand Bassa, and so on. Regarding future biomass resources, the quantity and their respective bioenergy potentials are highly dependent on the available cropland in each county. The ranking is slightly different—Bong County is leading, followed by Nimba, Grand Bassa, Lofa, Gbarpolu, etc.

The local production and use of biomass resources as substitute for fossil-based fuels offers many attractive benefits for Liberia. The socio-economic benefits include attracting investment opportunities, job creation, rural development, and poverty reduction. Benefits to the environment include offsetting the GHG emissions associated with burning fossil fuels, waste utilization, and erosion control. However, if not managed properly, biomass resource development could have negative environmental impacts such as deforestation, increased GHG emissions, loss of biodiversity, and soil erosion. The socio-economic and environmental implications briefly described in this paper should form the basis of a more detailed study on the impact of biomass resources development in order to guide appropriate national policies and measures.

Table 13. Bio-Power and Biofuels from Existing and Potential Biomass Resources

Existing Resources	Bio-power (GWh/yr)	Biodiesel (dam3/yr)	Ethanol (dam3/yr)
Food Crop Residues	188	-	-
Cash Crop Residues	5,889	-	-
Biogas from Animal Manure	219	-	-
Forest Residues	15,248	-	-
MSW (biogenic material only)	52	-	-
Total	21,596	-	-
Potential Resources			
Vegetable Oils*	4,946	2,473	-
Sugarcane**	-	-	1,527
Crop residues***	26,923	-	5,385

"-" Not Applicable; * Includes palm and coconut oil – using 10% of available cropland for oil palm and 10% for coconut; ** Using 10% of available cropland; *** Includes oil palm, coconut, and sugarcane residues – using 30% of available land (10% for each crop); 1 liter of vegetable oil = 2 kWh at 21% conversion efficiency; 1 tonne of lignocellulosic biomass yields ~ 300 liters of ethanol. Note: Currently, Liberia produces vegetable oils, which are mostly used in food consumption, medicinal, and few other purposes. Thus, it is unlikely that these resources would be used as a diesel substitute in the near future.

Table 14. Bio-Power and Biofuels from Existing and Potential Biomass Resources by County

County	Existing Resources				Potential Resources			
	Bio-Power from Food Crop Residues (GWh/yr)	Bio-Power from Cash Crop Residues* (GWh/yr)	Bio-Power from Forest Residues (GWh/yr)	Rank	Biodiesel** (dam3/yr)	Ethanol*** (dam3/yr)	Bio-Power from Cash Crop Residues**** (GWh/yr)	Rank
Bomi	1.4	25.1	0	11	152	94	1,660	6
Bong	32.6	105.5	0.04	3	499	308	5,435	1
Grand Bassa	8.2	66.2	0.15	5	318	196	3,465	3
Grand Cape Mount	1.6	32.5	0.15	10	147	91	1,604	8
Grand Gedeh	6.4	9.8	3.88	12	21	13	231	14
Grand Kru	1.6	5.5	1.15	15	93	57	1,012	9
Lofa	18.9	46.9	0.88	6	287	177	3,121	4
Margibi	8.8	114.7	0	4	148	92	1,614	7
Maryland	8.8	32.2	0.24	8	73	45	793	10
Montserrado	35.8	184.9	0	2	0	0	0	15
Nimba	45.6	213.3	1.76	1	464	286	5,053	2
River Cess	2.1	8.5	2.88	14	57	35	620	11
Sinoe	5.1	32.1	0.97	9	27	17	292	12
River Gee	3.9	12.0	2.19	13	24	15	261	13
Gbarpolu	7.4	40.5	0.98	7	162	100	1,764	5

1 dry tonne of biomass = 1.5 MWh of electricity (20-40% efficiency); * The total doesn't add up to total for the whole country. The analysis by county excludes residues from replanting. There would be different removal rates depending on local tree stock conditions; * Includes palm and coconut oil - using 10% of available cropland for oil palm and 10% for coconut tree; *** Using 10% of available cropland for sugarcane; **** Includes oil palm, coconut, and sugarcane residues - using 30% of available cropland - 10% for each crop.

APPENDIX A. ESTIMATING FOOD CROP RESIDUES BY COUNTY

County level crop production data is only available for rice and cassava from organizations such as FAO and the United Nations. Other crop data is available at a national level. The method described below is used in this study to disaggregate the national level statistics of crop production to county level. Then, crop residues are calculated using a crop-to-residue ratio as illustrated previously in Table 1.

The assumption is made that all families in any one county growing a particular crop have the same average yield and corresponding residue. Therefore, by knowing the number of farming families in a county and the percentage of families that grow a particular crop (Table 15), that county's contribution to the entire country's production can be calculated and the resulting residues estimated. For example: There are about 1,556 families growing rice in Bomi County (2,551 * 0.61). Dividing that number by the total number of families growing rice in Liberia (206,503) gives us the percentage of rice growing families in Bomi County from all rice growing families in Liberia (0.75%). This percentage is then multiplied by the country's rice production of 110,000 tonnes/year to give us the production of rice in Bomi County (829 tonnes/year). Further, applying crop to residue ratios (Table 1) gives us the amount of rice straw (325 dry tonnes/year) and husk (197 dry tonnes/year) in Bomi County, or total of 521 dry tonnes of crop residues per year (Table 2).

Table 15. Farming Families Growing Food Crops in Liberia, 2005

County	Number of Farming Families	Average Farm Size (ha)	% of Farming Families Growing Food Crops				
			Rice	Cassava	Other Roots and Tubers	Maize	Groundnuts
Bomi	2,551	0.73	61	84	8	8	1
Bong	37,736	1.42	86	62	17	19	4
Grand Bassa	18,850	1.54	60	87	2	0	0
Grand Cape Mount	4,572	1.13	53	50	9	1	0
Grand Gedeh	11,515	1.13	93	35	3	6	0
Grand Kru	2,945	0.77	82	82	10	11	0
Lofa	31,477	2.19	95	17	6	7	1
Margibi	24,117	1.21	33	79	1	12	0
Maryland	14,864	1.13	74	78	10	14	0
Montserrado	108,366	1.54	16	90	8	16	0
Nimba	62,862	1.05	80	78	22	6	3
River Cess	3,436	1.70	84	77	5	1	1
Sinoe	8,396	1.09	83	72	14	10	0
River Gee	7,268	0.77	98	17	1	2	0
Gbarpolu	13,753	0.93	83	33	3	3	1
Total	**352,788**	**1.22**	**71**	**67**	**10**	**9**	**1**

Source: FAO 2006; UNWFP - CFSNS 2006

Another method to estimate the food crop production and residues by county is using the number of farming families, the farm size for each crop, and average crop yield. However, farm size and yield data in Liberia is available only for rice and cassava with a great uncertainty. Because the available information on average farm size (Table 15) doesn't indicate what portion of the farm is used to grow each crop, the results using this method may be misleading, and is therefore presented only as a reference.

APPENDIX B. ESTIMATING CASH CROP RESIDUES BY COUNTY

Considering that cash crops in Liberia, other than rubber and oil palm, are grown predominately on a range of small-, medium-, and large-scale production systems, the study uses a similar method for estimating the cash crop residues by county as the one described in Appendix A for food crops. Table 16 illustrates the number of farming families in Liberia growing different cash crops.

Rubber. Rubber residues are estimated on land occupied by large-scale plantations. As mentioned earlier, rubber residues generated by small-scale (household) farms are most likely used as firewood or in farm applications. The study estimates that large-scale rubber plantations in Liberia today cover an area of approximately 58,000 hectares. This land area was calculated using information from government publications and media releases, as summarized below.

In February 2008, the Liberian government signed a new lease agreement with Firestone on the 25,000 ha plantation in Margibi County through 2041. The government is also reviewing agreements with other rubber companies, including the 14,000 ha LAC, owned by Sofinco of Belgium, and the 10,000 ha Guthrie plantation, owned by Synergy Drive Bhd of Malaysia (Bax 2008). Salala Rubber Corporation will receive long-term financing from the International Finance Corporation (a member of the World Bank Group) to rehabilitate and expand its existing plantation of 40,000 ha in Margibi County, of which about 2,500 ha were planted before the war (Global Security 1985). Cavalla rubber plantation (about 4,000 ha) commenced production in May 2006 under the auspices of an interim management team led by the Rubber Planters Association of Liberia (RPAL) and Firestone (MOA 2007). Sinoe rubber plantation (approximately 2,200 ha) is currently exploited in an unsustainable fashion due to the "slaughter tapping" by illegal tappers, and the county has called for investments and incentives to reactivate production (Paye-Layleh 2004; Executive Mansion 2008).

Table 16. Farming Families Growing Cash Crops in Liberia, 2005

County	Number of Farming Families	Average Farm Size (ha)	% of Farming Families Growing Cash Crops					
			Sugarcane	Bananas and Plantains	Oil Palm	Coconut	Coffee	Cacao
Bomi	2,551	0.73	17	52	17	3	3	14
Bong	37,736	1.42	21	26	17	1	9	26
Grand Bassa	18,850	1.54	28	53	8	11	2	18
Grand Cape Mount	4,572	1.13	0	18	49	18	15	18
Grand Gedeh	11,515	1.13	0	38	4	2	13	72
Grand Kru	2,945	0.77	27	65	5	12	1	20
Lofa	31,477	2.19	2	12	10	0	82	53
Margibi	24,117	1.21	14	34	14	14	0	10
Maryland	14,864	1.13	33	50	4	9	2	19
Montserrado	108,366	1.54	11	49	5	19	3	5
Nimba	62,862	1.05	34	45	19	1	16	37
River Cess	3,436	1.70	7	50	12	16	4	19
Sinoe	8,396	1.09	8	59	17	21	8	29
River Gee	7,268	0.77	1	64	5	19	4	54
Gbarpolu	13,753	0.93	6	23	19	5	28	52
Total/Average	352,708	1.22	19	40	13	6	20	32

Source: FAO 2006; UNWFP - CFSNS 2006

Oil Palm. Most palm oil is obtained from wild groves and because many of the state-owned plantations, largely abandoned during the war, were taken over by the local population for its own use, the study mainly considers small household production and it disaggregates it to county level using the approach described above. For industrial scale, state-owned plantations, the study estimates only the amount of residues that could be available during replanting (trunks and fronds).

APPENDIX C. ESTIMATING FOREST RESIDUES BY COUNTY

Some of the existing and pending logging contracts spread over two or more counties, in which cases GIS and the information presented in Table 6 were used to disaggregate the total contracts' area to county level. Figure 11 illustrates the analysis methodology. Calculations are based on the areas suitable for FMCs and TSCs, and include lands that are outside of the national forests, existing and proposed protected areas.

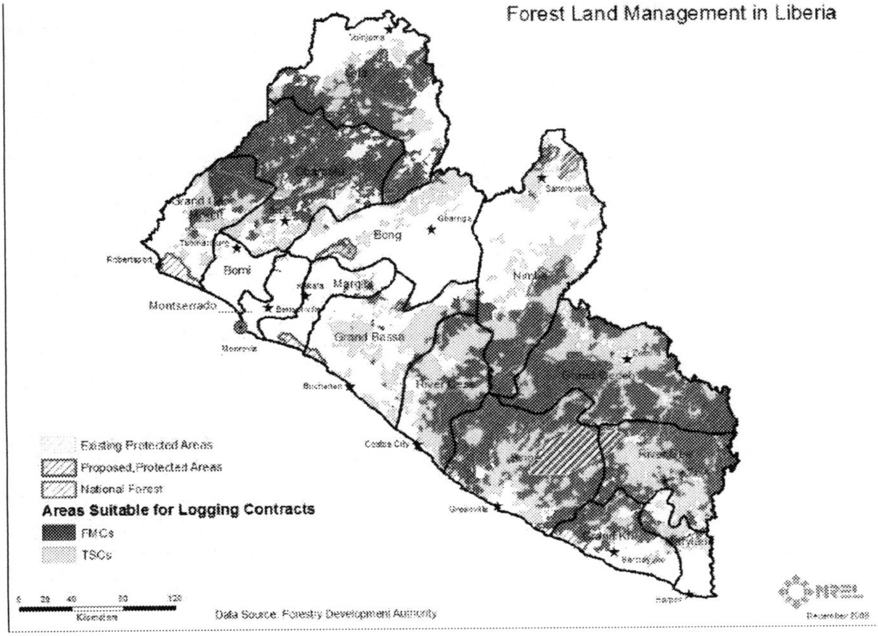

Figure 11. Forest Land Management in Liberia

REFERENCES

[1] Adams, M. & Dougan, J. (1981). "Biological management of coffee processing." *Tropical Science, Vol.123*, 178-196.

[2] African Agriculture in Liberia (July 2007 - August 2008). Accessed October 2008. *http://africanagriculture.blogspot. com/search/label /Liberia*

[3] Bax, P. (February 27, 2008). *Liberia Signs Accord with Firestone; Raises Taxes, Cuts Term*. New York, N.Y.: Bloomberg. *http://www. bloomberg.com/apps/news?pid=20601116&sid=aNM4h3HMD8Ss&refe r=afri* ca

[4] Brandolini, G. & Tigani, M. (December 2006). *Liberia Environmental Profile*. Created for the Government of Liberia and the European Commission. http://ec.europa.eu/development/ icenter/repository/liberia CEPpreliminaryreport.pdf

[5] Central Intelligence Agency. *Electricity Consumption by Country*. The World Factbook online. Accessed October 2008. https://www.cia.gov/

library/publications/the-worldfactbook/fields/2042 . html

[6] Duke, J. (1983). *Handbook of Energy Crops*. Purdue University. Accessed October 2008. *http://www.hort.purdue.edu/newcrop/ duke energy/theobromacacao.html*

[7] Executive Mansion, Republic of Liberia (July 2008). County Development Agendas. Executive Mansion online. Accessed October 2008. http://www.emansion.gov.lr/content.php?sub=County%20Development %20Agendas&rel ated=CDAs

[8] Food and Agricultural Organization (FAO). Commodities by Country – Liberia. Accessed October 2008. http://www.fao.org/es/ess/top/country. html?lang=en

[9] Food and Agricultural Organization (FAO) (February 2006). *Crop and Food Security Assessment for Liberia.*

[10] Food and Agricultural Organization (FAO) (December 2000). *Crop and Food Supply Assessment Mission to Liberia.*

[11] Food and Agricultural Organization (FAO) (January 1999). *Crop and Food Supply Situation in Liberia.* Accessed October 2008. http://www.fao.org/docrep/004/x1015e/x1015e00.htm

[12] Forest Resources Management (FRM), Land-cover data in GIS format, 2004

[13] Forestry Development Authority (FDA) (March 2008). Available Logging Contracts. Accessed December 2008. Accessed October 2008. http://www.fda.gov.lr/content.php?sub=Bids&related=Bids

[14] Forestry Development Authority (FDA) (2007). *National Forest Management Strategy, Monrovia.* Accessed October 2008. http://www.fda.gov.lr/doc/NFMgmtStrategy.pdf

[15] Global Security (1985). *Commercial Crops in Liberia,* Accessed October 2008. http://www.globalsecurity.org/military

[16] Index Mundi, Liberia Oil Consumption, Accessed December 2008, http://www.indexmundi.com/liberia/oil consumption.html

[17] Integrated Framework (IF), *Liberia - Tapping Nature's Bounty for the Benefit of All,* Diagnostic Trade Integration Study, June 2008, http://www.integratedframework.org/

[18] ITTAS Consultancy (May 2008). *Post Harvest Crop Assessment in Liberia (Rice and Cassava).*

[19] Jubah, K. (2007). *Interim Rubber Plantations Management Performance,* November 2007. Ministry of Agriculture (MOA). http://www.moa.gov.lr/doc/Guthrie Cavalla Final Report 07. pdf

[20] Koopmans, A. & Koppejan, J. (January 1997). "*Agricultural and Forest Residues – Generation, Utilization, and Availability.*" Presented at the Regional Consultation on Modern Applications of Biomass Energy conference at the Regional Wood Energy Development Programme, Kuala Lumpur, Malaysia.

[21] Krypton Systems Pvt. Ltd., Commercial Opportunity of Jatropha, Accessed December 2008, http://www.jatrophabiofuel.com/Commercial%20Opportunity%20-%20Project%20Cost. htm

[22] Liberia Institute of Statistics and Geo-Information Services (LISGIS) (June 2008). *2008 National Population and Housing Census: Preliminary Results.* Executive Mansion, Republic of Liberia. http://www.emansion.gov.lr/doc/census2008provisionalresults.pdf

[23] Manapol, P. (November 2007). "*SRE President Speaks At Liberia Workshop.*" Sustainable Rural Enterprise (SRE) blog. http://coconutsgalore.blogspot.com/

[24] Mano Properties & Investment, Inc. (MPI) (2007). *Logging and Timber in Liberia.* Accessed November 2008. http://us-africa.tripod.com/mrbc/logging

[25] Ministry of Agriculture (MOA) (2007). "Comprehensive Assessment of the Agricultural Sector – Synthesis Report." MOA, *Vol. 1.*

[26] Monrovia City Corporation (August 2004). *Waste Management Plan for Monrovia.* United Nations Children's Fund.

[27] Morris, G., Bioenergy & Greenhouse Gases, Pacific Institute, May 2008, http://www.usabiomass.org/docs/legislative/One%20pager%20--%20Morris%20F I NAL%207-24-08 .doc.

[28] Paye-Layleh, J. (February 17, 2004). "Liberian rebels take over, loot rubber plantation." *Associated Press (AP).* http://www.highbeam.com/doc/1P1-91188698.html

[29] PÖYRY Environment GmbH (November 2007). "Solid Waste Management in Greater Monrovia." Draft report prepared for the Monrovia City Corporation and the World Bank.

[30] Sajjakulnu kit, B., et al. (2005). "Assessment of sustainable energy potential of non- plantation biomass resources in Thailand." *Biomass and Bioenergy Journal*, *Vol. 29*, 214–224.

[31] Republic of Liberia (October 2006). *Comprehensive Food Security and Nutrition Survey.* Monrovia, Liberia: United Nations World Food Programme. http://www.reliefweb.int/rw/rwb.nsf/db900sid/RMOI-6VK3RV?OpenDocument

[32] Sheikh, N. (1989). *The preservation of banana crop residues through ensiling process*. Department of Animal Production, Faculty of Agriculture, Somali National University. http://www.fao.org/wairdocs/ILRI/x5490E/x5490e0v.htm

[33] Smillie, I. & Brownell, A. (July 2007). *Land Grabbing and Land Reform: Diamonds, Rubber and Forests in the New Liberia*. Partnership Africa Canada (PAC) and the Association of Environmental Lawyers of Liberia (Green Advocates). http://www.pacweb.org/e/images

[34] Smith, E. (May 2008). *Assessment on the Small-scale Livestock Sub-sector in Liberia*. Report for the Food and Agricultural Organization.

[35] Taylor & Francis Group (2003). *Africa South of the Sahara 2004*. London: Routledge.

[36] United Nations Environmental Programme (UNEP). *Atlas of Our Changing Environment, Harbel Rubber Plantation – Liberia*. Accessed October 2008. http://na.unep.net/atlas/

[37] United Nations Environmental Programme (UNEP) (July 2007). *Assessment of Solid Waste Management in Liberia*. UNEP Post Conflict Assessment Web site online. Accessed October 2008. http://postconflict.unep.ch/publications/Liberia waste. pdf

[38] United Nations (May 2006). *Human Rights in Liberia's Rubber Plantations: Tapping into the Future*. United Nations online. Accessed October 2008. http://unmil.org/documents/human rights li beriaru bber. pdf

[39] Woods, J., Blundell, A. G. & Simpson, R. (January 2008). *Investment in the Liberian Forest Sector: A Roadmap to Legal Operations in Liberia*. Washington, D.C.: Forest Trends. http://www.forest-trends.org/documents/publications/LiberiaGuidelinesEng.pdf

[40] The World Bank (June 2008). Liberia - Tapping Nature's Bounty for the Benefit of All, Diagnostic Trade Integration Study.

[41] The World Bank (1999). *Solid Waste Landfills in Middle- and Lower-Income Countries: A Technical Guide to Planning, Design, and Operation*. Washington, D.C.: The World Bank. Technical Paper No. 426, 248.

[42] Worldwatch Institute, Jobs in Renewable Energy, July 2008, http://www.worldwatch.org/node/5821

End Notes

[1] The amount of energy produced from biomass depends on the energy conversion technology employed and the scale of operation. However, in general terms for electricity generation, each tonne of dry biomass can generate between 1 and 2 MWh_e with efficiency in the range of 20 – 40%. This study uses an average conversion of 1.5 MWh per tonne of dry biomass.

[2] In the wet method, after harvesting and cleaning, the pulp is removed from the cherry before the drying stage. In the dry method, the entire cherry is placed in the sun to dry.

[3] Biogas is the gaseous product of the anaerobic digestion (decomposition without oxygen) of organic matter. The composition of biogas varies depending upon the origin of the anaerobic digestion process. Typical composition is CH4 (50% to 70%), CO2 (30% to 50%), and traces of gases such as H, CO, and N.

REPORT DOCUMENTATION PAGE

Form Approved
OMB No. 0704-0188

The public reporting burden for this collection of information is estimated to average 1 hour per response, including the time for reviewing instructions, searching existing data sources, gathering and maintaining the data needed, and completing and reviewing the collection of information. Send comments regarding this burden estimate or any other aspect of this collection of information, including suggestions for reducing the burden, to Department of Defense, Executive Services and Communications Directorate (0704-0188). Respondents should be aware that notwithstanding any other provision of law, no person shall be subject to any penalty for failing to comply with a collection of information if it does not display a currently valid OMB control number.

PLEASE DO NOT RETURN YOUR FORM TO THE ABOVE ORGANIZATION.

1. **REPORT DATE** *(DD-MM-YYYY)*	2. **REPORT TYPE**	3. **DATES COVERED** *(From - To)*
April 2009	Technical Report	

4. TITLE AND SUBTITLE
Assessment of Biomass Resources in Liberia

5a. CONTRACT NUMBER
DE-AC36-08-GO28308

5b. GRANT NUMBER

5c. PROGRAM ELEMENT NUMBER

6. AUTHOR(S)
A. Milbrandt

5d. PROJECT NUMBER
NREL/TP-6A2-44808

5e. TASK NUMBER
WTD3.1000

5f. WORK UNIT NUMBER

7. PERFORMING ORGANIZATION NAME(S) AND ADDRESS(ES)
National Renewable Energy Laboratory
1617 Cole Blvd.
Golden, CO 80401-3393

8. PERFORMING ORGANIZATION REPORT NUMBER
NREL/TP-6A2-44808

9. SPONSORING/MONITORING AGENCY NAME(S) AND ADDRESS(ES)

10. SPONSOR/MONITOR'S ACRONYM(S)
NREL

11. SPONSORING/MONITORING AGENCY REPORT NUMBER

12. DISTRIBUTION AVAILABILITY STATEMENT
National Technical Information Service
U.S. Department of Commerce
5285 Port Royal Road
Springfield, VA 22161

13. SUPPLEMENTARY NOTES

14. ABSTRACT *(Maximum 200 Words)*
Biomass resources meet about 99.5% of the Liberian population's energy needs so they are vital to basic welfare and economic activity. Already, traditional biomass products like firewood and charcoal are the primary energy source used for domestic cooking and heating. However, other more efficient biomass technologies are available that could open opportunities for agriculture and rural development, and provide other socio-economic and environmental benefits. The main objective of this study is to estimate the biomass resources currently and potentially available in the country and evaluate their contribution for power generation and the production of transportation fuels. It intends to inform policy makers and industry developers of the biomass resource availability in Liberia, identify areas with high potential, and serve as a base for further, more detailed site-specific assessments.

15. SUBJECT TERMS
NREL; Anelia Milbrandt; biomass; Liberia; biomass resources; biomass technologies; agriculture; rural development; transportation fuels; environmental benefits;

16. **SECURITY CLASSIFICATION OF:** a. **REPORT**	b. **ABSTRACT**	c. **THIS PAGE**	17. **LIMITATION OF ABSTRACT**	18. **NUMBER OF PAGES**	19a. **NAME OF RESPONSIBLE PERSON**
Unclassified	Unclassified	Unclassified	UL		
					19b. **TELEPHONE NUMBER** *(Include area code)*

Standard Form 298 (Rev. 8/98)
Prescribed by ANSI Std. Z39.18

CHAPTER SOURCES

The following chapters have been previously published:

Chapter 1 – This is an edited reformatted and augmented version of a Congressional Research Service publication, report RL33185, May 19, 2010.

Chapter 2 – This is an edited reformatted and augmented version of a United States State Department publication dated, February 2009.

Chapter 3 – This is an edited reformatted and augmented version of a National Renewable Energy Laboratory publication, report NREL/TP-6A2-44808, April 2009.

INDEX

C

D

E

F

G

H

M

N

O

P

Q

R

T

U

V

W

Y

Z